Inscribed for
Paul & Helen Crane
recalling the good days of
Elderhostel '86

Jerry L. Surratt

GOTTLIEB SCHOBER OF SALEM

Gottlieb Schober
(1756-1838)

Gottlieb Schober of Salem

*Discipleship and Ecumenical Vision
in an Early Moravian Town*

by JERRY L. SURRATT

MP

MERCER UNIVERSITY PRESS / MACON, GEORGIA 32107

ISBN 0-86554-083-7

Parts of chapters 2, 3, and 4 appear also in the author's
"The Moravian as Businessman: Gottlieb Schober of Salem,"
North Carolina Historical Review 60:1 (Winter 1983).

All books published by Mercer University Press are produced
on acid-free paper that exceeds the minimum standards set by the
National Historical Publications and Records Commission.

Library of Congress Cataloging in Publication Data
Surratt, Jerry L., 1936-
    Gottlieb Schober of Salem.

    Bibliography: p. 229
    Includes index.
    1. Schober, Gottlieb, 1756-1838.   2. Moravian Church—
North Carolina—Salem—Clergy—Biography.   3. Salem
(N.C.)—Biography.   4. Salem (N.C.)—History.
1. Title.
BX8593.S3S95   1983   284'.6'0924   [B]   83-983
ISBN 0-86554-083-7

TABLE OF CONTENTS

DEDICATION

To Alice, Andrea, Emily, and Maria,
Wife and Daughters,
Who have been patient and loving
beyond expectation.

LIST OF ILLUSTRATIONS

PREFACE

THE COMPLETION OF this study of Gottlieb Schober was made possible by the encouragement and cooperation of many individuals over a long period of time. An initial fascination with the man emerged from my graduate study of Salem's evolution. At many significant points Schober's name and influence appeared as I worked through the records. Long after the dissertation was completed, I began this second project centered around Schober, but very soon my leisurely investigation uncovered the immensity of the task. I considered abandoning the project, but some of Schober's descendants, especially Charles N. "Pete" Siewers, John Fries Blair, and Esley O. Anderson, Jr., provided continuing encouragement. The project was further enhanced with the restoration of Schober's home by Old Salem, Incorporated, and its acquisition of a significant body of Schober's personal papers which had been unavailable for research. Funds to support the research and writing were granted by the Robertson-Farmer Fund of the Southern Baptist Education Commission. As the manuscript neared completion and publication approached, the Wachovia Historical Society, under the leadership of William East, granted funds to help underwrite the costs of publication. To all of these individuals and agencies, I am deeply grateful.

A special word of appreciation must be conveyed to certain persons. R. Arthur Spaugh, Jr., President of Old Salem, Incorporated, has been a continuing source of help and encouragement. Miss Mary Creech, Archivist of the Moravian Church in America, Southern Province, has contributed most generously of her time and expertise in locating numerous records and in reviewing the completed manuscript. Colleagues and staff members of Wingate College have been supportive in a project that required far longer to complete than initially anticipated. Finally, I am grateful to Mercer University Press for their willingness to bring this project to its completion. My greatest debt of all is to my wife and daughters, to whom this book is dedicated.

From beginning to end this study has been an exciting and personally rewarding adventure. It is my hope that the work will help to preserve and interpret the life of Gottlieb Schober and the history of the Moravian Church in America.

Jerry L. Surratt
Wingate College
February 1983

CHAPTER 1

Moravians
and Schobers

O F THE PIONEERS who settled and civilized the wilderness of the eighteenth-century North Carolina backcountry, one of the most interesting and noteworthy was Gottlieb Schober. Traveling to the village of Salem as a boy of thirteen, this man labored for sixty-eight years to transform frontier into habitation and to convert ignorance and meanness into enlightenment and justice.

Schober's career is of interest for several reasons. First, he spans an enormous range of community evolution in Salem. When he entered the town in 1770, it was almost exclusively a religious community, a theocracy in which the Moravian church owned the land, managed the affairs, and completely controlled community membership. Practically untouched by the swirling forces which involved colonists in a struggle for independence, and unconcerned with emerging concepts of national destiny, Salem sought quietly to fulfill its mission. Moravians wished simply to evangelize the Indians and remote settlers and to establish a haven for the cultivation of the consecrated Christian life. However worthy that goal, Schober saw drastic, uprooting change during his lifespan. At his death in 1838, Salem differed from its surrounding sister towns only in a few aspects and even these had been largely emptied of meaning. Of the social and economic individualism which largely brought about this change, Gottlieb Schober was Salem's most prominent embodiment. He was occasionally a leader, but more often a gadfly. Time and again he was cautioned, reprimanded, and censured as he found and exploited loopholes and ambiguities in community regulations. But he struggled in the face of frustration, adapted, and survived. In the life of this individual the adaptation and survival of Salem can be viewed in microcosm.

Schober is interesting also as a study in personality. A fiery disposition which was tolerated as youthful enthusiasm in early years became less welcome in a young adult. Schober seemed bound to antagonize others even when trying his best to serve them and the community honestly and creatively. Yet he was respected by many and continually elected to positions of leadership. He could be headstrong and totally unwilling to compromise on matters of practice as well as principle. Vitriolic language and pure character assasination were his tools for persuasion of the recalcitrant, especially if he felt wronged. Coupled with this explosiveness was a quiet appreciation of beauty, for Schober was an accomplished organist who was welcomed to play for worship even when church authorities felt it best that he not share in Holy Communion because of his disruptions in the community. His artistry made the German chorales beloved by Moravians majestically sing praises to the Almighty. He loved children and almost singlehandedly built the Sunday schools in the vicinity of Salem in which many first learned to read, write, and spell. Proudly the seventy-year-old man led the annual Sunday school parade in the 1820s as hundreds of youngsters followed him through the streets of Salem. In creative tension these attributes sparked the personality of Gottlieb Schober.

A third point of interest in Gottlieb Schober is the quality of intellectual insight which he possessed. As might be expected, he was primarily a doer rather than a thinker, and therefore his writings reveal more enthusiasm than originality. He authored several pamphlets on contemporary religious controversies and a history of the church following the Reformation. He was attracted to early German romantic authors and translated several works into English. But Schober's real genius lay in his translation of ideas into action, even if that action was sometimes impulsive. The world of the mind impinged directly on the work of the hand and on the speaking of the persuasive word. Schober arrived in Salem with no financial assets. In a society that steadfastly subordinated individual economic initiative he nevertheless embodied that concept so persistently that he became a man of considerable means. In a community that consistently discouraged social mobility he rose from apprentice to craftsman of leather and tin; to respected businessman who built Salem's first industry, to elected community leader; to lawyer and politician in the North Carolina Senate; and, in the final stage of his career, to respected pastor and president of the Lutheran Synod of North Carolina. In Schober, the individualism so prominent among adventuresome Americans found ready soil for root and blossom. In this sense he became an intellectual leader at least among his own people. Others in Salem saw the same vision but in no other person did the dream engender reality so clearly.

The ability of Schober to translate vision into reality held equally true in the theological dimension. Schober reflected largely the ideas of his early training; the ceaseless repetition of theological phrases in Moravian education and worship developed in him a German evangelical pietism built on the Augsburg Confession. In one dimension, however, Schober transcended both his Moravian and Lutheran contemporaries. He was absolutely convinced that the essentials of the Christian faith had priority over any ideas that might fragment Christianity into confessional or denominational groups. In this conviction, Schober was the spiritual heir of Nicholaus Ludwig, Count von Zinzendorf, on whose estate persecuted Moravians found asylum in 1722. The Count advocated a "Church of God in the Spirit" which would include all Christians. But even Moravians soon discarded the Count's idealism and, in 1748, considered themselves a separate church. Schober is the most notable link between Zinzendorf and the later ecumenical developments of the mid-nineteenth century. He defied church authorities by accepting Lutheran ordination while maintaining his Moravian connections. Without hesitation he advocated union in the face of steady opposition and even showed in writing how so venerable an expression as the Augsburg Confession could be interpreted in essentials to promote the unity of all Christians.

With these attributes the character of the man begins to emerge. It was his fate to live and work in obscurity on the frontier during a period of emerging nationhood. He was most at home with settlers from Europe who were slow to acclimate themselves to the mainstream of American life. But his impact on these people was considerable percisely because he combined a deep rooted European heritage with an American experience inspired by the advent of freedom.

Gottlieb Schober was the son of Andreas Schober, a Bethlehem, Pennsylvania stonemason, and Hedwig Regina Schober. Both parents immigrated in 1743 to America from the European Moravian communities. Andreas Schober was born in November 1711 in New Hoffmansdorf, Moravia.[1] In 1729 he became acquainted with some preachers of the *Unitas Fratrum*,[2] who had returned to their native Moravia on a missionary journey. Members of the Unity of Brethren had fled to Saxony and Silesia during the Thirty Years War (1618-1648) to escape religious persecution. The group scattered and almost perished until in 1722, a group was granted asylum on the Silesian estate of Nicholaus Ludwig, Count von Zinzendorf. Five years later the *Unitas Fratrum* was reconstituted and rapidly prospered in its new-found freedom. The Brethren built the communities of Herrnhut and Herrnhaag as congregation towns from which missionaries traveled widely and colonists journeyed to specific locations to build new communities. It was a group of these missionaries that Andreas Schober met in 1729. Later visits by the Brethren to the Schober household strengthened this acquaintance and in 1734 Andreas came to Herrnhut. There he practiced his craft as a stonemason and three years later joined the congregation. He lived in Berthelsdorf and Herrnhaag as a member of the single brother's choir[3] until 1743 when he sought permission to emigrate to America. He could have undertaken this arduous journey as a single brother, but at thirty-two it was time for marriage. Moravians viewed marriage within the context of the individual's fulfillment of God's will for his life. To remain unmarried was quite honorable since it allowed a person to serve God fully without family responsibilities. If one wished to marry, church leaders were much involved in the choice of mates, although individuals could always decline a proposed connection. On 19 June 1743 Andreas

---

[1]Andreas was the son of Johannes Schober, a merchant, and Catharina, nee Kuntschner. According to family research and tradition, Johannes was a refugee from France who fled religious persecution and changed the spelling of his surname from Joubert to Schober.

[2]Translation: Unity of Brethren or Brethren for short. In America they became known as the Moravians. See J. Taylor Hamilton and Kenneth G. Hamilton, *History of the Moravian Church: The Renewed Unitas Fratrum 1722-1957* (Bethlehem, Pennsylvania: Moravian Church in America, 1967).

[3]Moravians organized their communities in terms of age and marital status into groups called "choirs." The choir shared religious services and instruction and, in the case of single men or single women in some communities, it was an economic and social unit providing housing and means of livelihood.

was married to Hedwig Regina Schubert in a ceremony shared with eleven other couples. Baron Johannes von Watteville, a prominent church leader, performed the group ceremony and Count Zinzendorf himself pronounced the benediction. All the couples together composed the second "sea congregation" for the journey to America. Sailing together as a group, the "congregation" quickly developed bonds of friendship and common purpose which lasted many years, even though the settlers scattered to various Moravian towns in America. The first sea congregation had sailed in 1742 and settled in Pennsylvania to build the town of Bethlehem. Now Andreas and his new bride were among those destined to civilize the wilds of the new world.

Hedwig Regina Schubert was born on 13 September 1721 in Landberg, Pomerania. When Hedwig was about ten years old, her father died, and she traveled with her mother to Berlin to live with an aunt, her mother's sister. A few years later, Widow Schubert and young Hedwig met several Moravians including Count Zinzendorf, and in 1737 the Schuberts came to live at Herrnhut. The mother stayed only a year, but Hedwig joined the children's group and assumed full membership in 1740. She traveled to Herrnhaag in early 1743 and was there married to Andreas Schober in preparation for the journey to America.[4]

On 12 September 1743 the Schobers were among seventy-five colonists from Herrnhaag and Marienborn, and another twenty from Herrnhut who boarded the ship "Little Strength" in Rotterdam.[5] The vessel was commanded by Captain Nicholas Garrison and manned by eleven seamen, all but two of whom were themselves Brethren. The anchor was weighed on the 16th, and seven days later the "Little Strength" first breasted the waves of the North Sea. After picking up a few more passengers in Cowes, England, the band of 117 pilgrims finally faced

---

[4]Hedwig was the daughter of Christian Schubert, Provincial Chancellor of Pomerania and Dorothea, nee Raunch. Family tradition maintains that Hedwig was reared among Prussia's upper social class and that there were connections between her parents and relatives and Prussian rulers. This account of the early lives of Andreas and Hedwig Schober is based on memoirs of each, written at their deaths in 1792 and 1800 respectively, and filed in the Archives of the Moravian Church, Bethlehem, Pennsylvania. A minister or close friends wrote such a life summary for most Moravians who died during the eighteenth and nineteenth centuries.

[5]John C. Brickenstein, "The Second 'Sea Congregation' 1743," *Transactions of the Moravian Historical Society* (1:107-24), p. 112.

westward. They were frustrated by several days of uncooperative weather, but on October 2, winds carried them beyond sight of land; for the next fifty-five days Andreas and Hedwig Schober sailed toward the new world.

By this time, life on shipboard was well organized. The women were quartered in tiny staterooms on the middle deck while the men swung hammocks on the lower level. The leaders organized mess-companies for eating and cleaning and assigned specific duties for cooking, management of provisions, tending the sick, and night watches. During the long days most passengers were far from idle: Germans studied the English language while the English Brethren struggled to master German. Evenings were given to worship, with services conducted on the middle and lower decks simultaneously. According to the journal:

> The sisters sit on the benches, each before her stateroom; the brethren each near his hammock, whilst the Liturgus takes his stand near, or on, the stairs which connect the two decks, thus becoming audible and in part visible to both. Lovefeasts, both regular Sabbath lovefeasts and occasional ones on birthdays, & c., are celebrated on deck, if wind and weather permit; ... They are mostly prepared from the ship's stores, and are distinguished from other meals chiefly by the social manner of enjoying them, and the religious feature they bear; singing, short addresses, reading of missionary and other reports, and religious conversation forming part of the entertainment.[6]

As the "Little Strength" moved smoothly under full canvas, most passengers began to enjoy the trip. They spoke with keen consciousness of their dependence upon God and a belief in His special providence over this group. But not everything was enjoyable. First seasickness, then monotony threatened equilibrium; to these was added a real physical threat when leaks were discovered in fresh water casks. Then on 1 November, the voyagers were enveloped in a furious storm.

> The hatches were closed and secured; the quarters on the middle and lower decks were shrouded in midnight darkness, and lights were kept burning all day. During the regular and irregular tossing and rocking of the ship, it often seemed as if she was on the point of turning over completely, when those who were standing or sitting on one side of the deck found themselves next moment sprawling at the feet of those on the other side, to be transferred in company with them back to their former position ....Whilst the waves were thumping and washing the deck, and during the roaring and hissing of thunder, tempest and ocean, the different class or mess companies were

---

[6]Quoted from the diary of George Neisser by Brickenstein, "The Second 'Sea Congregation' 1743," pp.118-19.

sitting together in semi-darkness, engaged for the most part in singing. A temporary lull in the tempest would enable all to chime in with the singers.[7]

Through this crisis the Brethren perservered. On 20 November soundings established the proximity of land but storms, fog and adverse wind kept the ship off the coast. Finally on 26 November, the Schobers and their shipmates first saw America. Within a few hours, the "Little Strength" rode safely at anchor just off Staten Island. The Brethren gave thanks for a successful voyage.

Meanwhile, the citizens of Bethlehem, Pennsylvania, were excited to hear of the arrival of the second sea congregation to American shores, and were especially delighted when the weary travelers began to appear. Bethlehem was the first successful attempt of Moravians to build a community in America. The first Brethren crossing the Atlantic had settled in Savannah, Georgia, in 1735. Civil authorities there, needing help in battling the fearsome Spanish in Florida, declared that all citizens must be willing to bear arms and that only citizens could preach to the Indians. The Brethren disavowed the new regulation and, in 1740, the ten remaining colonists accepted George Whitefield's offer of work and land in Pennsylvania. After arriving in the Quaker colony, however, theological disagreements between the revivalist and Brethren led to the latter's purchase of land on the Delaware River. It was on this tract that the Georgia settlers and the first sea congregation of 1742 had begun to build the town into which Andreas and Hedwig Schober walked on 6 December 1743. Here where the Schobers were to spend most of their lives, the congregation celebrated a lovefeast, after which "we welcomed our new brethren and sisters with the kiss of love and washed their weary and wounded pilgrim feet. (For they had had bad weather, roads, and lodging on their journey, and at times were short of food.)"[8] The Schobers, along with most of the new arrivals, were designated as the first settlers for the new town of Nazareth, located on the original Whitefield tract. Whitefield had encountered financial problems forcing the cancellation of his plans for colonization, so he sold the land to the Moravians in 1741. Workmen from Bethlehem had already almost completed the first build-

---

[7]Paraphrased from the journal of Johann Hopfner by Brickenstein, "The Second 'Sea Congregation' 1743," p. 121.

[8]Kenneth G. Hamilton, trans. and ed., *The Bethlehem Diary, 1742-1744* (Bethlehem, Pennsylvania: Archives of the Moravian Church, 1971), 1:171.

ing in Nazareth, making stonemason Schober anxious to get to the new village as soon as possible. After a restful Christmas season in Bethlehem, they traveled the last few miles of their long trek to Nazareth on 2 January 1744. Their sojourn in this village was short, however. Andreas helped in construction, but since Nazareth was primarily an agricultural community, his talents must have been needed in the commercial town of Bethlehem. In any case, by late 1744 or early the following year, the Schobers were back in Bethlehem. Sister Schober in 1745 became the teacher for small girls, responsible primarily to instruct them in reading and writing.[9] Brother Schober became the warden of the congregation charged to supervise the general social and economic welfare of the people. This was a most responsible position in an area of critical importance, and it occupied most of Schober's time and effort for the next few years. The warden's function was included in Hamilton's description of Moravian towns like Bethlehem.

> A Moravian settlement consisted normally of a village, the inhabitants of which belonged without exception to the Church, for only they were permitted to reside there permanently or to acquire property within it. A conference of elders superintended the spiritual affairs of the community. The local minister acted as its chairman; its membership consisted of all other ordained servants of the Church who resided in the settlement together with those sisters who had oversight over the women. The village government was vested in a warden, with whom were associated the members of the *Aufseher Collegium*, a committee elected by church council. Matters of primary importance were referred for decision to the church council itself, which consisted of a somewhat larger group of male communicants.[10]

The contributions of Andreas Schober to the development of Bethlehem are at present hidden in the very difficult Old German script in which church records were recorded. A translation of this immense store of information has only begun; and it is beyond the scope of this study to explore in depth the career of Andreas. At the moment he can only be acknowledged as a leader in the mother community of all American Moravians.

Among the happenings in the Schober household in these early years was the arrival of children. Johanna Sophia was born on 16 December

---

[9]Bethlehem Diary, 7,12 April 1745. Manuscript in the Archives of the Moravian Church, Bethlehem, Pennsylvania. Hereinafter cited as Moravian Archives (Bethlehem).

[10]*History of the Moravian Church*, p. 169. The *Aufseher Collegium* is usually translated as Board of Overseers.

1744, but died within sixteen months. Another daughter also named Johanna Sophia made her appearance on 25 May 1747. Two years later Johann Andreas was born, followed by Joseph, then Samuel, then Gottlieb, and finally a son who died in infancy. All of the children were reared in Moravian communities, but only Gottlieb maintained a lifelong connection with the church.[11]

Gottlieb Schober was born on the first day of November 1756. Other than his baptism shortly thereafter, very little is known of his early childhood. But a clue to the character of Schober's rearing he himself provided in a statement some years later.

> Even in my childhood years [Jesus] drew me to himself so that I loved him tenderly and often prayed to him with trust. I could often say to him the childish prayer "Keep me with you." Especially when I left the stage of childhood and was to be received in the boys' choir, my tears flowed the whole day because I feared what would happen to me in the world. I promised myself to the Saviour and asked for [death] if he saw that I did not want to be his. This day remains unforgettable to me.[12]

Gottlieb stated that until his thirteenth year he studied at Nazareth Hall, a boarding school for boys operated by the Moravians. In 1755, the Brethren constructed a building in Nazareth of beautiful native limestone in which they hoped Count Zinzendorf would live upon his return to America. The structure was eighty by forty feet, three stories high with a gambrel roof and belfry.[13] It was modeled after a Silesian manor house and was an imposing structure suitable for a nobleman. When Count Zinzendorf decided not to return to America, the Moravians in 1759 converted the building into a boys' school to complement a similar institution for girls already existing in Bethlehem.

On 6 June 1759, 111 boys, with nineteen tutors and attendants left Bethlehem for a happy trip to their new home. During four years under

---

[11]Johanna Sophia married Christian Franz in 1773 and they went as missionaries to Jamaica. Franz died in 1781 and Johanna remarried, but details of her later life are unknown. Johann Andreas married Rosina Thomas and was organist for Lititz congregation from 1763 to 1769, when he was dismissed from the church. He lived until 1805. Joseph never married, and lived his adult life in Philadelphia. Samuel disliked the restraints of the Moravians and moved to Philadelphia.

[12]Memoir of Gottlieb Schober, Moravian Archives, Winston-Salem, North Carolina. Hereinafter cited as Moravian Archives. See footnote number one of chapter 2 for complete bibliographical discussion of manuscript sources.

[13]William C. Reichel, *Historical Sketch of Nazareth Hall from 1755-1869* (Philadelphia: J.B. Lippencott Co., 1869), p. 24.

the principalship of John Michael Graff the school continuously enrolled more than 100 students, but changes in the financial system in Bethlehem in 1763 made it necessary that the school begin to charge tuition. It was probably about this time that Gottlieb Schober entered as a little boy of six. Separation from the parental household at a tender age was not unusual among Moravians, although it was never forced. The school assumed the roles of both teacher and parent and balanced religious training with the traditional classical education of the day. The new principal in 1763 was Francis C. Lembke, a profound scholar who had studied in the Universities of Erfurt, Leipsig, Jena, and Strassburg. He held the degree *Magister Philosophiae* and had taught in the Strassburg Gymnasium.[14] This man, along with other tutors, opened the world of learning to young Schober. His parents paid ten pounds per year to provide tuition, board and lodging, light, and fuel. Musical and manual training was available for those wishing it. The school was to be "an educational institution of the Church" in which "were to be educated not only skillful mechanics, but also assistants in the work of the Lord."[15] While the enrollment was not as large as when the community treasury of Bethlehem had paid all expenses, the school prospered modestly and in 1770 sixty-seven students lived, studied, and worked at Nazareth Hall. Altogether young Schober probably had at least four and possibly seven years there. No records reveal details on the curriculum, but a book inventory of 30 April 1771 gives an idea of what the boys studied. The 394 volumes embraced seventy-seven different titles, including grammar texts and lexicons for Latin, Hebrew, Greek, German, English, and French; Greek Testaments; Discourses on Augustine's Confessions; several volumes of Moravian sermons and doctrinal expositions; world history texts; Julius Caesar; Cicero's Epistles; Castelliani's Dialogues; English history; Biblical history and antiquity; studies of Old and New Testament; texts on grammatical and oratorical styles; and workbooks for mathematics, arithmetic, and geography. The inventory also mentions "a keyboard inst. in the boy's room" on which young Gottlieb

---

[14]H. H. Hacker, *Nazareth Hall* (Bethlehem, Pennsylvania: Times Publishing Co., 1910), p. 31.

[15]Levin T. Reichel, *A History of Nazareth Hall*, (Philadelphia: J. B. Lippincott Co., 1855), p. 21.

doubtless began to acquire the musical skills which he displayed early in life.[16]

Student life in Nazareth Hall was carefully disciplined. Each group of boys lived with two adult house-fathers who awakened them by 6:00 a.m., supervised room cleaning, and checked "cleanliness and orderliness during dressing, proper washing, combing of the hair, changing of underwear, shoes, etc."[17] Before breakfast the group gathered in a circle for prayer, scripture verses, and singing. After the meal,

> with the sound of the bell, the young people must be ready for their lessons or meetings. For the meetings they will file in and out, according to their rooms, in a respectful manner, and in the accompaniment of their two brothers.[18]

The lessons were regular and demanding. Tutors were forbidden to omit any "individual school lessons without first the prior knowledge and permission of the inspector." Even after lessons they were to be "usefully occupied" running errands or helping the craftsmen and professionals of the village. The house-fathers were expected to know each boy well and to promote his spiritual as well as physical and intellectual growth. They helped the boys maintain cleanliness and orderliness with their belongings, write letters home, learn good manners and politeness, and manage the "pocket-money from their parents." House-fathers were expected to be good examples of cleanliness, including

> daily combing of the hair, washing of the skin and face, rinsing out of the mouth, keeping the teeth clean, regular changing of linen and underclothing, washing of the feet, in the summer at least once weekly, in the winter, at least once monthly.

---

[16]Book Inventory for Nazareth Hall, 30 April 1771. Manuscript in Moravian Archives (Bethlehem). Translation by Del-Louise Moyer.

[17]The discussion of student life and the quotations are drawn from the document entitled "Draft for the House Regulations of the Educational Institution at Nazareth," manuscript in Moravian Archives (Bethlehem). Translation is by Del-Louise Moyer. The document contains no date but several reasons support a conclusion that it comes from the 1750s or 1760s. First, it was recently discovered in the Archives among documents of that period. Second, the language and ideas are consistent with other such documents of that period. Third, Nazareth Hall declined in the early 1770s and ceased to function during the Revolution. It was reconstituted in 1785 and a complete set of house regulations, properly dated, exists for the later period.

[18]Ibid.

Each was expected to possess a love for the young and a genuine concern for their care. Punishment of boys with "curse words, slapping, beating with a stick or rod, or the removal of necessary food and drink" was forbidden, but reprimands consistent with the problem were allowed. "For example 'Since you've been lazy today, you won't need any recess to recuperate. If, however, you persist in being lazy, one will have to use other means to make you diligent.' "[19]

Above all, said the regulations,

> seriousness and faithfulness for God's work must shine forth from the entire being of each brother, who desires to work usefully in the education of the youth in this institution. The young people must notice in all that we do that nothing is more important or greater for us than to rightfully serve God our Lord and His congregation.

Young Gottlieb valued his educational experience at Nazareth Hall highly. Later in life his familiarity with the classics of Greek and Latin literature, his musical ability, and his skill as a speaker testified to the quality of his instruction. But at thirteen, he was ready to enter the first stage of adult life. It was decided that he should go to North Carolina to live and work in the new Moravian communities being constructed in that distant state. With enthusiasm characteristic of youth, he turned his face southward.

---

[19]Ibid. Quotation marks indicate a quotation within the document itself.

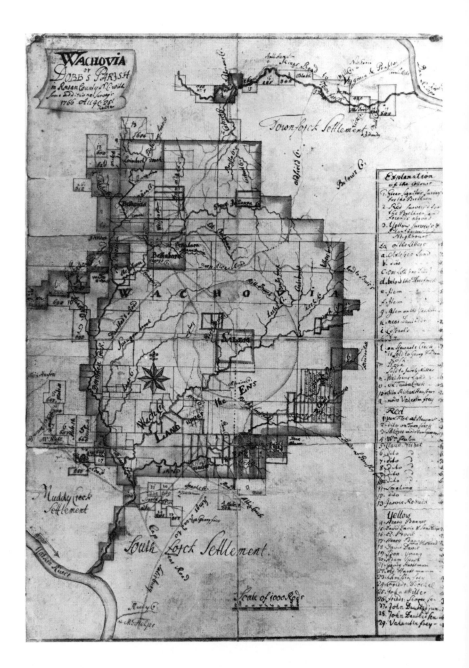

Map of Wachovia, 1766

CHAPTER **2**

Growing Up in Wachovia

THE MORAVIAN COMMUNITIES in North Carolina to which Gottlieb Schober traveled came into existence primarily because the Brethren wished to preach the Christian gospel among the Indians and settlers in the Southern colonies. In the early 1750s the Brethren investigated the possibilities of new settlements and were able to purchase from an Englishman, John, Earl of Granville, a tract of 98,985 acres in the backcountry of North Carolina.[1] In 1753, fifteen men from Pennsylvania arrived in this wilderness which had been named Wachovia[2] and began

---

[1]Information on the North Carolina Moravian communities is contained in diaries kept by the various ministers of the congregations as well as in minutes of the Elders' Conference, the Board of Overseers, and the Congregation Council in Salem. There are many manuscript volumes of these records, but an excellent selection has been published in Adelaide L. Fries, Douglas L. Rights, Minnie J. Smith, and Kenneth G. Hamilton, eds., *Records of the Moravians in North Carolina*, 11 volumes, Raleigh: North Carolina Historical Commission, 1922-1969), hereinafter cited as Fries and others, *Records of Moravians*. Research in the original documents for this study has gone beyond these published records. Those documents cited which are available in the *Records of Moravians* will be so indicated. Others are located in the Moravian Archives, Winston-Salem, North Carolina cited as "Moravian Archives." The repository in Bethlehem, Pennsylvania is cited as "Moravian Archives (Bethlehem)."

[2]German: Wachau. The name was taken from one of Count Zinzendorf's ancestral estates in Austria.

building the village of Bethabara. The first years in North Carolina were not easy, but the arrival of more colonists increased Bethabara's population and led to the establishment of a second village, Bethania, in 1759. Hard work and honesty won the confidence of scattered neighbors who were skeptical at first concerning these very religious people who spoke a strange language. Moravians were in North Carolina to stay, and after weathering the storms of the French and Indian War, they began in 1766 to construct a major town already named Salem.

While Bethabara and Bethania were designed from the beginning as agricultural communities, Salem was to be primarily a regional trading center with a relatively complex social and economic life. After locating several sites, each with fertile soil, construction timber, and fresh water, the Brethren left the final choice to God by use of the lot.[3] This practice was reminiscent of the New Testament Church by which Moravians believed that God would actively lead them in important decisions. After options were examined to the extent of human intelligence, the Elders' Conference would seek guidance by placing two or more possible answers on slips of paper, asking the question in a prayer, and then drawing one of the slips. This was considered God's will. In this manner the site for Salem was determined. Plans were drawn and surveyors laid out a public square, streets, and a graveyard. Workers commuting from Bethabara cleared land and constructed houses for families and shops for the trades. By 1769 a house for single brothers anchored the northwest corner of the public square. Soon a congregation house was built opposite the square's northeast corner, providing a hall for worship, living quarters for the minister and his family, and a separate section designated as the single sisters' house.[4] When Gottlieb Schober first saw Salem, it was already bustling with people and excitement.

Young Schober arrived in North Carolina in the middle of these happenings. A wagon rolled into Bethabara on 24 June 1769, carrying Brother Samuel Stotz and four boys, Petrus Glotz, Martin Schneider, Gottlieb Straele, and Gottlieb Schober. Church officials in Bethlehem had assigned the boys to the Bethabara plantation, but it soon appeared "that

---

[3]Bethabara Diary, 14 February 1765, Fries and others, *Records of Moravians*, 1:298. See Edward Rondthaler, "The Use of the Lot in the Moravian Church," *Salem's Remembrancers* (Winston-Salem: Wachovia Historical Society, 1976), pp. 198-203.

[4]Wachovia Memorabilia, 1769 and 1770, Fries and others, *Records of Moravians*, 1:384, 399.

some of their parents would like to have them in the trades."[5] After a summer's work, Gottlieb was convinced that farming was not his calling; even at thirteen he wrote a letter to Frederic W. Marshall, chief officer of the congregation, asking to be assigned to a trade.[6] There is strong evidence that his unhappiness was much deeper than simply the work to which he was assigned. Later in life he recalled that at Bethabara he became "very downcast concerning the future and wished to know what was ahead, whether I would finally go to the blessed habitation."[7] He realized that "my hot and stubborn head" continually created problems because "I was always headstrong and where I believed right to be, I did not yield regardless of the consequences."[8] But even then, Schober later wrote,

> I was ever concerned to live for the Lord and I know he often made himself known to me and afforded me abiding comfort. The first Elders' festival . . . that I celebrated in Bethabara I shall never forget. From then on I could say "The Lord is my shepherd. I shall not want."[9]

Before many months passed, the young boy's hopes were raised when Gottfried Praezel asked the Elders for an apprentice to learn linen weaving. Schober did not hesitate; on 12 March 1770 he prepared to move from Bethabara to Salem and enter the house of the single brothers to learn the trade of a weaver.[10] Already the talents of this youth had caught the attention of the adults: "The little Schober played the cabinet organ for the first time, for the singing of the liturgy 'O Head so full of

---

[5]Minutes of the Elders' Conference of Bethabara, 28 June 1769, Moravian Archives. The leader of this band of travelers, Stotz, became an important church official in the community until his death in 1820. Glotz died in Salem two years after his arrival. Schneider lived in Salem for many years, then moved to Friedberg where he died in 1806. Straele moved to Salem, then back to Bethabara until his death in 1806.

[6]Minutes of the Elders' Conference of Bethabara, 24 October 1769, Moravian Archives.

[7]Memoir of Gottlieb Schober, Moravian Archives. In the Moravian Church, it was customary at a person's death to compose a short summary of his/her life. Basically this was an obituary, not a memoir in the usual sense of the term. In Schober's case, some of the material was written by him about 1815 when he thought he was about to die. It does, therefore, contain useful information about his early years.

[8]Ibid.

[9]Ibid.

[10]Wachovia Diary, 12 March 1770, Fries and others, *Records of Moravians*, 1:411.

bruises.' "[11] A small pipe organ had arrived in Wachovia in 1762; Schober was one of several who had instruction on the instrument and was the first of the young people to play for worship. This small event foreshadowed a lifetime of enjoyment and service to the church. In later years, Schober became one of the better organists in Salem.

In moving from Bethabara to Salem, Schober entered the mainstream of Moravian activity in North Carolina. Salem was a congregation-town, consistently reflecting the Brethren's mission in North Carolina. A permanent resident had to believe that "he has had a special call from the Lord to live in that place, and that the Lord has brought him to this people. . . ."[12] The church owned all land within a three-mile radius of Salem, leasing lots to individuals on an annual basis. Some businesses in the community, such as the tavern, store, tanyard, and pottery, were owned by the congregation and operated for its benefit. Other trades were assigned to individuals for private profit even though competition was strictly controlled. The dominant social unit in Salem was still the family, since most people lived in small homes. But a system of "choirs"— groupings by age, sex, and marital status—supplemented the family. If fully developed, a congregation had groups of little boys, little girls, older boys, older girls, single men, single women, married people, widowers, and widows. The groups met together for worship and religious instruction appropriate for their age and interests.[13] In some congregations, the single brothers' choir, the single sisters' choir, or the widows' choir might function as an economic unit, maintaining housekeeping and possessing the right to engage in certain trades. When young Gottlieb Schober came to Salem, he took up residence in the single brothers' house where the linen weaving was located. Since Brother Praezel served also as business manager for the choir, Schober's workday was full. In the apprenticeship

---

[11]Wachovia Diary, 2 March 1770, Fries and others, *Records of Moravians*, 1:411.

[12]Minutes of the Salem *Helfer Conferenz*, 30 November 1772, Fries and others, *Records of Moravians*, 2:725. Hereinafter cited as *Helfer Conferenz*. In English translation, the group's title is misleading, so it is left in German. It was an advisory board of ex-officio and elected members to observe and discuss matters to enhance the well-being of the congregation. See Salem Diary, 27 April 1772, Fries and others, *Records of Moravians*, 2:679.

[13]Adelaide L. Fries, *Customs and Practices of the Moravian Church*, revised edition, (Winston-Salem: Board of Education and Evangelism, 1973), p. 53.

agreement he promised to serve his master faithfully, obey instructions, and behave respectfully. In return, Praezel provided clothing and necessities, paid the room and board expenses for his apprentice, amounting to six shillings per week, and taught him the skill of weaving.[14] A work day in the choir house began with morning prayers and concluded with evening worship. When questions of spiritual growth and welfare arose a choir spiritual adviser was available. But young boys and certainly teenagers like Schober found time for activities other than work and worship. Boyish pranks were mentioned in the records frequently. They chased the community cats, had pillow fights with feathers flying, sneaked downstairs to ring the bell in the dead of night, and occasionally hid cockleburs in the supervisor's bed.[15] Although associations with single sisters across the square were strictly forbidden, both the young men and the young women seemed to need the leisurely exercise of early evening strolls, and Salem was a very small village.

Young Gottlieb probably participated in all these activities, but there is some evidence that he was still not altogether happy. There was much discussion in late 1772 of dissatisfaction among several apprentices. Some wished to choose what work they would perform; others took extra long lunch breaks. Some apprentices worked by the hour; others on piece work gained extra leisure by finishing quickly.[16] This lack of consistency threatened community order and upset some of the young workers. Was Schober unhappy? Suddenly in May 1773, a letter arrived from Andreas Schober in Bethlehem complaining heatedly that his son had been apprenticed without the father's knowledge.

> Brother Marshall replied to him that the boys from Bethlehem had been sent to us at our expense, and with the recommendation that this [Elders] conference should be as parents to them and help them in the learning of a trade, which has been done in the most faithful manner according to our congregational order.[17]

---

[14]Julius A. Lineback, "The Single Brethren's House of Salem, North Carolina," *Salem's Remembrancers* (Winston-Salem: Wachovia Historical Society, 1976), p. 95.

[15]Lineback, "The Single Brethren's House of Salem, North Carolina," p. 89.

[16]Minutes of the Salem Board of Overseers, 1 December 1772, Moravian Archives. Hereinafter cited as Board of Overseers.

[17]Minutes of the Salem Elders' Conference, 18 May 1773, Moravian Archives. Hereinafter cited as Elders' Conference.

Had young Schober written home? In an autobiographical sketch written many years later, Gottlieb recalled his unhappiness and fears in this period.

> I was once frightened greatly about my [spiritual] condition. I was then about seventeen years old and believed there was no help for me. I did not cease weeping until the friend of sinners appeared to me as if I could take hold of him and he spoke: "Peace." I was at the time half awake, half asleep, but as I wanted to lay hold on him, there remained nothing but the peace that filled the heart of the sinner with heavenly joy. Now it was settled. But alas! only for a few days. The joy passed. Faith was demanded; love of sin showed itself gradually again but always with anxiety.[18]

Three weeks after his seventeenth birthday, Schober first partook of Holy Communion. "I expected heavenly things, and prepared myself for them. I believed that through prayer, singing, church going, etc. I would become worthy of enjoying it."[19] But nothing happened. It was only when "I came as a poor unworthy creature that my heart enjoyed what I cannot describe."[20] The strong Moravian religious consciousness and expression was becoming conspicuous in Schober's life. He struggled to determine how he should use his life; he was inclined toward congregational service in the ministry but unable to decide. Evidently, he received no encouragement in this direction from church officials. Finally Schober determined to serve the congregation in music while pursuing a livelihood by other means.

Until 1776 Gottlieb stayed with his loom, although at the same time he also was learning the skills of the tailor. The authorities recognized his unhappiness and reluctantly considered another apprenticeship. In April he was bound for two years to Johann Christian Fritz in the leather goods shop. There his tailoring experience helped him quickly to master the art of making leather trousers and pouches which were in great demand. Fritz expected to contract in the usual manner, but the Overseers advised him to offer a salary. The final agreement gave the young apprentice ten shillings weekly from which he had to pay his own room and board. The usual suit of clothes at the conclusion of the contract was omitted.[21] Fritz

---

[18]Memoir of Gottlieb Schober, Moravian Archives.

[19]Ibid.

[20]Ibid.

[21]Board of Overseers, 24 April 1776, Fries and others, *Records of Moravians*, 3:1083-84.

soon recognized the abilities of his new helper; more and more he was away from Salem on preaching missions, and before the contract expired, Schober was doing much of the leather work for the community.

Despite his newfound maturity, Schober allowed his impetuousity to involve him in one more boyish prank. In the fall of 1776, a fence was built around the public square which irritated several of the men. They argued that the gates were dangerous for the pregnant sisters of the congregation. One morning the community awoke to find the gateposts torn out and sections of the fence damaged.[22] Rumors pointed to several of the young men but when the Overseers questioned some of them privately, including young Schober, each vigorously professed innocence. The matter was referred to the Elders' Conference, who declared that unless "this Godless band" was discovered, they themselves would not participate with the congregation in Holy Communion. The whispers continued to implicate the young men, and finally on 12 November

> The Elders' Conference assembled alone. The letter of Gottlieb Schober and Rudolf Christ to the Conference was read. They confessed to their unseemly behavior before the Board of Overseers and apologized . . . .[Martin] Scheider [in a letter] confessed that he tore out the post and pedestals at both gateways simply because there were so many complaints about them.[23]

The Elders were doubly sorrowful. The prank, itself a subtle rebellion by youth against community authority, had now led to blantant falsehoods before the Overseers. Such behavior should not occur in Salem, and the Elders' Conference discussed an upcoming celebration of Holy Communion. Should it be held, the Elders asked God in the lot? The slip of paper drawn said "No." A boyish prank thus became a cause for community sorrow.

Although an unhappy experience, the effect of the fence incident on Gottlieb Schober was ultimately beneficial. He seemed genuinely ashamed of his actions, especially his attempt to conceal his complicity from community leaders. To make amends he concentrated in succeeding months on learning the leather business, playing the organ, and substituting for Brother Fritz as teacher of the boys' school. This last activity attracted Schober greatly. During his years in the single brothers' house, drills on writing, arithmetic, and spelling helped him maintain the skills

---

[22]Elders' Conference, 5,8 November 1776, Moravian Archives.

[23]Elders' Conference 12 November 1776, Moravian Archives.

he had mastered at Nazareth Hall. Now came a chance to expand his abilities by teaching English, reading, and writing to the young boys while Fritz was away on preaching trips.[24] As these trips became longer in 1778, Schober assumed even more responsibility, soon establishing his ability as a schoolmaster.

Despite Salem's relative calmness during Schober's youth, events around the town were far from stable. The Revolution which had burst upon the colonies in 1776 was rapidly enveloping the lives of all settlers regardless of political inclination. The Moravian Church affirmed that a person should not be forced to bear arms against his conscience, and although all did not agree on this policy, the community united in neutrality lest any be forced to compromise. Moreover, the Brethren followed the Biblical admonition to obey constituted civil authority, which at this time meant the royal government of England. But Moravian neutrality was suspected by both loyalist and patriot. As a community, Salem supported neither side, but helped both out of necessity. The armies of Nathaniel Greene and Lord Cornwallis passed through Salem in 1780, each demanding housing and food for men and horses.[25]

Long before dusty and battle-worn armies walked the streets of Salem, the realities of war had touched Gottlieb Schober and his community. In a commercial village, a stable currency was imperative, but the Revolution wrecked the economy. Moravians tried to equate paper currency and hard money but soon that paper flooded the community. Moreover, they found themselves with fixed salaries within the community and rising prices outside. By January 1778, the currency ratio outside Salem was three and one-half to one and rapidly becoming worse. The boards decided to increase the annual salaries of single brothers from eight to fourteen pounds or four shillings per day. The price for the noon meal was also raised and the one dissenting voice was squelched.[26] When the single brothers returned to their house "such bickering broke out especially among the boys born among us and recently received into the single brothers' choir that we thought an evil spirit had descended upon

[24]Elders' Conference, 8 November 1777, Fries and Others, *Records of Moravians*, 3:1179.

[25]Salem Diary, 21 April, 5,29 June, 1780, Fries and others, *Records of Moravians*, 4:1536, 1542, 1549.

[26]Salem Diary, 1 April 1778, Fries and others, *Records of Moravians*, 3:1225.

them."[27] The next day, without warning, about a dozen young apprentices walked away from their work, despite the admonitions of masters. Gottlieb Schober left his leather work in hopes that this strong protest would cause church leaders to recognize the effect of currency devaluation on wages. According to the congregation diary, the boys became "the laughing-stock of the town,"[28] but the Elders saw the walk-out as an attempt to pressure community leaders. No compromise was offered; the young men were "reproved and warned against rebelling against leaders in conferences which the Lord had approved [by the lot] as constituted authority."[29] The letters of apology expected from the young men were slow in arriving. By 7 April five letters were in hand, but Gottlieb Schober's did not come until the 10th. Three were still missing and must have been received later, although the final conclusion of the matter did not appear in the records.

There is no way to measure the effect of this experience upon Schober. Definitely he learned that overt dissent would not effect change, even when circumstances seemed to indicate a need. The penalties for active disagreement were so clear and devastating as to debilitate internal dissent. The spirit of American freedom which had inspired a declaration of independence was considered inappropriate in the internal affairs of Salem.

That declaration led to another event which must have occupied Schober's thoughts on sleepless nights for many years. On 8 November 1778 Captain Henry Smith of the Surry County militia drew four slips of paper each bearing the name of an able-bodied Salem citizen eligible for active service. The first one read: Gottlieb Schober.[30]

Early in the war, the Provincial Assembly at Halifax had recognized the Moravian refusal to bear arms and exempted them from service. By 1778 that easement was wavering. Brethren were subject to conscription and were expected to serve or hire and equip substitutes. Church leaders viewed the latter alternative as indirect service and informed military authorities that "neither directly nor indirectly would we serve in the

---

[27]Elders' Conference, 3 April 1778, Moravian Archives.

[28]Salem Diary, 2 April 1778, Fries and others, *Records of Moravians*, 3:1226.

[29]Elders' Conference, 3 April 1778, Moravian Archives.

[30]Elders' Conference, 10 November 1778, Moravian Archives.

war."[31] When Schober heard his name called for a campaign to the south, he must have experienced a momentary surge of excitement mixed with fear. His own sympathies probably lay with the colonists since it would have been inconsistent for the impulsive young man not to admire the adventuresome spirit of the patriots and to yearn for the personal freedom for which they fought.[32] But was he prepared to shoulder a rifle and fire it at the enemy? Whether anticipation or fear dominated his emotions, Gottlieb was spared the test. Once again the Brethren stood united behind a principle; this time Schober was the beneficiary rather than the culprit. With reluctance Captain Smith accepted a fine of twenty-five pounds to exempt each of the four single brothers who were drafted.[33] One hundred pounds was no small sum even for the entire community when the average annual wage for a journeyman was fourteen pounds; seventy-nine brothers were each assessed one pound, six shillings to make up the total. No murmur was heard, and for once Schober was likely grateful for the manner in which the Brethren stood together. Thirty years later, the event was clear in his memory although the details had faded. His friend Rudolph Christ signed the following affadavit:

> I do hereby certify that during the last war Gottlieb Schober was drafted to serve a tour of duty and that Captain Smith who was then the captain for the district was requested to hire a substitute for him, which he did and Schober paid him the price agreed on.[34]

When this was written in 1808, a wealthier Schober had forgotten that a community assessment, not he alone, had covered the fine. The twenty-five-pound fine would have almost equalled two years' total wages of Schober as a journeyman leather craftsman.

---

[31]Salem Diary, 24 May 1778, Fries and others, *Records of Moravians*, 3:1233.

[32]It is impossible to determine conclusively Schober's political feelings. Open discussion of the matter was discouraged since the congregation officially professed neutrality. The older generation seemed to prefer English government, according to a contemporary account written by Traugott Bagge. Most younger men evidently differed with their elders and were more attracted to the concept of independence. See the manuscript of Traugott Bagge, 1777, Fries and others, *Records of Moravians*, 3:1129-30.

[33]Elders' Conference, 10 November 1778, Moravian Archives.

[34]Document in the Gottlieb Schober papers owned by Old Salem, Incorporated, Winston-Salem, North Carolina. Hereinafter cited as "Schober Papers, Old Salem Incorporated Archives."

If the Brethren did not complain of the assessment for Schober's benefit, within a few months some likely questioned the wisdom of their efforts. Just before being conscripted and at the age of twenty-one, Gottlieb became a free man. The apprenticeship under Johann Fritz expired, and Schober could ask the wages of a journeyman. It was agreed that for every pair of leather breeches completed, he would receive eight shillings, while other work continued to earn him four shillings per day.[35] The incentive of piece work enabled Schober to capitalize on his own industry and initiative. Before long the new freedom began to cause problems. First, Schober requested to work in the choirhouse rather than at Fritz's house because the latter was away so often and the change would better facilitate the supervision of the boy's school. Within a month, the true reason appeared. Fritz complained that when he assigned Schober work, the young man was already busy because he had accepted extra work from outsiders.[36] This practice was strictly forbidden by community regulations. In order that every person could earn a living, a trade was assigned to one master; and all who practiced that trade worked as journeymen under him. For making a pair of leather breeches, Schober received two-thirds of the retail price and Fritz one-third. According to Fritz, Schober was circumventing this arrangement by accepting orders himself. Moreover, the quality of Schober's work had deteriorated badly, Fritz reported, so that the trousers had to be sold at discount.

The Board of Overseers listened also to the journeyman's side of the story. Fritz only allowed him to make two pair of breeches per week, Schober testified, and that gave him a smaller salary than most journeymen and left too much free time. The Board concluded that fault lay on both sides. Fritz was told to assign three pair of trousers per week, while Schober was admonished to produce quality work and to refuse direct dealings with outsiders.[37] Within two months relations between the master and his journeyman were again strained. The same charges and countercharges were aired again before the Overseers. It soon became obvious that the strong personalities of Fritz and Schober hampered cooperation. The master's increasing absence from town on preaching

---

[35]Board of Overseers, 6 May 1778, Fries and others, *Records of Moravians*, 3:1260.

[36]Board of Overseers, 7 July 1779, Moravian Archives.

[37]Board of Overseers, 14 July 1779, Moravian Archives.

trips allowed Schober too much flexibility so that the latter's initiative immediately emerged.

Fortunately, the impasse was resolved when Fritz was called as minister and teacher of a new congregation that was organized in the southwest corner of Wachovia.[38] Schober immediately suggested to the Overseers

> that he himself take over the leather goods shop and that he take on [Johann] Nilson as journeyman. He thinks he can then make enough money with his profession. There was no objection except that if another master should come or if Brother Fritz should return, Schober would be a journeyman as before.[39]

The move of Brother Fritz from Salem to Hope congregation opened still another opportunity for Schober. The young man had frequently watched over the school for larger boys while Fritz traveled and preached. Assumption of the entire teaching responsibility was more than Schober wanted, but when Christian Heckewälder agreed to take the older youths, an opening was created in the school for little boys. Schober could manage this responsibility and continue his leather work. "As to his fitness for the school, we have no doubts. We asked by the lot, 'Should we consider Gottlieb Schober as teacher for the small boys?' We received 'yes'."[40]

Early in January 1780, Schober became the teacher of about nine little boys. School was held six days a week beginning at eight in the morning when parents brought their youngsters to the single brothers' house in time for an opening hymn. The day was spent in basic instruction and practice in reading and writing, with meager beginnings in arithmetic. Some time was occupied in religious instruction, and when the minister visited the school he urged the boys "to be true in heart, and daily renew their baptismal covenant with the Savior."[41] Excepting a two hour break at midday, work continued until four or five o'clock when the teacher delivered his pupils either to home or to congregational worship.[42] The

---

[38]This congregation, organized in 1780, was named Hope.

[39]Board of Overseers, 11 January 1780, Moravian Archives.

[40]Elders' Conference, 29 December 1779, Moravian Archives. The little boys' choir consisted of children ranging from five or six years of age to about twelve. The older boys were from twelve to seventeen years old.

[41]Salem Diary, 31 August 1780, Fries and others, *Records of Moravians*, 4:1562.

[42]Salem Diary, 10 January 1780, Fries and others, *Records of Moravians*, 4:1521; Elders' Conference, 8 January 1780, Fries and others, *Records of Moravians*, 4:1581.

tuition of the school was four shillings per month, which made Schober's salary rather small. The leather work helped, and by April Gottlieb was made the master of the leather goods trade and given Nilson as a journeyman. After a month of instruction, Nilson would be salaried and could help Schober meet the leather needs of the town.[43] There was no lack of demand and under this arrangement Schober could profit from the labor of his subordinate. Unfortunately, the arrangement was short-lived.

By summer, Nilson's fondness for whiskey emerged. Despite the efforts of Schober and others, matters steadily deteriorated so that soon Nilson was asked to leave Salem.[44] The master of leather goods again faced financial straits, and the school work became even more demanding when Heckewälder went to Pennsylvania. Schober then assumed responsibility for the older boys and was assigned Martin Schneider as an assistant. Unable to spend time with his leather, Schober was forced to apply for a salary supplement of eight shillings per week. He still felt himself financially pressed and decided to try reducing his expenses for raw materials. Immediately, a storm descended.

> It will be necessary to remind Brother Schober that he must stop all his negotiating. He should rather make his living from his trade and from the school. . . . We think that he should not buy deerskin in the rough, but that he should leave that business to the white tannery and the store. He also must not swap all different kinds of articles for payment; but should send people who want to sell and swap to the right place.[45]

With this declaration, there was initiated a running conflict between community authorities and Schober which continued, sometimes muted, sometimes loud and bitter, for forty-five years. The Brethren were persistent in their prohibition of open competition, since allowing a free market would encourage the profit motive to become an end rather than a means. Time after time the people were admonished to be industrious and faithful in their work, "laying aside all desire for convenience or profit which would impair or spoil their work."[46] This monopolistic system effectively guaranteed every willing worker a living wage while other sanctions guarded against laziness or an unwillingness to work. The

---

[43]Board of Overseers, 4, 11 April 1780, Moravian Archives.

[44]Board of Overseers, 28, 30 September 1780, Fries and others, *Records of Moravians*, 4:1604-1605.

[45]Board of Overseers, 6 February 1781, Moravian Archives.

[46]Board of Overseers, 15 April 1772, Fries and others, *Records of Moravians*, 2:695.

system afforded Moravians maximum efficiency in supporting those engaged full time in teaching and preaching in the area.[47] Schober accepted this arrangement in principle, but in practice he was not always cooperative. In the case of the deerskins, Schober reluctantly conformed to the demands of the Overseers. He was encouraged to take another apprentice and was offered Jacob Meyer. But after a week's trial, Schober concluded that the boy was too young to learn the leather business.[48] The school salary was reinstated, and Gottlieb struggled along as best he could through the winter.

With the coming of spring, 1782, Schober gained permission to visit his family in Pennsylvania. Young Gottlieb had not seen his father and mother for twelve years. He had left Bethlehem as an adolescent and now returned an articulate individual full of ideas and ambitions. Physically, the little boy had become a man. Inferring from an adult portrait, Schober was of medium height and somewhat slight of build. His nose was rather long, serving to attract attention to dark, intense eyes which captured and held the attention of those around him. Andreas and Hedwig Schober would scarcely have recognized their son had they not known of his coming. It must have been a happy occasion for the family. For Gottlieb, it was a chance to share problems and concerns with kinfolk who could understand the frustrations of a dedicated but ambitious young man. Gottlieb would certainly have discussed with his father the financial pressure he was experiencing and perhaps his ideas for a change of profession. In any case, within two months of Gottlieb's return to Wachovia he was again involved in a new venture.

During the trip to Bethlehem, Schober escaped a sharp reprimand directed generally at Salem's young men. It seems that some of the younger generation came out with ruffs and leggings, immediately prompting the Congregation Council to declare that

> dress fashions, especially among our young people, should be prevented as much as possible. The tailor can contribute much to this. Anyone who lives

---

[47]The congregation granted monopolies to individuals in the minor professions, but reserved for the community treasury (Ger. *Diacony*) monopolies in the more profitable enterprises such as the tavern, pottery, and the store. In addition to paying salaries to persons who preached and taught, the treasury covered general community expenses, such as the nightwatchman's salary, and special projects like the water system which piped fresh spring water to the town from a source several miles distant. Firefighting equipment was purchased by the treasury after the tavern burned in 1784.

[48]Board of Overseers, 6, 13 September 1781, Moravian Archives.

in our community should show by his clothes that he is a Brother. Other people can wear their clothes as fancy as they wish.[49]

Schober was not the community tailor, but he definitely possessed those skills. He tended to be a free spirit as a youth and was known in later years to appreciate the ruffled shirt front. It is more than possible that some of the fancy outfits came from his hand and more than probable that he wore them. Church leaders adamantly maintained that a true brother "must not put his pride in dressing up," lest he be "carried away from [his] actual mission in the Lord."[50] Perhaps the temporary absence of Gottlieb at this time was a fortunate turn of events.

When Schober returned to Salem, events which usually evolve slowly in the lives of most people developed at a dizzying pace. Evidently Gottlieb decided that he would never advance himself as a schoolmaster. When the position of assistant clerk in the community store opened, he immediately asked for the job. The Overseers granted his request, and by late August 1782, Schober was a salesman.

The store position posed for Schober an interesting set of possibilities. He would labor under the supervision of Traugott Bagge, a prominent community leader generally recognized as relatively wealthy by Salem standards.[51] The exact nature of Bagge's financial arrangement is unknown. Some managers of community enterprises worked for a salary and then in addition received a percentage of profits above a certain level. Since the store was the source of many articles needed in the community, its profits were consistent in Salem's early years. This could account for Bagge's personal prosperity. Equally important, his frequent contact with outsiders may have given him knowledge of good investment opportunities. Or perhaps he just managed his personal affairs well. In any case, Schober was keenly aware of how well the store experience had treated

---

[49]Minutes of the Salem Congregation Council, 1 May 1782, Moravian Archives. Hereinafter cited as Congregation Council.

[50]Congregation Council, 30 May 1782, Moravian Archives. A few years later the Brethren were more specific concerning prohibited modes of dress. Among the men, they censured waistcoats with short sleeves or without sleeves, fine pleated shirts with silver shirt buttons, scarlet waistcoats, big buttons, and boots with tops made to hang down. Sisters were not to wear high heels on the shoes and ribbons on the sleeves. *Helfer Conferenz*, 1 February 1787, Fries and others, *Records of Moravians*, 5:2178.

[51]Traugott Bagge was born in Gothenburg, Sweden, in 1729. He came to Wachovia in 1768 and was Salem's only store manager until his death in 1800.

Bagge, and he himself was not immune to the hope of prosperity. Perhaps he imagined Bagge would in a few years be offered the managership of the Bethlehem store, leaving his assistant as an experienced heir to the top position in Salem. Even if he remained an assistant the assignment included some management responsibilities with the branch store in Bethabara. His work would involve frequent trips to Cross Creek (later renamed Fayetteville), Charleston, and Philadelphia purchasing supplies and making new friends. Most important of all, Schober's travel would reveal to him first hand the kinds of business activities and opportunities that were occurring in the cities and towns of America. It would be valuable experience.

With these considerations in mind, the decision to join Bagge in the store was not difficult at all. The salary was set at £60 annually plus free living quarters.[52] Even in the days of inflated currency, the arrangement was the best Schober had known. But his situation changed so quickly that he never knew any financial relief. The 1782 minutes of the Elders' Conference told the story dramatically.

> November 28: Circumstances in the store here and in Bethabara demand that Brother Schober be married. We received in the lot that the Saviour approves that we propose to Brother Schober that he marry Single Sister Elizabeth Dixon . . . .
> December 2: Brother Schober did not accept the proposal that he marry Sister Elizabeth Dixon. He proposed Sister Maria Transou. The Saviour approved this in the lot . . . .
> December 4: Sister Maria Magdalena Transou has accepted the proposal to marry Brother Schober. . . .[53]

On 17 December they were wed.

---

[52]Elders' Conference, 21 August 1782, Fries and others, *Records of Moravians*, 4:1806.

[53]Elders' Conference, 28 November, 2, 4 December 1782, Moravian Archives.

Maria Magdalena Schober (1758-1835)

CHAPTER 3

A Family
and the Search
for Security

MARIA MAGDALENA SCHOBER reflected on the events which had so rapidly changed her life. Only a few weeks ago she had lived and worked in the single sisters' house as a member of that choir. Then Brother Frederich Peter spoke the words which formalized her marriage to Gottlieb Schober. In that ceremony the pink ribbon of a single sister that had tied her white linen cap for religious occasions was replaced with the light blue ribbon of the married people's choir.[1] Perhaps also her thoughts returned to earlier years.

Although Maria Schober had lived in Salem less than three years, she was essentially a child of Wachovia. She was born in Friedensthal, near Nazareth, Pennsylvania, on 18 June 1758, the daughter of Philip and Magdalena Transou.[2] As a child of four, she moved with her parents to Wachovia, settling in the new community of Bethania. Her memories of

---

[1]These events are inferred from accounts of other marriages among Wachovia Moravians. For example, see Bethabara Diary, 1, 2 March 1772, Fries and others, *Records of Moravians*, 2:730.

[2]Philip Transou was born 2 October 1724 at Mutterstadt in the Palatinate. He came to America at seven years of age with his parents and grew up in Pennsylvania. He joined with Moravians in Bethlehem in 1745 and ten years later married Magdalena Gander. In 1762 they moved to Wachovia, settling in Bethania where Philip worked as a farmer and wagonmaker. Transou was known as a kind man and affectionate husband and father. At

the journey to North Carolina were primarily the result of hearing her parents tell the story of the passage by sea. According to them, a company of fifteen Moravians—three couples, four single sisters, a widow, a single brother, and three children—left Bethlehem on 20 April 1762.[3] Maria was almost four years old; her brothers were six and one. The group traveled to Philadelphia where they boarded the sloop "Elizabeth" for the voyage to Wilmington, North Carolina. The group saw themselves as especially protected by God's providence, when, on the first day, Sister Transou narrowly escaped serious injury from a discarded iron pin which fell from the mainsail and grazed Maria's mother's head.

When the ship finally reached open water, the passengers became so seasick that some yearned even for a bumpy wagon. On 4 May an unseasonably cold wind and rain lashed waves across the decks, wetting everything above and below.

> Nothing worried us as much as the poor children, who had to stay in the dark, wet hold all day, with nothing warm to eat, and those who took care of them could hardly hold up their own heads on account of seasickness and the tossing of the sloop.[4]

Despite the security of a mother's arms, it must have been terribly frightening for four-year-old Maria. If she remembered anything of the trip, it was that day.

On 12 May the "Elizabeth" crossed Frying Pan Shoals and entered the Cape Fear River. The next day the ship made anchor at Wilmington, and plans for the river journey were arranged. After traveling up the Cape Fear by flatboat, battling huge mosquitoes all the while, the company

---

times he was severely ill with gout, ultimately weakening him and causing his death on 19 April 1793. See his memoir, Moravian Archives.

Magdalena Transou, nee Gander, was born 18 February 1729 in the Palatinate. She moved with her parents to Pennsylvania in 1738. Her mother died on the voyage and her father bound her to a man who treated her harshly. Later the father redeemed her and she ultimately became associated with the Moravians in Bethlehem about 1747. After her marriage in 1755, she moved with her husband to Wachovia. She lived her last years in Salem with her children and died 12 November 1803. See her memoir, Moravian Archives.

[3]This summary of the Transou's journey is taken from a travel diary probably written by the group's leader, John Michael Graff. Significant portions are translated in Fries and others. *Records of Moravians*, 1: 255-63.

[4]"Diary of the Colony which on April 20, 1762, set out from Bethlehem, by way of Philadelphia and Wilmington, to Bethabara in the Wachau," 4 May 1762, Fries and others, *Records of Moravians*, 1: 257.

finally reached a landing below Cross Creek where they welcomed the sight of Bethabara wagons ready to take them to Wachovia.

Maria's father was a farmer and planned to settle in the new community of Bethania. The land there was fertile and had quickly attracted a population of seventy-two persons by 1762. In this community Maria lived until her twenty-first year, when her father forwarded to the Salem Elders' Conference her request to move. As required by a new regulation from the last Unity Synod in Europe, her request needed the approval of the lot, a requirement which confirmed the Brethren's belief "that we do not so much care for a great quantity of brethren in Salem, but more for their quality."[5] An affirmative lot brought Sister Maria Transou to the single sisters' house in Salem on 10 February 1780.

The single sisters of Salem lived in the second story of the congregation meeting hall which was designated the single sisters' "house." About twenty-seven sisters and older girls shared several sleeping halls at night and worked together in the day weaving linen and cotton, dying and spinning yarn, making buckskin gloves, and laundering. For her labor, each received a salary of three shillings per day and paid a board fee of six shillings per week.[6] According to its regulations, the choir was to be

> a garden of the Holy Ghost, where he may produce people for all kinds of service; it may be for marriage or for service in the Choir, among children, or in families, or as Choir Sisters passing their days in quiet and union of heart with the Friend of their soul, thinking with deep interest on the things of the Lord, and praying for them.[7]

The strength and reputation of the choirs of the single men and women offered a fulfilling concept of life without the necessity of marriage. But neither male or female was discouraged from the latter state if they so desired. Moravians viewed marriage as a spiritual institution, designed to enhance the relationship of men and women to God. The Elders' Conference sought the guidance of God in considering proposed marriage unions, and, reaching the limits of human discernment, they looked for God's blessing as indicated in an affirmative lot. Then the individuals were consulted. According to one Moravian writer, the Elders'

---

[5]Congregation Council, 10 February 1780, Moravian Archives.

[6]Salem Diary, 13 May 1778, Fries and others, *Records of Moravians*, 3:1231.

[7]Principles of the Single Sisters' Choir, quoted in Adelaide L. Fries, "History of the Single Sisters' House, Salem NC." (Typescript, Moravian Archives), p. 32.

Conference conferred with individuals before using the lot, but the records do not substantiate this as a predominant practice.[8] In any case, before or after an affirmative lot, either person could decline a proposal and the matter would end. For example, in late 1781 Sister Transou was given the proposal of marriage to Matthew Oesterlein—a proposal initiated by him to the Elders' Conference and approved by them and by God through the lot—but "after careful consideration she ... declined the proposal."[9] A year later she accepted the proposal to marry Gottlieb Schober.

The newlywed couple set up housekeeping in a small dwelling originally built by Christian Gottlieb Reuter in 1771, and located on the southwest corner of Main and West Streets.[10] With the store just next door, the house was ideal for the new assistant clerk. The Elders' Conference regretted losing Schober as a teacher and complimented his work with the declaration that the little boys "have progressed so far that they can read English with the older ones."[11] They also expected good things to result from Schober's new responsibility and recognized his additional financial needs by giving him an extra fifteen pounds per year in exchange for the store's assuming the retail sales of leather breeches.

While the new store duties kept Gottlieb busy, he always found time to participate in Salem's musical activities. One such opportunity was the signing of the peace treaty terminating the war and assuring the independence of Americans. The congregation was grateful for the prospect of peace and, upon learning of Governor Alexander Martin's proclamation that 4 July 1783 would be a "Day of Solemn Thanksgiving to

---

[8]A marriage proposal could be initiated by an individual to the Elders' Conference or by the Elders' Conference itself. Regardless of the source, a negative decision of the Conference was final. If the Conference approved and God's blessing was given through the lot, either person could accept or decline the proposal. See, for example, Elders' Conference, 5, 12 December 1781, Fries and others, *Records of Moravians*, 4:1737-38. See also Edward Rondthaler, "The Use of the Lot in the Moravian Church," *Salem's Remembrancers*, pp. 198-203.

[9]Elders' Conference, 12 December 1781, Fries and others, *Records of Moravians*, 4:1738.

[10]Reuter's widow, Anna Catherina, later married Johann C. Heinzmann and the house was known by his surname. Eventually the house was purchased by John Vogler and moved to the back of the lot so he could build a two-story dwelling on the corner.

[11]Elders' Conference, 18 December 1782, Fries and others, *Records of Moravians*, 4:1810.

Almighty God," immediately began preparations for the celebration of the independence of Americans. The Governor's proclamation required

> all Ministers of the Gospel of every Denomination to convene their congregations [on the 4th of July next], and deliver to them Discourses suitable to the important occasion, recommending in general the practice of Virtue and true Religion as the great foundation of private blessing as well as National happiness and prosperity.[12]

Salem's celebration was therefore a day of religious Thanksgiving. Men, women, and children gathered in the congregation house during the morning hours for a worship service featuring a sermon on Psalm 46 and the *Te Deum.* The afternoon was given to a community Lovefeast and an elaborate program of music. The evening program featured a liturgy of thanksgiving and praise.[13] Schober was involved in the musical program, probably playing the organ for at least one of the services. Musicians for the day were unidentified, but the program called for organ, flutes and horns, brasses led by trombones, and two violins, a viola, a cello, and a bass.[14]

The remainder of 1783 passed quietly for Schober, marked only by a trip late in the year to Charleston, South Carolina, to buy goods for the store. But the following year was a memorable one. One of the fearsome hazards of eighteenth-century living was fire. In cold weather, the open fireplaces and ceramic stoves posed a threat to every building. Salem was fortunate in its earliest years probably because of strict fire regulations. But on 31 January 1784, the tavern burned to the ground. It was a tragedy which not only cost the community financially, but also struck a note of fear in every heart. Since the tavernkeeper Jacob Meyer and his family had no roof, it was decided that the Schobers would move into a part of Tycho Nissen's house so that the Meyers could have the Reuter house. The move was especially hard on Maria because she was expecting a child. But the

---

[12]Proclamation of Alexander Martin, 18 June 1783, Moravian Archives.

[13]Elders' Conference, 2 July 1783, Moravian Archives. Adelaide L. Fries argues convincingly that the first celebration of July 4th occurred in Salem. North Carolina was the only state to proclaim 4 July 1783 as a day of thanksgiving and Moravians were the only group known to have planned a special celebration. See Adelaide L. Fries, "An Early Fourth of July Celebration," *Journal of American History* 9 (July 1915): 469-74.

[14]For more detail see Marilyn Gombasi, *A Day of Solemn Thanksgiving: Moravian Music for the Fourth of July, 1783, in Salem, North Carolina* (Chapel Hill: University of North Carolina Press, 1977).

new house was likely nicer and warmer and was the scene of celebration when Gottlieb wrote on 2 May 1784, "In the morning, at half past three o'clock, God gave us a son. Brother Benzien baptized him with the name of Nathaniel."[15] Mother and child were well and healthy, and the dawn of the new day was a time of rejoicing.

The expanding family of the Schobers called for a new arrangement so that Gottlieb decided to build a house. He was interested in the lot across from the southeast corner of the square at the joining of West and Church streets. The lot was just across from the Nissen house and beside the dwelling of Traugott Bagge. It was a prime location because it faced the public square along with the congregational buildings and the choir houses.[16] Since he and Maria began housekeeping "in poverty," according to his memoir, he was unable to finance the construction entirely, but gained permission to borrow 150 pounds from the store. At first a log structure of one story was proposed, but later Schober changed to brick and added sleeping rooms in the attic. It measured thirty-two by twenty-nine feet. Springtime seemed a good time for him to be away from the store, so on 1 February 1785, Schober signed a lease for his lot and construction plans were finalized.[17] The lease extended for twelve months "and so from year to year, as long as both the said parties shall please . . ." at an annual rent of ten shillings, eight pence in hard money. Schober retained the right to sell his improvements to anyone "qualified to possess, and with his Family to live in a House at Salem" who was also approved by the directing boards. If the congregation terminated the lease it promised to purchase the improvements should a suitable buyer not be found. Any disagreement on value would be resolved by arbitrators.[18] Most North Carolinians of that time would have seriously questioned the wisdom of investing in buildings on land which could only be leased. But for Schober and Salem Moravians the arrangement worked

---

[15]A leaf pasted in Gottlieb Schober's Bible recorded the birth and baptism of each of his children. Gottlieb Schober Papers, Moravian Archives.

[16]Construction of the single sisters' house was already planned on the northeastern corner of the square, east of Church Street, but was delayed until the new tavern was completed.

[17]Board of Overseers, 4 January 1785, Moravian Archives. The lot measured eighty-five feet east and west by 132 feet north and south.

[18]Copy of lease agreement between Gottfried Praezel, Salem Warden and Gottlieb Schober, 1 February 1785, Schober Papers, Old Salem Archives.

well; it gave the community an effective method by which to control the realization of Salem's ultimate purpose, yet it provided for equitable settlement in case a citizen departed. Schober was happy to have his plans approved[19] and to see Salem's leading mason, Gottlob Krause, hard at work. But progress lagged. The sisters' house was going up across the street, and some workers were involved in both projects. Schober soon experienced the frustration of delays and was slightly scolded for giving too many drinks to the workmen. It was unclear whether he was trying to keep the workers at his place or to attract them back across the street. As the summer grew hotter, tempers also rose. Both Schober and Krause were temperamental men given to outbursts of anger, and on 29 June it was reported that

> Schober and Gottlieb Krause have had such a severe altercation on the building scaffold that our reputation as a people of God suffered greatly. That in consequence they remain away from Holy Communion is understood, but we considered what further steps must be taken in the matter, particularly since Krause expressed himself so very unseemly against the congregation.[20]

The disagreement could have occurred over wages which Krause received. Three years earlier, the request of Krause and several others for an increase in wages to offset inflation had been denied.[21] In mid-June, during the construction of Schober's house and the sisters' house, he further expressed dissatisfaction with his masonry trade in the town. Again the boards advised him to continue. The actual circumstances leading to the fight were not recorded, but evidence would suggest an unhappy worker who was not as careful of the quality of his work as his employer expected. Perhaps Schober expected too much. In any case the matter was viewed as serious, since it challenged the community economic management and order. A hearing before the Overseers led to a most revealing comment by the Elders:

---

[19]Plans of all buildings required the approval of the Overseers prior to the beginning of construction. The Overseers viewed the size of the dwelling in relation to a family's anticipated needs and the ability to pay for the structure without excessive debt.

[20]Elders' Conference, 29 June 1785, Moravian Archives.

[21]Congregation Council, 28 October 1782, Moravian Archives.

> In the congregation a spirit has become evident which seeks to have *American freedom.* This should be taken up in Congregation Council and thoroughly investigated, so that so dangerous a thing may be put away from us.[22]

The discussion proposed for the Congregation Council probably occurred immediately, but no record was kept. Moravians were very sensitive concerning their reputation in the surrounding area. Many people were jealous of their obvious prosperity and would be happy to discredit them. Only by an act of the General Assembly in 1782 was the title to Wachovia cleared from possible confiscation.[23] So soon after this victory the Brethren could not afford tales of public fistfights among members of the congregation. Consequently, Schober and Krause were fortunate to escape with only a sharp reprimand.

Construction continued on the Schober residence, and finally in October moving day arrived. It was a happy Gottlieb and Maria, who, with sixteen-month-old Nathaniel, spent the night of 14 October 1785 under their own roof.[24]

The Schober dwelling cost 356 pounds to build. In addition to his savings, Gottlieb borrowed heavily from the store, and thus the financial pressure increased. During the fall of 1785, relations between Schober and Traugott Bagge deteriorated steadily. The exact problem was never mentioned, but it probably involved Gottlieb's salary and his work. He was dissatisfied with his financial progress, but he knew that the demand for leather products, especially breeches, was declining because the store had a sizeable inventory.[25] So his sharp eye spotted another craft which

---

[22]Elders' Conference, 6 July 1785, Fries and others, *Records of Moravians*, 5:2096. The fact that this comment comes as a result of the Schober-Krause altercation is not explicit in the published records but is quite clear in the original manuscript. Emphasized words are in the original.

[23]When the Moravians purchased Wachovia, the deeds were placed in the name of an Englishman, James Hutton, in trust for the *Unitas Fratrum.* After the Confiscation Act of 1777 declared land vacant which was owned by Englishmen, neighbors around Salem began filing claims on Wachovia land. The deeds had by this time already been transferred to Wachovia's administrator, Frederic William Marshall, but there remained a question of whether a power of attorney had been properly registered. See discussion of Mulberry Fields case in Chapter 5. Since a court decision favoring dispossession of the Moravians was possible, action by the General Assembly was necessary.

[24]Salem Diary, 14 October 1785, Fries and others, *Records of Moravians*, 5:2087.

[25]Board of Overseers, 8 February 1785, Fries and others, *Records of Moravians*, 5:2091.

promised a healthier income. The demand for tinware in Salem was substantial, causing Schober in December 1785, to ask to establish himself as a tinsmith.[26] That product, he felt, in addition to the leather business, would provide a livelihood. The directing boards were sorry to lose his services in the store, and even offered him complete charge of the Bethania store, but Gottlieb declined.[27] His request was granted with the clear restriction that he could retail only the goods which he made; under no circumstances was he to bring finished items into Salem, thus acting as a community store. The boards also approved his request to borrow an additional fifty pounds from a non-Moravian neighbor named Mazinger for the establishment of the trade.[28] Years later, Schober reflected upon his gamble:

> In spite of all hinderances, I was unwearied and fortunate. If I suffered loss here and there, I saw plainly that it served for my best so that worldly treasure should not be my chief purpose. After my kind of effort, that could happen only too easily.[29]

From this time until his death, Schober worked "on his own account." His business expertise needed a degree of freedom and flexibility; during the next ten years he was entirely absorbed with business dealings and the development of financial security.

Schober organized his business affairs carefully. Since he himself planned to concentrate on tinware, an apprentice for the leather work would be a good investment. In February 1786, Schober took a young boy, Johannes Steinmann, into the leather trade.[30] The youngster attended school in the morning and spent the remainder of his time with his new master. This arrangement was perfect for Schober to develop his craft in tinware. Most tinware in Salem was very utilitarian in design and manufacture. The American tinsmith of this period generally tended to be unoriginal in his craft. Seldom did he develop new styles or shapes but

---

[26]Board of Overseers, 13 December 1785, Moravian Archives.

[27]Elders' Conference, 30 November 1785, Moravian Archives.

[28]Board of Overseers, 13 December 1785, Moravian Archives.

[29]Memoir of Gottlieb Schober, Moravian Archives.

[30]Elders' Conference, 15 February 1786, Fries and others, *Records of Moravians*, 5:2131.

usually contented himself with meeting the popular demand.[31] After 1750, tin items became especially useful in the kitchen, rapidly replacing utensils of iron, pewter, and wood. The process of applying tin to thin sheets of iron was perfected in England; most American tin was shipped across the Atlantic in 9x12- or 12x18-inch sheets.[32] The tinsmith used handtools for cutting and shaping the thin sheets and on many articles inserted stiff wire under rolled edges for strength. A good tinsmith could offer a multitude of merchandise: pans for baking and roasting; molds for stuffing sausage and making candles; collanders, graters, measures, and cake cutters; coffee and tea pots with cups for drinking; lanterns, candlesticks, sconces, and snuffers; and even specialty items such as mousetraps.[33] When Gottlieb applied all his energy to a task, he learned quickly. By July he advised the Overseers that he could now provide Salem's tinware needs and that the store should stop selling it. The community establishment complied, but soon the true motive of Schober's arrangement became evident. Complaints were lodged with the Overseers that Schober

> was trying to establish a small shop in addition to his trade; that he had recently brought in snuff boxes, silver shirt-buttons, and knives for sale; that he had ordered chocolate for sale; that he had offered to order all kinds of things for the Brethren and Sisters; that he had approached people on the streets who had brought tallow and wax to town, and had offered a higher price than was being paid by others, whereby the price of those articles was raised; and that he planned to export those things.[34]

The same week, the *Helfer Conferenz* discussed the problem in general and concluded:

> It must be understood that a Brother who is a craftsman shall abide by his business, and not indulge in trading and chaffering. . . . A man is more blessed when he follows his calling faithfully and industriously. A man who tries too many things and mixes in matters which do not concern his business, loses his sense of order and becomes restless under steady work; and his business goes backwards.[35]

---

[31]William L. Warren, "Foreword," in Shirley S. DeVoe, *The Tinsmiths of Connecticut* (Middletown CT: Wesleyan University Press, 1968), p. xviii.

[32]DeVoe, *The Tinsmiths of Connecticut*, p. 36.

[33]DeVoe, *The Tinsmiths of Connecticut*, pp. 61-85.

[34]Board of Overseers, 7 November 1786, Fries and others, *Records of Moravians*, 5:2145.

[35]*Helfer Conferenz*, 2 November 1786, Fries and others, *Records of Moravians*, 5:2144.

Schober was summoned to respond to the charges and describe his general purpose. At a special meeting of the Overseers, Gottlieb asserted that he had ordered tin from Philadelphia, but the buyer who had carried the order could find none and he had bought a number of other things instead. He produced the invoice which showed the articles not related to his trade, saying that people in town had ordered them. "From what he said, however, it was evident that he had gone around the town and had solicited the orders."[36] He denied raising the price for tallow but admitted he paid a penny more per pound for beeswax . He maintained that he could ship it to Pennsylvania more safely than money and there exchange it for tin.

After hearing this explanation, the Overseers directed Schober to cease his trading and concentrate only in tinware and breeches. He was to transfer the other items he possessed to the store to settle the thirty-five pounds still owed on his house. The decision of the Overseers was not satisfactory to Schober although there was no official record of his response. Evidently, he just sulked and did nothing. A month later Traugott Bagge complained to the Overseers

> about the rude behavior of Schober upon his question concerning the payment of thirty pounds owed to the store. Schober did not give him any answer except bad words. We thought it necessary to talk to Schober about that in the Collegium and called him. He answered that he was still in such a rage that it would be better not to call him today because it would be useless. The Collegium let him alone for that day.[37]

A week later it was still considered best that Schober not be summoned before the whole board and two members were asked to talk with him privately. By the first of January, a note came to Bagge from Schober apologizing for his conduct and promising the money as soon as possible.[38]

In this matter, Schober was clearly in violation of congregational regulations. The ordering of items in the mercantile category belonged exclusively to the community store. Trading in raw materials unrelated to a profession was also prohibited. Schober did have a point that it was safer to transport beeswax than money, but his argument was weak. More

---

[36]Board of Overseers, 18 November 1786, Fries and others, *Records of Moravians*, 5:2145.

[37]Board of Overseers, 22 December 1786, Moravian Archives.

[38]Board of Overseers, 2 January 1787, Moravian Archives.

important to him than safety was the probability of extra profit in trading beeswax in Philadelphia. Schober's seemingly excessive anger over this reprimand was likely because it presented a major snag in his plans. From the very beginning, he probably planned more business than converting sheet tin into utilitarian kitchen utensils. Tinware gave him a highly marketable set of products, and by using his ingenuity profits could be made in several ways. The Overseers were quick to see this development and to stop it. When he asked permission to make a business trip to Pennsylvania, the Elders were skeptical. They did not oppose his going but "if, as we hear, he wants to buy goods on commission and sell them here" he should stay at home.[39] The Overseers declared further that they were quite doubtful about his whole way of life lately.[40] Nevertheless, Gottlieb made the trip, leaving Salem on 6 March and returning two months later. If Schober made arrangements in Pennsylvania in pursuit of his mercantile business, he had the good sense not to bring anything back with him. The Brethren thus had reason to hope that their stern warnings had caused Gottlieb to respect the community order and regulations.

Almost nothing was recorded of the events on this trip to Pennsylvania. Certainly the reunion of the family would have been a welcome event, especially since there was so much personal news to share. Since his last visit, Gottlieb had married, built a house, developed a new trade, and become a father. Young Nathaniel now shared his parents' attention with a sister, Johanna Sophia, who was born on 11 August 1786. Surely Gottlieb would have been full of stories to tell eager grandparents so that the days of visiting passed rapidly. It is possible that Schober made at least one business trip to Ephrata, Pennsylvania, where he looked over the paper manufactory there. Two years later, his knowledge of the Ephrata establishment helped him to crystallize plans for a similar venture in North Carolina.

The months following Schober's return to Salem were quiet. Gottlieb tried his hand at painting houses in the summer, but this whim was quickly satisfied.[41] He also asked for a sign to identify his business on which a lion would appear, but was advised that a sign with "a sample of

[39]Elders' Conference, 7 February 1787, Moravian Archives.

[40]Board of Overseers, 27 February 1787, Moravian Archives.

[41]Board of Overseers, 24 July 1787, Fries and others, *Records of Moravians*, 5:2187.

finished goods, or a picture of one, or the name of the business in large letters, is the easiest to read and most suitable for us."[42] Generally, business was good and Schober prospered.

In early 1788 he submitted an inventory to the Overseers which revealed that his "status has improved very much."[43] For the first time, assets equaled liabilities and, if called upon, Schober could pay all his debts. But even that happy state of affairs became a problem. When Brother Peter Yarell encountered difficulties paying his debts in 1788, Schober advanced him a sum of money to help. No interest rate was mentioned, but in all probability, it was present. This transaction prompted the Overseers to declare: "Since Brother Schober is able to lend money to others, it would be good for him to pay his debts to the community treasury."[44] Further discussion revealed that other people were starting "little deals" and when questioned about it, responded: "If Schober can do it, why can't we?" The board came to the conclusion that Schober "knows to start his things off so well that we cannot catch him."[45] Obviously, Schober was walking a very narrow edge; his survival in Salem was a testimony to his ingenuity. More than that, however, it also revealed a fundamental weakness in Salem's economic system. The Brethren knew that unless a person voluntarily subscribed to the community economic philosophy, real compliance could never be enforced.

Schober's recalcitrance convinced most that he was trying to take advantage of the system, an attitude which usually led to immediate exclusion. But Schober also displayed real piety and participated regularly and strongly in the religious life of the community. Was it possible for a true Moravian Brother to seek personal economic advancement? The continuing toleration of Schober would seem to indicate the persistence of that question in the minds of some.

Actually, in the midst of his conflicts, Schober continued to make recognized contributions to the strength and vitality of the community. In 1788 he was suggested for the position of curator of the single sisters

---

[42]Board of Overseers, 4 September 1787, Fries and others, *Records of Moravians*, 5:2188.

[43]Board of Overseers, 9 January 1788, Moravian Archives. The purpose of the inventory was not recorded. It may have come as the result of Schober's violation of trade regulations the preceding year.

[44]Board of Overseers, 15 July 1788, Moravian Archives.

[45]Ibid.

choir but a negative lot prevented his being considered.[46] The same year he accepted, although with some reluctance, the responsibility of caring for beggars on behalf of the congregation. A special account was supported by all citizens from which Schober would give to the poor so that beggars would not solicit from door to door. Most likely the collection of this account was not pleasant, nor could he give any destitute person enough to make a real difference.[47] In early 1789 Schober assumed responsibility for securing and placing gravestones in God's Acre. He continued to help regularly with the music in worship, especially at Bethabara and Bethania. Gottlieb's efforts in this regard must have caused ambivalent feelings among those on the directing boards. Was he an asset or a liability?

For Schober, the answer to that question was clear. He believed that he was a faithful Moravian and that he should be allowed reasonable financial rewards for his efforts. But he knew that he was testing the patience of the boards. In February 1789, Gottlieb wrote the Overseers to explain how he had again emerged from the barter system with a shipment of gunpowder and other items from Petersburg, Virginia, which he had no permission to sell. The reaction of the Overseers was predictable. Other tradesmen in the community made a reasonable profit without the trading of merchandise and so must Schober. Clearly once more, Schober was given a directive.

> If Br. Schober receives the products of the land or paper money for his tinware, and spends the paper money to buy products which he can ship to the seaport and there exchange for tin or hard money, or if he finds it more profitable and ships to England for exchange there for tin or other necessaries, the Collegium has no objections. But if for the products he bought he brings in goods for resale, that is contrary to the spirit of the congregation rules which provide that no one shall overstep the boundaries of his own business.[48]

Schober acquiesced orally to the arrangement, but by July it was asserted that "Brother Schober is still taking new wares into his house."[49]

---

[46]Elders' Conference, 2 April 1788, Moravian Archives.

[47]Board of Overseers, 9, 23 December 1788, Moravian Archives.

[48]Board of Overseers, 10 February 1789, Fries and others, *Records of Moravians,* 5:2274.

[49]Board of Overseers, 17 February, 7 July 1789, Moravian Archives.

Investigation substantiated the charge and Brother Frederic Marshall was directed to deliver to him a letter.

> With much patience, we have tried to wait and see what Brother Schober will do in his merchandising, even after several reminders from the Brethren of this Board. Now our daily experience shows that his trade instead of stopping . . . is expanding more and more. . . . The Board of Overseers is forced, therefore, to demand from him through this letter, a final declaration whether he is now going to stop immediately this buying and selling together with the commission trade which he pursues besides his real trade.
> . . . If Brother Schober does not want to listen to our demand, he is violating the orders of the community, has no more the character of a brother and will have to suffer that we do not consider him as such any longer. Yes, it would be his own fault if we would have to make use of the last method in the lease to part from him.[50]

Finally, Schober knew that the Overseers would not yield. Every excuse he offered was pushed aside; his proposals for new ventures were tabled; his woeful tales of losses if he had to give up trading were disregarded. And then came this letter written in third person demanding absolute conformity or threat of exclusion from the community. One week later Schober's response was read to the Overseers. He agreed to the ultimatum and consented to sell his stock altogether, even though it meant no profit and some loss of shipping costs. Two board members were immediately dispatched to inspect his stock and to explain once again the difference between trading "with a merchant's profit by the pound or by the yard" and accepting wares in barter as a community service to be sold without attention to extra profit. He could certainly raise the price to cover shipping, but not to increase profit.[51] The store in Salem took some of Schober's inventory, and the Bethabara establishment agreed to pay him the regular wholesale price for his gunpowder. In each case, Gottlieb insisted that his goods were of superior quality and were worth more. But he had little choice. He probably did lose some money, but not nearly as much as he claimed. In any case, declared the boards, "he bought them consciously acting against the orders of the community" and if he loses some money "on the whole we think it necessary because of the bad example he has set for so many people who also want to trade."[52]

---

[50]Board of Overseers, 14 July 1789, Moravian Archives.

[51]Board of Overseers, 21 July 1789, Moravian Archives.

[52]Board of Overseers, 14 July 1789, Moravian Archives.

As harsh as the narrative of these events may sound, Schober's relations with the directing boards were not completely negative. They recognized his obstreperous manner and finally concluded that only the ultimate threat of exclusion from the community would be heard. Schober submitted and complied with the boards' demands. He still believed he was right but knew that the boards at this time held the final allegiance of the community. Consequently, during the middle of the controversy, Gottlieb was so bold as to propose a totally new venture. Because there was a need in North Carolina for good quality paper, and sources were scattered and undependable, Schober asked permission to build a paper manufactory on the western outskirts of Salem. The Overseers recognized the need and conjectured that "it might keep him from speculations of which we cannot approve."[53] Once Schober responded in writing to the ultimatum concerning his merchandizing, the boards encouraged him to proceed with his plans for a paper mill if he could avoid bringing in a non-Moravian craftsman. A mill pond to provide water power was no difficulty, and Christian Stauber expressed an interest in learning the art of papermaking. In early September 1789, the plans were approved and Stauber left for a six month stay at Ephrata, Pennsylvania. Before his return, he would also visit other mills, preparing himself to begin a quality establishment. In the *Fayetteville Gazette* there soon appeared an advertisement.

SALEM PAPER MANUFACTORY
LADIES SAVE YOUR RAGS

The Subscriber begs leave to inform the public that he is erecting a Paper Mill, in this town, which he hopes, in a short time, to have completed; and at the same time humbly makes known to the ladies of Fayetteville, Hillsborough, Salisbury and Morgan Districts that without their assistance, he can do nothing—without rags, paper cannot be made. The economical housewife, who supplies the paper mill with rags, serves the country in her sphere as well as the soldier who fights for it does in his. For all kinds of clean *Cotton and Linen Rags* a generous price will be given, and the favor particularly acknowledged of any person collecting a quantity.

Gottlieb Shober [sic]
Salem, Septr. 8th, 1789[54]

---

[53]Board of Overseers, 7 July 1789, Fries and others, *Records of Moravians*, 5:2278.

[54]*Fayetteville Gazette*, vol. 1, no. 4, Monday, 14 September 1789. Reprinted in the *North Carolina University Magazine*, November 1853 and in Fries and others, *Records of Moravians*, 5:2402. Schober increasingly dropped the "c" in his surname after this period and especially when the communication was in English.

CHAPTER 4

The Paper Mill
and Prosperity

For THE SPECULATIVE businessman, papermaking was an interesting gamble in 1790. The art was imported to America about 1700 when the Rittenhausen family came to Germantown, Pennsylvania. Mills proliferated in New Jersey and Massachusetts in the early eighteenth century to the point that the British expressed fears for their exports.[1] The Stamp Act of 1764 specified that all official documents must be on stamped paper or parchment, but public outcry led to repeal after one year. Another law in 1767 included paper as a taxed import, reducing consumption generally but encouraging domestic manufacture. By the time of the Revolution, paper was very scarce in the colonies, leading to many new establishments in the 1780s. By 1787 there were sixty-three mills in Pennsylvania, New Jersey, and Delaware. South of this immediate area, however, the craft was almost nonexistent. In North Carolina, only the small establishment near Hillsborough owned by John Hulgan produced paper products.[2] In a travelogue translated in 1792, J. P. Brissot de Warville observed that, because rags and labor were scarce, Americans

---

[1] J. Leander Bishop, *A History of American Manufactures from 1608 to 1860* (Philadelphia: Edward Young and Company, 1866), 1:196.

[2] Dard Hunter, *Papermaking in Pioneer America* (Philadelphia: University of Pennsylvania Press, 1952), p. 72.

would not be able to "furnish sufficient paper for the prodigious consumption caused by the increase of knowledge and the freedom of their
press."[3] On the other hand, in his 1790 report, Secretary of the Treasury
Alexander Hamilton declared that papermaking was very adequate to
meet the national demand. Such differences in evaluative opinion created
ripe opportunities for the speculator who guessed correctly on the true
situation. And Schober was a gambler. From appearances, however, the
young businessman had only limited investment capital. How much
better to find a partner to share the initial risk, especially one willing to
advance money without demanding a management voice. In November
1789 Schober petitioned "the honorable the General Assembly of the
State of North Carolina" to advance three hundred pounds "for a few
Years without Interest," so that he might establish this much-needed
manufactory. He cited the great expense of securing artists and machines
from other states and feared that he could not do it alone. He hoped "at
the next session of the General Assembly to produce paper, Sufficient and
nice whereon our own Laws may be printed."[4] Accompanying the petition was a letter signed by six prominent Salem citizens testifying that
Schober had in fact launched the enterprise with his own money, but "by
Letters received from Pennsylvania it is found more expensive than at
first expected." Should the Assembly grant the request

> we are assured that he will be punctual to his Engagements (which he always
> was) and that he will also have the Paper Manufactory in a reasonable Time
> compleated.[5]

The General Assembly hesitated, but after a vote of 25 to 12 in the Senate
with the House concurring, the Treasurer was directed to loan to Schober

---

[3]Jacques Pierre Brissot de Warville, *New Travels in the United States, Performed in
1788* (New York: T & J Swords, 1792), cited by Bishop, *A History of American Manufactures*, 1:208.

[4]Petition of Gottlieb Schober to the General Assembly of North Carolina. Dated by
another hand 7 November 1789 and filed among the Legislative Papers of the Senate,
1789, North Carolina State Archives, Raleigh, North Carolina. Hereinafter cited as North
Carolina Archives.

[5]Letter to the General Assembly of North Carolina, dated 31 October 1789, Salem,
Surry County signed by Jacob Blum, Samuel Stots, John Rightz, Fred. Wm. Marshall, John
Hanke and Peter Yarrell. Legislative Papers of the Senate, 1789, North Carolina
Archives.

Three hundred pounds, clear of interest, for three years, for the purpose of
encouraging a paper manufactory in this state, taking bond with sufficient
security for the punctual payment thereof. . . .[6]

The young man returned from Raleigh flushed with his success and
ready to bargain for the land on which to build a mill pond. The site was
already tentatively selected: the meandering course of Peters Creek just
south of the main road leading west from Salem provided an excellent site
for a dam and mill pond to supply the power for the mill.[7] Schober liked
the location, but he wanted to buy the land for the pond rather than lease
it. The congregation regulations mandated that the church should own all
land within a three-mile radius of the community and only lease to
individuals who were granted use of the property. But Gottlieb believed
that the investment was too large to risk termination of a lease and forced
sale. He probably remembered well the curt letter from the Overseers
threatening to cancel his house lease if he failed to follow community
regulations. Ownership of the land would give him a measure of security
should the paper business open other opportunities frowned upon by
community leaders.

However, Schober's attempts to circumvent the regulations were also
fresh in the memories of others.

Brother Schober is still violating all the limits of trade and commerce for
which the paper mill, where he also wants to build his house, will give him
even more opportunity. Therefore the Collegium thought it advisable not to
sell him the land, but to give it to him through a lease and have him promise
all the necessary conditions through a bond.[8]

Schober balked. He knew that the community at large liked his proposed
manufactory, and the Overseers' response seemed to indicate that the
only real barrier to the sale was Schober's own past activities. He offered
to accept a forty-year lease with a thousand dollars bond to guarantee his
proper behavior. Still the Overseers would not compromise. They were
suspicious of Schober's voluminous arguments and his fear of the one

---

[6]Walter Clark, ed. *The State Records of North Carolina*, vol. 21, 1788-1790, (Goldsboro, North Carolina, 1903), p. 581. A few similar loans were made during this period to
encourage various business enterprises in the state.

[7]The millpond was located just south of the place where today Academy Street crosses
Peters Creek. At that time the Shallowford Road ran westward from Salem.

[8]Board of Overseers, 16 February 1790, Moravian Archives.

year lease. Perhaps he intended to pursue his own business goals and avoid repraisal.

> Even if he contracts himself with a large sum of money, [we are still unsure of] his intentions. It is mainly a question of conscience that would keep him from [illegal] trading. He would always be able to [make excuses] before the court though he may have violated his [obligation] constantly. [In light of our past] experiences [with him,] we cannot believe that he honestly wants to follow community principles in every way. . . .[9]

Therefore the Overseers insisted that the contract contain no special terms, but they did agree to eliminate local competition if he could supply the community's needs. Still Schober was not satisfied. He argued for lower rent payments on the flooded land and objected to the strict application of specific community regulations to an enterpise located outside the village. But the Overseers parried every thrust. In seeming exasperation the Overseers finally declared:

> If Brother Schober is therefore not willing or does not believe that he is able to follow the conditions of the lease in their true sense, and if he does not think that we act brotherly and righteously with him, he will do good to look for another place.[10]

Probably sensing that he had gained as much as possible, Schober gave an oral assent. There was surely annoyance on both sides, but given Schober's disposition, such negotiation was without permanent rancor. Gottlieb wanted the best arrangement possible and worked to that end. The issues were not insignificant; rather they illustrated the main points of conflict between a philosophy of economic individualism and a concept of management of economic enterprises for the benefit of the community.

The contract was prepared for signatures, and a plat of 196 and three-fourths acres was measured. Schober finally signed although he formally protested some of the provisions in a written statement. Evidently even the Overseers were not unanimous. Several men backed Schober's protest with their own signatures. He believed that "he was forced to the conditions of the contract since he could not retreat any more because of the money already invested in the project."[11] But the majority of the Board held firm and judged the protest as "unreasonable

---

[9]Board of Overseers, 20 February 1790, Moravian Archives.

[10]Board of Overseers, 2 March 1790, Moravian Archives.

[11]Board of Overseers, 14 July 1790, Moravian Archives.

and not to be accepted."[12] The Overseers were probably correct in their cautious dealings with Schober at this time. In an invoice dated 8 September 1790 the Philadelphia firm of Statt and Donaldson acknowledged Schober's order of gunpowder and some necklaces for which in exchange Schober had sent one cask of tallow and six hogsheads of tobacco. Only a wide imagination could include these items in the trade of a tinsmith and breeches maker or in the business of paper manufacturing.[13]

Meanwhile, work was in fact proceeding rapidly at the mill site. Christian Stauber returned from Ephrata, Pennsylvania, where he had acquired the necessary skills in papermaking. Schober employed Johann Krause as chief carpenter for the project and rented slaves for the manual labor.[14] The only negative incident recorded was the frequent "cursing, use of bad words and songs" by the paper mill workmen which Schober was requested to control because it was influencing the younger brethren.[15] The dam was completed, land flooded, and the mill itself constructed. Early in 1791 Schober proudly exhibited his products, first, simple blotting paper and, by June, a fine quality writing paper of double folio size with a watermarked "NC" on the left page and "S" on the right in nine-sixteenths inch letters.[16] Schober had every reason to be proud, because, according to a twentieth-century Scholar,

> the quality of the North Carolina paper made by the Moravian Brotherhood is equal to that of any paper manufactured in America during the latter part of the eighteenth century.[17]

---

[12]Board of Overseers, 20 July 1790, Moravian Archives.

[13]Invoice in Schober Papers, Old Salem Inc. Archives.

[14]Board of Overseers, 6 December 1790, Moravian Archives. Schober and other Moravians used slaves for heavy labor but usually rented them from neighbors. A few were owned by community enterprises, such as the tavern, but private ownership required authorization by the governing boards. Permission was granted only when the need for ownership was clearly demonstrated and when it would not interfere with the apprentice system for training the youth. See Philip Africa, "Slaveholding in the Salem Community, 1771-1851," *North Carolina Historical Review* 54 (July 1977): 271-307.

[15]Board of Overseers, 22, 29 June 1790, Moravian Archives.

[16]Salem Diary, 30 June 1791, Fries and others, *Records of Moravians*, 5:2326. The "S" could have stood for "Schober", but combined with "NC" likely signified "Salem". There is some question whether the watermark existed on the early paper. See Adelaide L. Fries, "First Paper Mill in Salem Started in 1791," *Employment Security Commission Quarterly* 6:1 (Winter 1948): 30-32. But watermarked examples have been discovered among the Schober papers indicating an early if not initial use of the symbols.

[17]Dard Hunter, *Papermaking in Pioneer America*, p. 75.

In the 1790s most paper was made by hand. The process began with old rags of cotton or linen. The cloth was reduced to a finely chopped mass, mixed with water to form a pulp, and bleached with chloride of lime in a large vat. The sheets were formed in a wooden mold the bottom of which consisted of fine interlaced wire. Schober's molds usually had twenty-four horizontal wires to the inch and vertical wires one and one-eighth inch apart. A "vatman" gradually poured a dipper of pulp into the mold, shaking it gently to allow the water to pass, leaving the fibrous particles on the wire in the form of a sheet. This was blotted between felts and dried in an airy room.[18] Paper was thus produced one sheet at a time. The quality, of course, depended on the pulp and the bleaching process. Extant examples from Schober's mill are light weight, sturdy, and of a cream color. It could be folded once for folio size, twice for quarto, or three times to form eight pages.

Despite the apparent success of the venture, the paper manufactory was not without its problems both for Schober and the community. The main road leading west was covered by the mill pond, and since there was no other suitable place to ford Peters Creek either the road had to be completely rerouted or a bridge built over the mill race. Since the former would involve the county court, the Brethren decided on a bridge. This required the hauling of fill dirt, large quantities of stone and timbers, and continuing maintenance. Schober offered to supply the initial materials and four dollars in money or labor if the community would supply the remainder and maintain the structure along with other town roads. The fact that this matter was accomplished in June 1791 without significant bickering between Schober and the community authorities pointed to a more amicable relationship. Actually two significant events had occurred. First, in October 1790, Schober himself had been elected by the Congregation Council to the Board of Overseers. Secondly, the first renewal on the paper mill lease had solved some concerns on the part of both parties.

Schober's election to the Board of Overseers was not unexpected. The heated negotiations over the lease likely reflected personal antagonisms rather than community consensus. Gottlieb had long been entrusted with the administration of the Salem "poor fund" and in the middle of the lease negotiations was commended for his efforts and commissioned to

---

[18]Edward Hazen, *The Panorama of Professions and Trades* (Philadelphia: Uriah Hurt and Son, 1836), pp. 191-92.

supervise the matter so that "no beggar should be allowed to go to the houses unless he has a ticket from Br. Schober."[19] In July 1790 the Elders asked Gottlieb to be one of three organists for worship services, each rotating one week at a time.[20] In October of that year the Congregation Council, in an obvious show of support for this young entrepreneur, elected him to the Overseers, a council of seven men charged to manage the economic affairs of the entire community. Such an expression of confidence would not have been easily given. An affirmative lot confirmed the election of each member, and Schober became a member of the body which had been to this point his most severe critic. In a division of duties, Schober was designated to collect and administer the school fees for the town. For older children in Salem, parents paid one shilling per week; those in Bethabara and Bethania paid eight pence. The children of four or five years were charged six pence weekly.[21] Schober also participated in the deliberations and decisions of the entire body, a responsibility which doubtless smoothed the way for the lease renewal in May 1791, although the renewal was far from automatic.

The anniversary of the initial lease gave both Schober and the Overseers a chance to amend offending sections. Schober renewed his request to be the sole supplier for the community, but his colleagues felt that it must first be determined whether "we can get from his mill all different sorts of paper of good quality and quantity for a good price."[22] The board encouraged Schober to expand the variety of his product and promised that the store would not compete when he could meet the need. In the new lease the acreage was altered, since the dam had been built eight feet high and had flooded more land than originally expected. Schober paid rent of £6.9.4 in gold or silver. He promised to conform with community regulations and to sell his improvements to a buyer approved by the community authorities should he terminate the lease. He was not to use the land for any trade or commerce besides paper making.[23] Gottlieb was evidently happier with this contract—or at least realized he could do no

---

[19]Board of Overseers, 18 May 1790, Fries and others, *Records of Moravians*, 5:2305.

[20]Elders' Conference, 7 July 1790, Fries and others, *Records of Moravians*, 5:2308.

[21]Board of Overseers, 15 October 1790, Moravian Archives.

[22]Board of Overseers, 19 April 1791, Moravian Archives.

[23]Lease agreement between Gottlieb Schober and Samuel Stotz, warden of the single brothers' choir, signed 1 May 1791. Schober papers, Old Salem Inc. Archives.

better. He also decided about this time to reduce his own risk by taking a partner, an unlikely turn of events if Schober was sure of future profits or if he had been able to use the venture as a base for more diversified operations. He had already tried to manage the mill himself with his father-in-law as the primary supervisor. Phillip Transou, Sr. moved with his family to Salem in April 1791, to live at the mill but returned to Bethania in July for reasons of health.[24] In October, Schober entered a partnership with Christian Stauber, the man who had learned the skill in Pennsylvania and who was already the chief operator. Schober believed that Stauber would develop a better product if he himself could share potential profits. The contract established salaries for both Schober and Stauber with each sharing equally the expenses and future profits or losses. A clause was added to the lease granting Stauber the same rights and responsibilities as Schober possessed.[25]

With these matters seemingly settled, Gottlieb proceeded with the development of the business. He was given permission early in 1792 to purchase a slave named Stephen for work at the mill on condition that he would be sold if his conduct became bad and provided that he "does not spend his [free] time here in the community and returns to the mill on Sundays when he comes here to the sermon."[26] Another Moravian, Johann Volz, came to work at the mill and built a house nearby. But soon trouble began to develop between the partners. The details of the difficulty were not recorded, except Schober's charge that Stauber's management of the business was so haphazard as to drive both of them to bankruptcy. The Overseers tried to mediate the dispute, suggesting that Schober himself become more active "in the employment of workers and also the whole direction of the business."[27] The mediation seemed successful at first; both agreed for Schober to repurchase Stauber's share and dissolve the partnership, but the latter would continue making paper for

---

[24]Salem Diary, 29 April, 22 July 1791, Fries and others, *Records of Moravians*, 5:2323, 2326.

[25]Board of Overseers, 4, 11, 25 October 1791, Moravian Archives.

[26]Board of Overseers, 10 January 1792, Moravian Archives. The arrangement revealed that Salem Moravians in this early period welcomed blacks to attend worship but did not encourage the development of social relations. But it should also be pointed out that no non-Moravians were allowed to loiter in the community except the paying guests at the tavern.

[27]Board of Overseers, 5 February 1793, Moravian Archives.

an annual salary of forty-nine pounds plus housing for his family. Soon matters deteriorated further, causing Schober to tell Stauber that "he should do better to look for another working place and another living quarter because he is neglecting everything."[28] Again the Overseers tried to settle matters because Stauber's other skill as a tailor promised him only a meagre livelihood. But Stauber appeared satisfied if he could only escape from the mill and the dominance of his employer. Schober reissued paper mill notes and obligations over his own name to clear Stauber of any liability and in July the latter moved his family to Bethabara to resume his trade as tailor.[29] The reorganization at the mill was not described. Schober evidently assumed total financial responsibility for the mill and employed supervisors. Johann Volz already had sufficient experience to run the operation; then Johann George Wageman emerged after 1794 as a key figure in the business. It is doubtful that Schober himself was ever heavily involved in mill operations because his personal business affairs became increasingly complex in the mid-1790s.

The tinsmith business expanded rapidly during this period. Early in 1792 Schober took William Eldridge on a three-year apprenticeship to learn the craft. The apprentice was to have a regular salary but detailed arrangements were included in case of sickness, indicating that the young man did not likely possess a hearty constitution.[30] More important was Schober's request to build a shop between his house and that of Traugott Bagge. This was necessary for several reasons. First, Schober's family had expanded considerably since his house was built. In addition to Nathaniel, Johanna Sophia had arrived on 11 August 1786 at 9:30 in the morning, Emmanuel on 12 February 1789, and Anna Paulina at 3:30 on the morning of 6 December 1791.[31] Four small children left little space for even a tinsmith! A one room frame and weather board shop was built and soon became the scene of even more community activity. In July 1792 Schober became Salem's first postmaster.

The Postal Act of 1792 of the United States Congress reorganized the system and provided for an expansion of service. One result of this action

---

[28]Board of Overseers, 12 March 1793, Moravian Archives.

[29]Board of Overseers, 2 April 1793, Moravian Archives; Salem Diary, 6 April 1793, Fries and others, *Records of Moravians*, 6:2472.

[30]Board of Overseers, 24 July 1792, Moravian Archives.

[31]Gottlieb Schober's Bible, Gottlieb Schober Papers, Moravian Archives.

was a postal rider who traveled from Halifax to Salisbury once every two weeks, the first arriving in Salem on 1 July 1792.

> Our Br. Gottlieb Schober was appointed postmaster, and we made the first use of the post to send letters to Pennsylvania, and hope by it also to keep in touch with the political news.[32]

The Congregation Council subscribed to a regular newpaper, and soon reports from the Unity Elders' Conference in Pennsylvania began to arrive regularly. A letter by post to Philadelphia cost two shillings or twenty-five cents, and only six pence more would carry it all the way to Europe.[33] The advent of this system did much toward eliminating the isolation of this backcountry community. The fortnightly arrival of letters and newpapers soon became an important event. Regular communication increased Salem's knowledge of and involvement in the affairs of the nation. The community was also drawn closer to the Brethren in Pennsylvania and Europe, since the postal system's regularity was more dependable than the old way of using travelers to carry letters and reports between communities.

Salem's inclusion in the system was likely influenced by the growing reputation of the town among North Carolinians. Certainly the visit of President George Washington to Salem in 1791 while on his tour of southern states did much to help that reputation.[34] Washington was most impressed with the cleanliness and order of the community as well as the unexpected musical abilities of these people of the backcountry. He inspected with approval the engineering of Salem's water system which piped spring water up and down several hills to empty in the community square. This was accomplished with wooden pipes through which large holes were bored for downhill flow and small holes for uphill flow. Schober himself played a distinct role in the growth of Salem's reputation. After 1789 he was a regular visitor at sessions of the North Carolina Assembly, usually going "on his own business."[35] There he doubtless had no difficulty making friends with prominent North Carolinians— relationships which well served both Schober and Salem over the next

---

[32]Salem Diary, 1 July 1792, Fries and others, *Records of Moravians,* 5:2362.

[33]Congregation Council, 20 July 1792, Moravian Archives; Board of Overseers, 24 September 1792, Fries and others, *Records of Moravians,* 6:2481.

[34]Salem Diary, 1 June 1791, Fries and others, *Records of Moravians,* 5:2324-5.

[35]Salem Diary, 7 December 1792, Fries and others, *Records of Moravians,* 6:2474.

few years. Before pursuing these developments, a review of Schober's business dealings will reveal his progress toward his goal of financial self-sufficiency.

Reflection upon the early business career of Schober reveals that he exemplified on a small scale a particular group of men in American business history. He started with almost no financial capital; yet within a very few years and despite Moravian regulations aiming at financial egalitarianism and opposing individual accumulation, Schober became wealthy measured by standards of his own community. To be sure, he continued to work for his livelihood for many years; but after 1795 increasing amounts of Schober's time would be given to non-commercial pursuits.

To say that Schober was an exceptional individual in his business career requires some explanation. Despite several rags-to-riches careers in American business history, studies have shown that most successful businessmen came from substantial business or professional backgrounds and therefore had distinct initial advantages. Most merchants and planters in colonial America were born into the upper class. That pattern was equally pervasive from the mid-nineteenth century forward. The exception to this pattern in business history occurred from 1780 to about 1820 when "the number of businessmen coming from humble origins increased markedly."[36] So Schober put forth his great effort at a time propitious for success. Moreover, his choice of a field by which to reach financial independence was especially discerning. According to one scholar, the vocation of general storekeeper in this period was the best route to success. This, he wrote, was a position of great influence necessary in the rise of towns and villages. The storekeeper became a middleman for the predominantly agrarian society, bartering merchandise for farm crops and participating in the growth of a region. Storekeeping offered subsidiary opportunities for profit in sawmills or gristmills. In a period before banks, the storekeeper functioned as a bank, extending credit and profiting from several sides of a single transaction. The merchant's connections often gave him knowledge of land speculation possibilities or participation in maritime ventures. "Storekeepers constituted the central

---

[36]Elisha P. Douglass, *The Coming of Age of American Business* (Chapel Hill: University of North Carolina Press, 1971), p. 10.

group in the development of interior villages and towns in the ante-bellum period."[37]

Schober was not *the* Salem storekeeper, but studies of his activities reveal that he attempted to operate in that dimension. The wealthiest and probably most respected citizen in Salem, apart from church officials, was Traugott Bagge, who operated the store for the community on a monopolistic basis. Yet Schober managed to wedge himself into this business, much to the displeasure of community governance. Both the tinsmithy and the paper mill gave opportunity for barter operations necessitating a flow of attractive merchandise through Schober into the community; moreover, both operations afforded possibilities of multiple profits in storekeeper fashion. A brief sampling of Schober's business journals for the early 1790s revealed the variety of his operations. In October 1791 he sold to Daniel Christman one ream of paper, twelve papers of pins, ten pair of buckles, four pairs of knee buckles, one dozen knives, and six spelling books. For labor, Schober paid a man with one quart whiskey, a half-dozen spoons, and four needles. In February 1792 Schober bought rags with needles, English books, buckles, lace pins, and knives. Other items mentioned in the journal for 1792 were pills and drops for medical uses, wire, sausage, grain, water, pots, cups, all kinds of paper, nails, shoes, thread, thimbles, indigo cloth, tobacco, butter, and two copies of *Robinson Crusoe*.[38] He was indeed a merchant.

Thus Schober made his mark in the business world. On a national or regional scale, he was an unknown, but in Moravian Salem he exemplified aggressive economic individualism. It may be that the restrictive economic environment of Salem magnified Schober's success unduly, and it could be argued that this environment created the chance for his success by holding back more reticent persons. But the predominant evidence seems to reveal Schober as an aggressive and perceptive businessman who consistently tried new ideas and new means and who persistently sought to modify institutions in the face of opposition not simply for profit, but to satisfy an inner drive to exercise his inherent talents.

---

[37]Lewis E. Atherton, *The Southern Country Store* (Baton Rouge: The Louisiana State University Press, 1949), p. 193.

[38]"Journal wherein all Transactions concerning my Paper Mill are justly recorded and serves also as a Journal for my other businesses for 1790" [to 1795] Schober Papers, Old Salem Inc. Archives.

The Gottlieb Schober House built in 1785
(artist's conception by Stewart Archibald)

CHAPTER **5**

Practicing Law
and Speculating
in Land

WHILE THE LIFE of an independent businessman appealed to Gottlieb Schober in many ways, from his early years he viewed this pursuit as a means rather than an end. Or so it appeared to him at least in retrospect. When writing an autobiographical summary in 1815 he declared:

> After we were having somewhat better times and were free of debts my wish to serve the Lord in some way was roused again. In a spiritual way it was not possible and I finally believed when I was involved in a small law suit that I could serve my people perhaps in external matters. I studied law, acted some years as advocate and helped with the lawsuits of the brothers in their difficult land troubles in the belief that it was being done for the Lord—not for man.[1]

Had Schober been granted more freedom in business affairs, the result might have been different. As a businessman, he was certainly prospering even under adverse circumstances. He was becoming aware of new opportunities as the North Carolina backcountry slowly developed. He knew that with modest capital, the insightful and energetic person could make for himself a very comfortable if not abundant life and leave for each of his children a handsome legacy. In this effort, Schober was

---

[1]Memoir of Gottlieb Schober, Moravian Archives.

successful, and many people knew it. In 1791 it was suggested that several citizens like Brother Schober and Transou, "who have good incomes from their professions" might contribute more to the support of the night-watchman.[2] Nevertheless, this goal which motivated so many of his period seemed not to satisfy the enterprising young man. Beyond his own statement, there is little to suggest why he was attracted to the study of law. Perhaps his contact with the Assemblymen, most of whom were lawyers, convinced him that the practice of law would open great opportunities for a young man who had become a leader in his community and who now aspired to the same on the state or national level. Perhaps Schober saw in the law an acceptable way to expand his business affairs without the harness imposed by community authorities. The profession did in fact open new avenues into which Schober in later years was quick to step. Perhaps he could supplement the income of a tinsmith through the increasing involvement of individual Moravians in external legal affairs. Or perhaps in fact he genuinely wished to serve the church in its legal problems. Whatever the reasons, Schober's interest was first captured by his involvement in several local lawsuits, one of which he mentioned in his autobiography. It was probably the matter of the Widow Aust.

Gottfried Aust, the prominent potter in the early Salem community, died on 17 November 1788. Schober and Johannes Mücke were named executors of the estate according to the will of the deceased. That will assigned the estate to the widow, Mary Aust, except for a clause providing transportation to America plus 200 pounds for Gottfried's niece still living in Europe. Should she choose not to come, she was to receive 100 Spanish dollars, and the remainder was to go to the widow. Three years after Aust's death, the matter was still unsettled and, at the request of the widow, the Overseers investigated. Schober testified to the difficulty in converting all the bonds and notes to cash and clearing all debts. Sister Aust seemed satisfied with the accounting at first but soon raised new questions. Despite efforts of the Overseers to mediate a settlement,[3] she insisted on taking the matter to court. Her petition in June 1792, to the Stokes County court argued that while the estate inventory showed a value of £1,457.17.6, she had not received any part of the legacy. The

---

[2]QBoard of Overseers, 22 March 1791, Moravian Archives.

[3]Board of Overseers, 10 January, 29 May 1792, Moravian Archives.

petition requested the court to examine Schober on this and several other matters relative to the estate.[4] Salem Overseers viewed her decision as a serious breach of congregational regulations; the Brethren believed the Biblical injunction that Christians should settle their differences without recourse to civil courts if possible. In July Widow Aust was advised that pursuit of the matter in court would jeopardize her continuation in the community. While this threat may appear excessive, a close reading of the record confirms that a more serious breakdown in personal relationships was just beneath the surface. Both Widow Aust and Gottlieb Schober were strong-willed and articulate persons; without doubt charges and countercharges were heatedly exchanged, and Moravians wished to avoid the precedent of Brethren using courts to solve internal personal problems. To assume that the Overseers were siding with Schober and against Sr. Aust would be a mistake; their censure resulted from the action of the widow's taking the matter outside the community. At first she promised to halt her civil action, but later decided to leave the community. The records do not clearly establish whether she was excluded from the Moravian congregation entirely or simply asked to leave Salem for one of the country congregations such as Bethania where community regulations were less demanding. It was only stated: "Concerning her whole way of life, we thought it better if she would live outside the community."[5]

While this decision concluded the matter for Salem Moravians, Schober was still involved. The county court appointed arbitrators who reviewed Schober's payments to the widow: in February, May, and October 1791, and September and November 1792, Schober paid a total of 1,584 pounds. The point of contention was the amount of interest Schober owed the estate for money collected during the period 1789-1792. It would appear that Schober had not kept estate accounts separated from his own assets and business dealings—a practice common in the period when the medium of exchange included barter and depreciated currency as well as hard money. The suit dragged on for another year until the court directed a final payment of seventy-one pounds be made by Schober to Sr. Aust. It was a compromise which favored neither side. While Schober was disappointed with the decision—as was also Widow

---

[4]Petition of Mary Aust to State of North Carolina, Stokes County, June term 1792. Schober papers, Old Salem Inc. Archives.

[5]Board of Overseers, 2, 9 October 1792, Moravian Archives.

Aust[6]—the experience proved very beneficial for the future. Schober had his first taste of law and the civil courts and evidently saw new possibilities for his own career.

It is not known exactly when Gottlieb began his studies, but established attorneys were frequent visitors in Salem. By 1792 Moravians were already involved in an important lawsuit which was to drag on for many years. As the Brethren's attorney, Colonel William R. Davie spent time in Salem in that year[7] and public discussion of the case could have excited Schober's interest in the study of law, especially since he was already unpleasantly involved in the Aust case. Since Salem was only a few miles from the local seat of justice, Germanton, Schober likely knew several lawyers of the area including George Hauser who had represented Widow Aust. Any of these could have directed Schober to the kinds of reading and study necessary to pass the bar examination and to practice on a local level. Schober himself provided only one glimpse of his study. Writing to a friend, he prefaced his letter with this comment:

> I am this evening tired of reading the antiquated processes of real Actions, especially the Assise of novel disseisin, [Assise of] mort d'ancestor, writ of entry in the per, & per cui & c.[8]

Schober was studying real estate law; in particular he was dealing with the recovery of lands where a tenant has been wrongfully dispossessed. To him, at least this part of his study seemed tedious. He concluded this letter in a humorous vein, asking his reader to remember "the maxim of Law, Mala Grammatica non vitiat chartam."[9] But Schober's study had a very practical and serious application. He was by 1793 involved in another lawsuit even more serious than the Aust case. Schober acted as his own attorney, soon learning that his own advice could be very expensive. It involved a piece of land and an angry woman.

---

[6]Despite the arbitration, Widow Aust two years later reopened the case insisting that she now had proof that Schober was a "cheater." The Overseers counseled Schober to settle with her outside court according to what was right. Schober insisted that he did not owe her more interest. There is no evidence of further litigation so it must be assumed that the matter was settled. Board of Overseers, 23 February, 3 March 1795, Moravian Archives.

[7]Salem Diary, 15 August 1792, Fries and others, *Records of Moravians*, 5:2363-64.

[8]Gottlieb Schober to Evan Alexander, 20 January 1793, Schober Papers, Old Salem Inc. Archives.

[9]Translation: Bad grammar does not vitiate a deed.

On 15 January 1793, five days prior to the letter cited immediately above, Schober purchased from Peter Volz a house and seven acres of land for forty pounds. Two years earlier Volz had bargained the house to its occupant, Catherine Hauser, only to discover that she could not legally hold title alone.[10] She continued to live in the house but paid no purchase money or rent. In October 1792, according to Volz, Mrs. Hauser threatened to kill his wife, so in January 1793 Volz sold the house to Schober and gave Mrs. Hauser sixty days to vacate. She refused. Then, in Schober's words

> I offered her any Terms if she would move, but no. I and Six other men went & uncovered the stable & plucked up fences knowing that I could do with my property as I saw cause.[11]

Mrs. Hauser indicted all seven men for trespassing and destruction of property. Charges began to fly in all directions. Volz believed that Mrs. Hauser and her daughters "kept a bawdy house upon the Land," had threatened his wife, and now resisted his possession and sale of his rightful property.[12] Salem Moravians became concerned and declared:

> We wish that the affair in which Brother Schober is connected with the widow Hauser at the South Fork would be quieted down and not brought before the court because we suspect that unpleasant things would be revealed on both sides which would harm the good reputation of the Brethren.[13]

Nevertheless, Schober prepared for the case. He developed each of the main points in writing, citing laws and precedents in his documentation. At the trial, Schober's motion for dismissal was denied by the presiding Jusitice of the Peace, and the court refused to hear his witnesses to substantiate purchase of the property. The prosecution produced six witnesses and won the case. The court awarded Mrs. Hauser £17.10 on 28 November 1793 and assessed the defendants the cost of court for seven indictments. Schober was furious. "Is all this not an unheard of &

---

[10]Hers was a condition known as *Feme covert* or married woman. Usually a husband, brother, son, or other male would receive the deed with a *feme covert* to enable her to hold property.

[11]Document entitled "Statement of the Law" in Schober Papers, Old Salem Inc. Archives.

[12]Ibid.

[13]Board of Overseers, 28 May 1793, Moravian Archives.

accumulating oppression in a Republic? but where is the remedy?"[14] He considered an appeal, but "I was advised that, if the Indictments are quashed, or I am found not guilty above yet I must pay cost [of court] below & above."[15] Even though he believed that he could impeach the action of the court at a higher level, the financial risk was far greater than the potential reward. So he paid the cost of court for himself and each of his six friends, plus the fine awarded to widow Hauser. It was expensive tuition, more in pride than in money, but Schober filed away his carefully prepared and documented "Statement of the Law" and "Reasons in Arrest in Judgment" with the final comment: "I can prove the unjust proceedings of the County Court as stated above."

Usually legal notations are of interest only to lawyers. But an examination of Schober's preparation for this case can reveal the progress of his legal study as well as something of the intellectual capability of the man. Schober saw three flaws in the court's decision:

> 1. That the Court has no jurisdiction of the offense as charged in the Bill of Indictment. . . .
> 2. That there is no actual force laid in the Indictment charging Breach of the Peace. . . .
> 3. That the Indictment charges the offense committed against the freehold of the prosecutrix, who is a feme Covert.[16]

A review of the detail developed by Schober to challenge jurisdiction showed the degree of his familiarity with the law.

> Jurisdiction is only given to C. Courts to
>   Action of Trespass Iredll page 547
> where quarter sessions have not original
>   Jurisdiction even consent of parties
>   dont give it IV Com Dig 155 Sal 202
> The State empowers Justices & they have their
>   Authority from Commission or Statutes
>   Wood. Inst 79
> Authority of Justices must be exactly pursued
>   2 Sal. 475

---

[14]Document entitled "Statement of Indictments," Schober Papers, Old Salem Inc. Archives.

[15]Document entitled "Statement of the Law," Schober Papers, Old Salem Inc. Archives.

[16]Document entitled "Reasons for Arrest of Judgement," Schober Papers, Old Salem Inc. Archives.

Justices have no authority but by express
  Words IV Com Dig 57
to usurp Jurisdiction & by colour thereof,
  imprision is punishable according to
  bill of Rights W. Inst 464
If the Court has no jurisdiction & gives
  Judgment it is not only erroneous but
  void Bull N. P. 66
where the Subject Matter is not within the
  Jurisdiction anything done is absolutely
  void & the officer executing it is a
  Trespasser B.N.P. 83, II E.N.P. 73
The Judgment must not be narrower or broader
  than the Court or Barr Co. Litt.
  p. 303ta[17]

Schober's second and third contentions were similarly outlined and documented. Whether Schober's argument was valid—evidently the court thought not—is secondary here; the important point is that Schober was in fact a serious and diligent student.

Matters of far more significance awaited the conclusion of Schober's early legal tangles and his study of the law. Frederic W. Marshall, Salem's administrator, wrote on 21 July 1794, that "For some years Br. Schober has been studying law, and has been admitted to the bar by the Court." Marshall further stated that Schober "has had charge of the law business [of the town] for a year and a day"[18] which would indicate that he assumed direction of Salem's legal affairs on 20 July 1793. His admission to the bar had already occurred by that time.

The matter to which Marshall referred was known as the "Mulberry Fields" suit and was indeed difficult litigation for an inexperienced attorney. After the Moravians purchased the Wachovia tract from Lord Granville, they discovered that some of the land was of poorer quality than anticipated. For compensation, the Englishman deeded to the Brethren two additional tracts in western North Carolina which had been surveyed in the original Moravian exploration for suitable land. Title was held by a Moravian leader, Henry Cossart, in trust for the *Unitas Fratrum*, just as James Hutton held title to Wachovia. In 1772 the Moravians decided to sell these 8,773 acres, and power of attorney was sent to

---

[17]Ibid.

[18]Frederic W. Marshall to Unity Vorsteher Collegium, Salem, 21 July 1794, Fries and others, *Records of Moravians*, 6:2514.

Frederic W. Marshall. From 1774 to 1779 Marshall was in Europe; he had only planned to attend the General Synod but was prevented from returning by the Revolutionary War. In 1778 Bishop John Michael Graff, acting with Marshall's power of attorney in hand, sold the Mulberry Fields tracts to Hugh Montgomery for $6,250, of which $2,500 was paid in cash and a mortgage given for the remainder. The same year in Europe, Marshall, a naturalized citizen, received deeds to all the North Carolina Moravian lands. But legality of the Moravian title came into question because of the North Carolina Confiscation Act of November 1777, which declared vacant all lands belonging to a person who was absent from the country on 4 July 1776 and still absent at the time of the act, unless he appeared at the 1778 Assembly session to substantiate his citizenship. In 1782 Moravians successfully petitioned the North Carolina Assembly to confirm title to Wachovia, but questions concerning whether the power of attorney from Cossart to Marshall to Graff was valid led to a slightly different treatment of the Mulberry Fields tracts. It was clear, however, that the Assembly intended to validate the Moravian claim, and that Hugh Montgomery held a clear title. In the ensuing years squatters had settled on the Wilkes County land, forcing Montgomery to sue to remove them. Moravians were unaware of this action until after the Superior Court in Morgan District in 1789 had refused to honor Montgomery's title. Moravians then felt honor bound to defend the title. Again the North Carolina Assembly was petitioned, and the bill seemed headed for passage in 1791 until it was blocked by parliamentary maneuvers by the president of the Senate, General William Lenoir. Since Brethren could now only resort to the courts to eject the tenants-in-possession, in 1793 they initiated *Frederick William Marshall vs John Lovelass and others*. Lenoir appeared for the defendants, claiming Cossart was an alien, the lands had escheated to the State at the Revolution, and state grants given to himself and others were valid. Moravians cited the parallel development of the Wachovia title with its confirmation by the Assembly and claimed that both Wachovia and the Mulberry Fields were free of encumbrance.[19]

---

[19]A more complete treatment of the case can be found in Fries and others, *Records of Moravians*, 3:1413-19, and in Adelaide L. Fries, *Forsyth County* (Winston: Stewarts Printing House, 1898), pp. 33-46. Records of the suit are included in Walter Clark, ed., 16 volumes, *The State Records of North Carolina* (Winston, Goldsboro, and Raleigh: State of North Carolina), 14:123-24, 466.

It was at this juncture that Gottlieb Schober rendered significant legal service to his community. Marshall, of course, did not leave litigation so complex and so important to an inexperienced attorney. William R. Davie continued on the case, but the Moravians found that an outsider easily became confused in trying to explain the complexities of Moravian property holding.[20] Schober's task was to gather evidence for the hearing, provide liaison between Marshall and Davie, and, when necessary, explain officially the nature of the community. In early 1794 he spent considerable time in Burke County taking depositions and interviewing those who were involved in the case. Whether Schober actually argued the case before the court in these early years of his career is doubtful; in any event, settlement of the case was delayed year after year. In 1795 the Moravians decided on a new maneuver. If the lands had escheated to the state, the title or benefits of sale now belonged to the University of North Carolina to which the Assembly had recently given all escheated land as a part of its endowment. Therefore, if Moravians could persuade the Trustees to renounce all claims, the case in court would become unnecessary. Gottlieb Schober was selected as the man to address the University Trustees—in itself a testimony to the confidence of community officials in Schober's abilities and to his familiarity with state politics and leaders. Gottlieb was well received by the Board in Chapel Hill and must have argued persuasively because the Trustees voted to relinquish all claims as beneficiaries to the land, even over the opposition of one of the Trustees, William Lenoir. All seemed settled until Schober was gone, when Lenoir persuaded the Trustees to reconsider the matter and to rescind their decision. Then it was back to the courts; but many years would pass before a final decision was rendered by the high court of North Carolina. At various times during this period, Schober was involved in representing Moravian interests in the case,[21] but detailing these activities belongs more to the history of the case than to a study of Schober himself. Schober's role on the case in the early 1800s will be treated in its proper place.

Fortunately for Schober's sanity, the Mulberry Fields case did not encompass all of his legal work for Salem. As the official community

---

[20]Frederic W. Marshall to the Unity Vorsteher Collegium, Salem, 21 July 1794, Fries and others, *Records of Moravians*, 6:2514.

[21]Salem Diary, 15 March 1798, Fries and others, *Records of Moravians*, 6:2604.

attorney, he was asked in 1794 to revise the lease by which new citizens would be able to hold local property. Gottlieb already had conflicted with the Overseers on the paper mill lease, but evidently there was no lingering antagonism on either side. After much work, Schober presented a new format to the Overseers which was acceptable, and plans were set for all leases to be revised.[22] The new lease provided for an upward valuation of property values. Since this was an internal matter not affecting taxation, several people objected that their houses were not valued high enough. If forced to leave Salem, the value stated in the lease would be the maximum that could be demanded. Schober's house, for example, was first reappraised at 200 pounds, then finally set at 250 pounds. Traugott Bagge's was identical. Only one house in town was set higher than Schober's, and most were valued between 100 and 150.[23]

Another local legal problem involved estate settlements. The possibility of unexpected death made most Brethren aware of the need of a will, but experience had shown that unusual formats were necessary for conditions peculiar to Salem. Many persons included minute details concerning the education and apprenticeship of children. As conditions changed, these provisions were difficult to fulfill, jeopardizing the validity of the entire document.[24] Since individuals in Salem owned houses, but leased the land on which they stood, the wills had to be consistent with the lease. Where individuals operated a community enterprise such as the store or tavern, personal assets had to be carefully separated. Such problems led community officials to ask Schober for sample wills to aid the citizens with these particular problems.[25] In 1796 Schober and Bagge developed documents which were approved by the Overseers and recommended to the Brethren. There are indications that Schober spent some time counseling heads of families in this regard. Although fees for these services were never mentioned, undoubtedly they contributed in a small way to Schober's growing prosperity.

At various times during this period, Schober helped the town in minor legal matters. In 1794 officials feared that the Brethren's exemption from military service would be lost. Schober wrote letters "to some of

---

[22]Board of Overseers, 18, 25 November 1794, Moravian Archives.

[23]Board of Overseers, 17 February, 2 March 1795, Moravian Archives.

[24]Board of Overseers, 31 May 1796, Moravian Archives.

[25]Board of Overseers, 24 May, 5 July, 11 October 1796, Moravian Archives.

our good friends in the assembly,"[26] in particular a Mr. Parsons, asking that the exemption be maintained while assuring the Assembly that Moravians would continue "to pay our part in money to the tasks of the country."[27] The exemption was continued. Community officials also petitioned the governor to make Schober a notary public to serve the community.[28] He was asked to aid in the collection of debts and to mediate in minor legal quarrels between Brethren.[29] In short, Gottlieb's legal service as a Salem resident became increasingly significant in the 1790s, both to the management of the community and to local citizens.

Along with these activities, Schober continued to rise in prominence as a town leader. He served on the Board of Overseers beginning in 1790 and was assigned tasks typical of all members of that body. He counseled Peter Yarrell and George Ebert about their debts and financial problems. He was directed to warn Heinrich Blum about possible exclusion because of a drinking problem. He counseled Charles Bagge who was disappointed at not getting the position of storekeeper when his father, Traugott Bagge, died. Schober was given continuing responsibility to collect funds to care for the increasing number of beggars who went from door to door asking for money.[30] He also collected fees for the local schools from parents who were sometimes a little slow in paying. While relations between Schober and church officials were usually congenial during this time, there was occasional friction. One such instance can be inferred from the following board discussion:

> Since Brother Schober is often absent from the Collegium, we came to talk about the necessity with which all members of the Collegium should regard their meetings and never be absent without serious reason. Otherwise, we cannot reach the purpose of this Collegium. It was also said that all the resolutions of the Collegium should be supported by all of its members.[31]

---

[26]Board of Overseers, 8 July 1794, Moravian Archives.

[27]Board of Overseers, 1 July 1794, Moravian Archives.

[28]Board of Overseers, 17 February 1795, Fries and others, *Records of Moravians*, 6:2537.

[29]Board of Overseers, 19 July 1796, Fries and others *Records of Moravians*, 6:2570; Board of Overseers, 19 December 1797, Moravian Archives.

[30]Congregation Council, 8 August 1792, Fries and others, *Records of Moravians*, 6:2480-81; Board of Overseers, 16 July, 15 October 1793, Moravian Archives.

[31]Board of Overseers, 14 April 1795, Moravian Archives.

Most disagreements of the period seem to have centered around Schober's speculation in land—an activity which consumed a great deal of his time in the 1790s.

During the years following the Revolution, speculation in undeveloped lands was a favored activity for Americans with excess money or good credit who wished to multiply their material prosperity rapidly. Many prominent planters were barely able to support their families by agricultural means, but made and lost great fortunes by dealing in undeveloped territory on the western frontier. George Washington, for example, even though political responsibilities limited his speculative participation, owned 71,000 acres of western lands at his death.[32] Richard Henderson of North Carolina owned vast tracts in what became Kentucky. For early aristocrats, land speculation was not gambling, but was the proper pursuit of the gentleman of English heritage. Timothy Pickering purchased Pennsylvania land in 1785 for one shilling per acre and valued the worst of it at two dollars per acre in 1796.[33] Even if extensive landholding was a badge of wealth and nobility, its purpose was usually a quick profit. Few speculators of this period intended to enhance land values by development or improvement. They depended on a growing population and America's material prosperity to add value to their holdings. Sometimes the lands were sold to European individuals or companies who in turn would distribute to prospective settlers. Profits could be high, but after 1795 laws limiting the size of grants along with higher taxes discouraged the larger speculators. If money was made on one deal, it was usually reinvested and many times lost on the next.

Although Gottlieb Schober could not begin to compare in wealth with a Washington, Henderson, or Pickering, it was certainly an evidence of general prosperity that he began to participate in these gambles in the 1790s. Moravian officials deplored the activity and were particularly concerned about Schober. In connection with the Board discussion quoted immediately above, the Overseers viewed Schober's external affairs as "rather expansive and confusing" and asserted that "all this speculation the cause of which is the greediness to become rich does not fit for

---

[32]A. M. Sakolski, *The Great American Land Bubble* (New York: Harper and Bros., 1932), p. 11.

[33]Octavius Pickering and Charles W. Upham, *The Life of Timothy Pickering* (Boston: Little, Brown and Company, 1867-73), 3:296.

brothers in this community at all."[34] It is quite possible that Schober's involvement with the Mulberry Fields suit brought to his attention the opportunities in state land grants. In 1793 Schober received four tracts totaling 1,249 acres and purchased another 100.[35] The next year he entered tracts of 600, 195, and 640 acres in addition to purchasing of a 200 acre claim filed by another individual. In January 1795 Schober paid 600 pounds entrance money and £33.12 processing fee on 40,000 acres, location unknown, but likely in Surry county.[36] Another 500 acres in Surry county was granted later that year. Schober usually had these tracts accurately surveyed at his own expense and then awaited the opportunity for resale at a profit. The activity did require investment money and was very risky, but the reward was also handsome. Much of the land was quickly resold through brokers in northern cities. In 1795, ten tracts containing 16,500 acres were sold to Timothy Pickering for $1,750. Three others went to Charles Cist of Philadelphia for £145.19, and another to William Gerhard of the same city for 15. Still another tract of 236 acres was sold to Joseph Billing for 150 pounds.[37] In 1797 Schober registered four grants totaling 770 acres and in 1800 two more of 100 acres each. His list of taxable real estate in North Carolina for 1802 showed 3,379 acres in Stokes County in twenty tracts, 35,379 acres in Surry county, and 100 in Cumberland county. In 1814 he still held 3,200 acres; in 1824, 2,860; and in 1827, 3,210 acres.[38]

Sometimes Schober profited, sometimes he lost. One land broker writing to William Lenoir concerning similar lands and complaining that Lenoir's price of twenty-five cents per acre was too high, declared

> You [Lenoir] seem to labour under the same Malady Mr. Shouber did, when he had his Land for Sale a couple Years ago—namely that of being afraid I

---

[34]Board of Overseers, 7 April 1795, Moravian Archives.

[35]Land grant, Schober Papers, Old Salem Inc. Archives; Stokes County Deed Book 1:373; 2:50, 60. State Archives of North Carolina, Raleigh, North Carolina. Hereinafter cited as North Carolina Archives.

[36]Receipts, Schober Papers, Old Salem Inc. Archives.

[37]Stokes County Deed Book 2:90, 115-20, 138, 142, 143, 247-50, North Carolina Archives.

[38]Taxable Property of G. Shober in Stokes County owned 1 April 1802; also tax lists for 1814, 1824, and 1827, Schober Papers, Old Salem Inc. Archives.

would make too much profit by it—in consequence he lost about £3000 himself.[39]

Sometimes Schober acted as an agent for other large speculators. In one such case, Gottlieb represented Christian J. Heeter of Philadelphia who was seeking land for a European investor. Schober approached a western North Carolina land company, owned by William Lenoir, Charles Gordon, and Hillair Rousseau, that held grants in Wilkes County for 700,000 acres. Schober visited the land to

> lay off in one or more Tracts such part of the seven hundred thousand acres aforesaid in such manner as he might think best, to include the most firtle [*sic*] land and Conveniently Situated for making Settlements for Farmers and Michanicks [*sic*].[40]

After two tracts of 100,000 acres each were laid off, Heeter was to offer the land to his Amsterdam company at twenty-five cents per acre. Schober would collect an agent's commission only if the sale was made. Negotiations continued on this transaction in 1797, but it would appear from Schober's letters that nothing materialized.[41]

By far the most valuable—potentially at least—of Schober's speculations was his tract of Indian land in Maryland. In 1796 Gottlieb became an equal partner of Valentine Arnett in a 10,000-acre tract in Dorchester County on Maryland's eastern shore which Arnett "bought of the Nantekoke tribe of Indians."[42] But the state had already claimed the land as vacant and sold it to other individuals, making Schober's investment very risky. The affair began with Schober acting as Arnett's attorney for the recovery and sale of the tract at a commission of fifty percent of the proceeds. A year later Arnett sold his entire interest to Schober who in turn earnestly set about to establish the validity of the claim. Through a minister friend who also had some legal connections, John Sergeant, Gottlieb sought to locate members of the Indian tribe who would testify to the land sale. Several had moved to New York, "near Niagara" and

---

[39]Christian Jacob Heeter to William Lenoir, Lancaster, 2 January 1797. Lenoir Family Papers, N426, Southern Historical Collection, University of North Carolina Library, Chapel Hill, North Carolina. Hereinafter cited as Southern Historical Collection.

[40]William Lenoir to Christian Jacob Heeter, Lancaster Town, Pennsylvania; 25 November 1796. Lenoir Family Papers N426, Southern Historical Collection.

[41]Gottlieb Schober to Mess'rs Hillair Rousseau and Co., Salem, 26 August 1796. Lenoir Family Papers N426, Southern Historical Collection.

[42]Document in Schober Papers, Old Salem Inc. Archives.

securing their legal testimony would be expensive. Another Delaware Indian, by then living in Massachusetts, "frequently went to Meriland [*sic*] and is well acquainted with all his people, and can give every testimony you wish."[43] Sergeant also mentioned a "Tusharara Indian" who might help in the case. Schober approved the gathering of depositions from these Indian sources at considerable expense and then retained a flamboyant young Maryland attorney, Patrick H. O'Reilly, to pursue the matter in the courts. How Schober came to employ O'Reilly is unknown. The young man was a member of the Maryland assembly and was eager to take the case. At the outset he wrote

> I am sorry to find you indulging in any apprehensions of my not begin able to attend your business. . . . If I were as full of business as I could wish to be I still could find time to attend to you especially as I feel myself particularly interested in preventing a distant gentleman who kindly honored me with his confidence (though a stranger) from regretting it. . . . At the end of the suit you will say that though I am a man of paultry talents, yet I am faithful, zealous and industrious, and whatever abilities I may possess were always exerted for the benefit of those who confide in me.[44]

In 1801 O'Reilly wrote that defendants did not appear at the preliminary hearing to establish their claim.[45] Since Schober's case depended in part on the testimony of several elderly people, O'Reilly began to take legally valid depositions in case they died before the suit was heard. In December 1801 the defendants asked for an out-of-court compromise, but O'Reilly judged that Schober's response was too generous and might convince the defendants that they could win the suit.[46] O'Reilly and Schober built their case around the fact that the Indians were actual occupants of the land with a valid title "elder and paramount to that of the English settlers."[47] Moreover, the Maryland assembly of 1698 and 1704 had recognized Indian rights, establishing their possession of the identical tract which

---

[43]John Sergeant to G. Shober, New Stockbridge, 10 March 1800, Schober Papers, Old Salem Inc. Archives.

[44]P. H. O'Reilly to Gottlieb Shober, Annapolis, 30 April 1801, Schober Papers, Old Salem Inc. Archives.

[45]P. H. O'Reilly to Gottlieb Shober, Annapolis, 19 November 1801, Schober Papers, Old Salem Inc. Archives.

[46]P. H. O'Reilly to Gottlieb Shober, Annapolis, 10 December 1801; P. H. O'Reilly to Gottlieb Shober, Annapolis, 29 January 1802, Schober Papers, Old Salem Inc. Archives.

[47]P. H. O'Reilly to Gottlieb Shober, Annapolis, 12 January 1802, Schober Papers, Old Salem Inc. Archives.

Schober now owned. The best witness uncovered was an Indian named Welch, although there was some question of the acceptability of his testimony in Maryland courts.[48] Still, O'Reilly was confident of the outcome and estimated the worth of the tract in excess of $200,000. The case was continued in 1803 as defendants retained counsel to prepare their case. It was scheduled for the 1804 term and Schober anxiously awaited news. Finally he heard: case dismissed because Schober had not provided security to cover the cost of court should he lose.[49] In a letter to Daniel Bussard, a friend and District of Columbia attorney who had declined to take the suit initially because of age and distance from Annapolis, Schober declared that the fault was O'Reilly's because "I remitted to O'Reilly $250 which he was to deposit in a persons hand to enable him to be my Security."[50] But he had failed to accomplish this task.[51] Schober was livid with anger; he was afraid to dismiss O'Reilly lest "he may betray the Secrets of my cause." Moreover, Gottlieb had paid over $500 in security money, expense reimbursements, and fees. He complained that he had already spent $2,500 on the suit, and it all seemed for nothing. Schober requested Bussard's help in locating another agent, promising as a fee one-eighth of the final recovery. O'Reilly was to be kept on the case at a similar fee, but inactive in the actual pursuance of the matter. Schober believed that his case was valid, and that early reinstatement would bring success. On hearing of Schober's displeasure, O'Reilly immediately wrote a bitter letter, declaring that the suit dismissal was not his fault and accusing Schober of misrepresenting the truth. "I do not deem it quite equitable that the *whole burden* of the miscarriage should fall upon me, as the unfavorable issue of the business was not fairly

---

[48]Schober expressed concern regarding a 1717 Maryland law which prohibited the testimony of Indians and blacks in any matter involving a Christian white person. O'Reilly assured Schober that this law did not apply to the case, since the matter in question pre-dated the testimony law. As a precaution, however, O'Reilly sponsored a bill in the 1802 Maryland assembly to allow Indian testimony. The bill was killed, but O'Reilly still believed that the suit was not hampered. P. H. O'Reilly to Gottlieb Shober, Annapolis, 30 January 1801; Annapolis, 12 January 1802, Schober Papers, Old Salem Inc. Archives.

[49]G. Shober to Daniel Bussard, Salem, 5 July 1805, Schober Papers, Old Salem Inc. Archives.

[50]G. Shober to Daniel Bussard, Salem, 5 July 1805, Schober Papers, Old Salem Inc. Archives.

[51]Daniel Bussard to Gottlieb Schober, George Town (date torn away but likely early 1805) Schober Papers, Old Salem Inc. Archives.

attributable to me."[52] He claimed that a proposal made to Gottlieb's son, Nathaniel, who traveled to Maryland to attend to the case, had been unduly rejected. Since now off the case,

> I deem it unequal that the expenses incurred by me in the course of my agency shall fall entirely on me, neither can it be reasonably expected that my immense trouble and fatigue should go uncompensated.[53]

He asked for a final accounting from Schober, but instead of demanding final compensation, said,

> as I cannot turn my hearts blood into dollars, and cannot collect money from those who owe me, so I cannot promise you the cash instantly, but will pledge myself to remit it or pay it to your order as soon as so much comes to my hand and must urge you not to press me unreasonably.[54]

O'Reilly insisted that all the money Schober had sent had been used on the case, but he never referred to the security guarantee which Schober alleged he was to arrange. He concluded with a veiled threat similar to what Schober had feared, demanding to be released from futher service "leaving me at perfect liberty to have whatever other Agency in the business the exigencies of other parties may require and my own inclination prompt."[55] It would seem that Schober had been ill-served by a young lawyer who was in personal financial straits. Schober's next agent in the matter, a Mr. Evans, wrote,

> I almost believe O'Reilly never attempted to go to N. York, and never was taken ill of the Yellow fever, where he said he was, and in short never concerned himself about the Suit, but only made out of you what money he could.[56]

Still confident of success, Schober himself traveled to Georgetown to confer with Brussard and Evans in October 1805. While there, a letter arrived from home revealing the family's outlook on the case. Johanna, Schober's nineteen-year-old daughter, did not want Gottlieb

---

[52]P. H. O'Reilly to Gottlieb Shober, Herring Bay, 5 November 1805, Schober Papers, Old Salem Inc. Archives.

[53]Ibid.

[54]Ibid.

[55]Ibid.

[56]Quoted in Nathaniel Shober to Gottlieb Shober, Salem, 18 October 1805, Schober Papers, Old Salem Inc. Archives.

to spend your Estate in prosecution of the Maryland business, and she joins
with us all to beg you not to loose any dinners on that Account, as we trust we
shall still be able to live, if even that should be eventually lost.[57]

The trip came to nothing. Although no reinstatement occurred, Schober
did not give up. In 1816 his son Emmanuel traveled to Baltimore on
another matter and checked on the status of the suit. Until his death,
Schober continued to assert the validity of his claim. He bequeathed to
Emmanuel "any thing . . . obtained, procured and recovered on my
purchase of Land in Maryland from the Nantekeke Indians as recorded in
Dorchester County there."[58]

The account of land speculation, especially the Indian land, has carried
Schober's life across the turn of the century. When the Moravian leaders
criticized Gottlieb's financial dealings in 1795, they could not have envisioned the difficulties that land speculation would ultimately cause him.
But they were perceptive enough to realize that activity of this nature was
detrimental to Gottlieb's service to the community. They could see easily
enough that Schober had all the problems he needed even within tiny,
uncomplicated Salem, without inviting others from outside.

[57]Ibid.

[58]Gottlieb Schober, Last Will and Testament, 19 June 1835, Moravian Archives.

The Congregation House in Salem, 1771
(artist's conception by Stewart Archibald)

CHAPTER 6

A Controversial Community Leader

GOTTLIEB SCHOBER WAS never an organized, logical person. His mind and his interests were constantly flitting from one thing to another. Driven by a desire to expend his talents well, he tackled new projects while leaving loose ends on other responsibilities. Yet he had a quick mind driven by tremendous energy. Perhaps all the affairs fit together in Schober's own perspective, but for the observer in 1795—or now for that matter—they seemed hectic.

The paper mill continued to prosper even though it required considerable attention. Schober was sole owner of the property, and Johann Volz was his supervisor and chief operator. Volz and his family occupied a house near the mill which had been purchased by the mill from Volz himself. He rented the house and seemed content until sometime in early 1794. After a disagreement with Schober, Volz determined to leave the mill but wanted to keep the house. Schober resisted, appealing to the Overseers to get Volz out.[1] Volz would not leave until Schober paid him for the house, but Gottlieb refused; he evidently had additional time on the note and maintained that he needed the house to attract a new

---

[1]Board of Overseers, 17 June, 14 October 1794, Moravian Archives.

manager. Even finding a new supervisor caused the owner difficulties; when Schober suggested a Mr. Rothhaas, the Overseers

> thought that it is not advisible that such people who have many connections to the community and yet do not have the right spirit of the Lord should not live so near to the community.[2]

Volz and Schober continued to negotiate. Gottlieb raised the house rent substantially to force Volz either to resume supervision of the mill or vacate the house. Only the objection of the Overseers prevented this tactic, but a stalemate ensued which lasted until 1802.

Schober also maintained his position as Salem's tinsmith. During this period business was consistently good, but Schober's apprentice probably did most of the actual work. William Eldridge labored for several years in this capacity until appointed an instructor in the boys' school in 1794.[3] Schober immediately took another young man, Christian Reich, to learn the trade.[4] Despite some unrest among several apprentices in Salem in 1795, Schober's relation with Reich seemed to have been agreeable. By 1796 the young man decided to establish himself as a householder. Schober was "willing to grant him £70 annually and free lodging as long as he continues the tinsmith shop on the account of Br. Schober."[5] Reich would essentially be a salaried journeyman under the monopoly granted to the master tinsmith. To accomodate the expanded business, Schober needed another house and suggested that of George Ebert. Ebert had at this time lost control of his financial affairs. He was heavily in debt and drinking badly, causing the Overseers to consider a civil suit for debts "so that he might be made willing to sell his house in peace and pay his debts with that and leave the community."[6] Schober offered to buy the property outright or would lease it if the community treasury bought it. The Overseers hesitated to allow any individual to own two houses in Salem; Schober's penchant for speculation gave them further pause. A complex compromise was finally reached. The house would belong to the community treasury, but Schober would provide the original purchase price of

---

[2]Board of Overseers, 17 November 1795, Moravian Archives.

[3]Minutes of Elders' Conference, 12 November 1794, Fries and others, *Records of Moravians*, 6:2511-12.

[4]Board of Overseers, 16 December 1794, Moravian Archives.

[5]Board of Overseers, 25 October 1796, Moravian Archives.

[6]Board of Overseers, 19 July 1796, Moravian Archives.

$500, for which he received a bond from the treasury, and would assume responsibility for repairs and outfitting as a tinsmithy. Schober received interest on his "loan" and then paid an annual rent of ten shillings, eight pence. He maintained total control of the Salem tinsmithing with Reich under him.[7] The arrangement showed the extremes to which the Overseers would go to protect established monopolies while providing ways for younger men to enter the village economy, and, on the other hand, their caution lest a monopoly should propel a master into affluence.

Schober's renovation on the house included painting the frame dwelling with a new kind of paint to "help make the house more fire proof from the outside."[8] The formula came from an Almanac and consisted of three parts unslaked lime, two parts ashes, and one part fine sand, all mixed with linseed oil. Gottlieb's experiment must have looked nice and weathered well, for the new paint was later discussed for the new church in Salem to replace the unsatisfactory paint made from white lead and varnish.[9]

The arrangement between Reich and Schober lasted for three years. In 1800, Gottlieb reported "that the small demand for tinware" required him to request permission "for the work of a coppersmith also."[10] It was soon determined that Reich would become the coppersmith, no longer under Schober's management. Perhaps Reich realized that the demand for tinware would remain limited, and that he would never prosper with Schober taking a portion of all profits. He bought the house in which he was making tin products and soon supplied new copper wares previously unavailable in Salem.[11] The willingness of Schober to allow the journeyman his independence appeared somewhat unusual. Schober probably saw in the separation still another chance to expand. Within three months of the break, Schober submitted plans "to build a new workshop for the tinsmith trade to which a room for the post office will be added."[12] Hardly a wise move if business was bad!

---

[7]Board of Overseers, 25 October, 1, 8, 22 November 1796, Moravian Archives.

[8]Board of Overseers, 28 February 1797, Moravian Archives.

[9]Board of Overseers, 17 April 1798, Fries and others, *Records of Moravians*, 6:2610.

[10]Board of Overseers, 27 May 1800, Fries and others, *Records of Moravians*, 6:2653.

[11]Board of Overseers, 3 November 1801, Moravian Archives.

[12]Board of Overseers, 6 October 1801, Moravian Archives.

The expansion of the tinsmithy was accompanied by growth in other aspects of Gottlieb's business affairs. In 1797 he employed a non-Moravian to work as a bookbinder, adding another product to his articles for sale.[13] At about the same time, the poor financial conditions of Johannes Reuz became a scandal in the community. He drank too much brandy and neglected his household. The Overseers, for the sake of his family, suggested that someone manage his affairs. Schober was given the task. He assumed Reuz's debts of 800 pounds and as security held the deed for his house and a claim on his tools and materials. He purchased raw goods from which Reuz would continue to make hats for Schober to sell in his tinsmith shop. From the proceeds, Reuz's community obligations were paid and his family provided for.[14] Schober received a manager's fee as well as adding still another item to what was rapidly becoming a store. Within a few years, Gottlieb was selling or bartering—in addition to tin, paper, and hat products—lace, beads, shawls, India calico, molasses, bandanas, scarlet flannel, black patent buttons, pins, thread, tapes, thimbles, fish hooks, rings, velvet, cloth bonnets, penknives, Sicily wine, French brandy, and plaster of Paris.[15]

Schober was still Salem's postmaster, although he tried to give it up in 1795 because, he said, "the income is too low."[16] He continued as warden for the poor: arranging for meals and lodging in the tavern, a horse for a destitute traveler, and transportation for a man trying to get to Pennsylvania.[17] He contined to be involved in community musical affairs, regularly taking turns with three others in playing the organ for worship services. In 1794 he supervised arrangements for the purchase of a new organ made in Lititz, Pennsylvania, by David Tanneberger and Johann Bachman and installed in the meeting hall in 1798. The cost was met by a freewill offering to which Schober himself contributed five pounds. The same year this respected musician was asked to teach piano lessons in the boys' school. By 1799 he was supervisor of all music in community

---

[13]Board of Overseers, 27 June 1797, Fries and others, *Records of Moravians*, 6:2591.

[14]Board of Overseers, 20 June, 4, 11 July 1797, 13 February 1798, Moravian Archives.

[15]These articles appeared on invoices from various wholesale merchants to Schober between 1800 and 1803, Schober Papers, Old Salem Inc. Archives.

[16]Board of Overseers, 1 December 1795, 27 January 1796, Moravian Archives.

[17]Board of Overseers, 17 May, 14 June 1796, Moravian Archives, 23 January 1798, Fries and others, *Records of Moravians*, 6:2608.

services and began preparing for a most significant community event.[18]

Since 1797 the Brethren had been constructing a new church on the town square just north of the meeting hall. The consecration was set for 9 November 1800. Over 2,000 members and visitors gathered to the musical welcome of trombones and a choir singing: "This is a day which the Lord hath made; let us rejoice and be glad in it. Let us come before His presence with thanksgiving and rejoice before him with psalms."[19] One especially appropriate hymn of Zinzendorf was chosen by Schober to voice antiphonally the dedication of the people:

First choir
The Saviour's blood and righteousness
Be of this house the glorious dress;
Here be His word to all made known,
His Sacrament blessed to His own.

Second choir
And may all who assemble here
Find peace, united hearts to cheer,
Together know their highest good,
His merits, and His precious blood.

All
O may this be a house of grace,
Where power from on high finds place,
That unto poor and sinful men
His pardon be proclaimed. Amen![20]

After sermons and hymns of dedication the Brethren had a lovefeast for the 2000 worshipers. Schober had earlier offered to provide tin cups for beer, although he probably had not anticipated so great a crowd. It was indeed a day to be remembered.

It was probably during this period of heavy involvement in musical affairs that Schober purchased a fine piano for his home. The instrument was made by Christian R. Heckewelder in Pennsylvania and described as "a Forte Piano of Wild Cherry Wood."[21] The piano was the most valuable article in the sale of household goods after Schober's death.

---

[18]Schober's musical activities were mentioned in the Congregation Council, 19 June 1794, Fries and others, *Records of Moravians*, 6:2508; Elders' Conference, 19 August 1795, 17 April, 25 May 1799, Fries and others, *Records of Moravians*, 6:2541, 2628-89, Congregation Council, 28 October 1800, Fries and others, *Records of Moravians*, 6:2656.

[19]Salem Diary, 9 November 1800, Fries and others, *Records of Moravians*, 6:2947-48.

[20]Ibid. Since Schober had charge of all music for the service, it seems valid to conclude that he had a role in the selection of this particular hymn.

[21]Receipt in Schober Papers, Old Salem Inc. Archives.

When Gottlieb purchased his piano he perhaps had in mind his growing family. After Nathaniel, Johanna, Emmanuel, and Anna Paulina, a third daughter arrived on 22 September 1794 and was baptized Hedwig Elizabeth. In 1797 Benjamin was born but died the same day. The family was completed with the arrival of Maria Theresa on 3 June 1799. It was no surprise to the Overseers when Schober requested to employ a young girl as a maid for his wife, to build an extra bake oven near his house, and to lease an additional outlot for pasture and an orchard.[22]

Nathaniel, the eldest son, was rapidly becoming a young man. From childhood his physical constitution was weak and his parents feared for his survival. Still he was a joy to the household and often delighted the family with "infantine plays . . . and loving expressions toward the Friend of Children."[23] Early he learned to read and write and at eight years of age requested to leave the home to lodge in the academy. Gottlieb and Maria reluctantly gave consent on condition "that he would solemnly covenant to become a Servant of the Lord, and apply all his acquirements to that purpose."[24] He entered the boys' school in Salem housed at that time in the single brothers' house and then moved to newly completed facilities in 1794. Nathaniel and five other older boys studied under William Eldridge, Gottlieb's former apprentice, until 1800. During this period his physical constitution was further weakened by a severe attack of pleurisy, significantly dimming his dream of seminary training and service to the church. But the Schobers were proud of this son of whom it was said that

> his honesty and punctuality in all his Transactions was proverbial, and his obedience to his Supervisors and particularly to his Teachers caused him to be beloved by them—and generally all that knew him esteemed him.[25]

In 1800, he moved into the single brothers' house to follow his father's footsteps as assistant room supervisor for the smaller boys.[26]

Johanna, the oldest daughter, also took advantage of the Moravian schools in Salem although she remained in the Schober household. Reading, writing, reckoning, geography, and the practical arts of a poten-

---

[22]Board of Overseers, 6 May, 1 April 1794, 9 August 1796, Moravian Archives.

[23]Memoir of Nathaniel Shober, 1818, Moravian Archives.

[24]Ibid. This was unusual because most Salem children resided with their parents until about fourteen years of age.

[25]Memoir of Nathaniel Shober, 1818, Moravian Archives.

[26]Salem Diary, 8 January 1800, Fries and others, *Records of Moravians*, 6:2642-43.

tial wife and mother constituted her early training. She was quick to learn and excelled in her studies so that when the Girls Boarding School opened in Salem in 1804 she was one of its first teachers. Hannah, as she was affectionately called, was the natural leader among the children of the household. She was more outspoken than the others and inherited the quick temper of her father.

The religious atmosphere of the Schober household made deep impressions on the children. Nathaniel responded early to descriptions of Jesus' love for children. Anna Paulina later wrote:

> At a very tender age I experienced the powerful influences of the Holy Spirit in my heart. I distinctly remember, at the age of three-four years an ardent longing I had to go to the Saviour, and be with him forever. How often have I wished that happy state of mind might have continued longer, but my natural lively and volatile dispositions soon effaced these impressions.[27]

For Emmanuel's twelfth birthday, Gottlieb composed a religious message in verse. It reminded Emmanuel that "the years are gone when one was guiltless," and he should "Be inscribed under Jesus' banner and not in jest; promise that you will love Him and be His forever more." The last verse bespoke a father's longsuffering love:

> So grow and become a noble man, so that we—in return for all the trouble we have taken with you—can be eternally happy that the Lord gave you to us, that we can joyfully call you [ours] until they lay us in the grave.[28]

While his own family was growing toward maturity, Gottlieb did not forget his aging mother. She still lived in Bethlehem and was alone since the passing of Gottlieb's father in 1792. She too died in 1800, but her son managed visits to her in 1794, 1795, and 1798 as he made business trips to purchase sheet tin and articles for trade in exchange for beeswax, ginseng root, and tobacco.

The happiness of a growing family stood at times in sharp contrast to Schober's public life. His quick temper and quicker tongue still plagued him; his occasional verbal altercations with several Brothers recalled the problems of his youth. For example, he quarrelled with Abraham Hauser regarding the latter's administration of community funds in maintaining public roads. Schober took the matter to the justice of the peace where

---

[27]Memoir of Ann Paulina Herman, 1867, Moravian Archives.

[28]Manuscript in verse dated 12 February 1801, Schober Papers, Old Salem Inc. Archives. Translation by Elizabeth Marx.

Hauser admitted his negligence, but then returned to Salem "making much ado about the matter and calling Brother Schober a perjurer throughout the neighborhood."[29] Gottlieb stood his ground and proved his testimony before the Overseers. He was ready to "sue the denunciations of Hauser" unless he apologized publicly and retracted his statements in every place they had been spoken. The Overseers agreed wholeheartedly and lectured Hauser on the true behavior of a Brother.[30] While Schober was right and was advocating the proper use of community money, the quarrel was unsavory and even a retracted charge of perjury had negative effects.

Schober's most serious disagreement occurred in 1798 with Gottlieb Strehle. The two men, both members of the Overseers, argued so forcefully, including very coarse language, that both were suspended from the Board and from Holy Communion.[31] According to Schober, hard feelings against him in the community had arisen because of his work as a lawyer, a vocation considered by some as unsuitable for a Moravian. In addition, Schober had several times mentioned to the Overseers that Strehle, the town butcher, treated people rudely. But the Overseers had done nothing. On this particular occasion, while Gottlieb was out of town, the Schober children went to Strehle to buy meat

> and in their presence he called me in effect a good-for-nothing deceiver; ... I went to him in order to tax him roundly. It happened that a Single Sister was present ... [and] I did not spare anything, but threw up to him his behavior without scolding. The consequence was that he first picked up a bone and when I turned that away, he then came at me with a knife, spit in my face and hit me in the face. All my power of recollection was required; I was fully conscious, spit after him and then he got Title—an individual of his own kind [who] grabbed me by the neck and dragged me out.[32]

Schober immediately resigned from the Overseers, expecting an impartial investigation and, with a witness present, anticipating no trouble. But

> instead of that, the Lot was misused (as I call it) and in spite of the unprecedented atrocity against me, he and I were publicly excluded from the

---

[29]Board of Overseers, 12 December 1797, Moravian Archives.

[30]Board of Overseers, 19 December 1797, Moravian Archives.

[31]Board of Overseers, 17, 24 July 1798, Moravian Archives; Elders' Conference, 25 July 1798, Moravian Archives.

[32]Gottlieb Schober to [Johann F.] Reichel, Salem, 15 September 1800, Schober Papers, Old Salem Inc. Archives. Translation by Elizabeth Marx. This account was written two years after the event as background to still another controversy.

brethren's fellowship and also from the Collegium. This gave me such a blow
that it will remain into eternity; I have said it and I continue to say that no
God can act in that way and therefore it is a card game and the work of man...

Church leaders talked to both men, especially regarding the need for good
conduct among community leaders. When the heat finally cooled, both
men were embarrassed about their actions. They ultimately returned to
communion but, in Schober's words, "the scar remains."[33] This petty
incident, even considered among a long list of positive contributions,
highlighted a trait in Schober without which the picture would be incom-
plete. He possessed a volatile personality, often speaking before he
considered the impact of his words. His tongue ruptured a number of
otherwise productive relationships and more than once gave church
leaders pause regarding Schober's fitness as a brother.

Above and beyond his roles as papermaker, tinsmith, postmaster,
musician, community leader, father, and sometimes congregation gadfly,
Gottlieb Schober was Salem's only attorney at law. The task involved
some unhappy experiences, illustrated by his administration of Johann
Reuz's affairs. Reuz began drinking again in 1798 and hiding money from
Schober's accounting. Gottlieb protested to the Overseers that he was
using his own funds to provide for the family and receiving nothing for
his services.[34] But the practice of law had its good days also. In 1799,
Stokes County reappraised taxable property. Joseph Kerner assessed
Salem's buildings and Moravians stated, "We have heard that the houses
in his county were taxed higher than those in the neighboring counties."[35]
Schober was requested to petition for redress and to seek a complete
exemption for the sisters' house. When other Moravians in Wachovia
also expressed resentment, a delegation went to Germanton and succeeded in reducing the assessment. The Salem sisters' house, but not the
brothers' establishment, was declared tax free. "We shall," the Overseers
opined, "hear more about the taxes on the occasion of the coming
elections."[36] Another petition was circulated by Schober the following
year to persuade the county court to declare the bridge over Peters Creek

---

[33]Ibid. See also Elders' Conference, 25 July, 5 September 1798, Moravian Archives.

[34]Board of Overseers, 1, 21, 28 August 1798, Moravian Archives.

[35]Board of Overseers, 23 July 1799, Moravian Archives.

[36]Board of Overseers, 30 July, 6, 20 August 1799, Moravian Archives.

west of Salem a public responsibility. Again Gottlieb's efforts were successful, relieving the Brethren of maintenance of the structure.[37] In July 1802 Schober was asked to research the law codes regarding the legality of contracts made by the community treasury, especially those existing with the administrative body of all Moravian's secular affairs in Europe.[38] Schober continued his involvement in the Mulberry Fields case, although at a reduced level. In 1799 he took depositions of several Moravians, including Traugott Bagge and Adam Steiner, designed to explore the nature of the Brethren's economy and policies on the holding and use of land. The extensive transcripts, written incidentally on Schober's own paper by Nathaniel Schober acting as secretary, included cross-examination by William Lenoir and other attorneys for both sides. As usual, the case was delayed again and again, much to the frustration of Schober and the Moravians.[39]

A new dimension of the legal profession emerged in 1801. Schober increasingly represented non-Moravians in matters relating to the community and its inhabitants. Letters from a David Marck of Petersburg, Virginia, requested that Schober secure the former's inheritance from his mother who died in Salem. Since settlement was delayed, Schober was asked to secure an advance of $500 to relieve Mr. Marck's financial straits. A few months later he wrote again, requesting another $500 with which to purchase a house. The source of these funds was not mentioned and since the estate was unsettled, they may have come from Schober himself. Marck trusted Schober to "take care of the terms [of the loan] and make them just and equitable."[40]

Despite occasional conflicts, the period around the turn of the century included Schober's most important services to the community and congenial relationships with church officials. He served on the Board of Overseers from 1790 through 1802. He became a member of the *Helfer Conferenz* when he replaced the deceased Traugott Bagge as official host to important visitors to the community. Schober's relationships with the

[37]Board of Overseers, 29 April, 22 July 1800, Moravian Archives.

[38]*Helfer Conferenz*, 24 July 1802, Fries and others, *Records of Moravians*, 6:2710.

[39]Reports to Unity Elders' Conference and Unity Vorsteher Collegium from Christian Ludwig Benzien, Salem, 11 February 1803, Fries and others, *Records of Moravians*, 6:2750.

[40]D. Marck to Gottlieb Shober, Petersburg, 22 May, 3 June, and 25 October 1801, Schober Papers, Old Salem Inc. Archives.

world outside and his acquaintance with important state officials made him a natural selection for this post. Since Moravians were always careful that visitors received a true impression of village life and attention to their needs, Schober's responsibility was an important one.

In financial matters, Gottlieb also had reason to be satisfied with his progress. When he married he needed to delay payment on existing debts and borrow more money to set up the tinsmithy. By the turn of the century he owned one of the finest homes in the village, a farm outside of town, several negro slaves, about 40,000 acres of undeveloped North Carolina land, 10,000 acres of valuable Maryland real estate, a new shop housing the tinsmithy and post office, and a paper manufactory. Since tax listings usually understated real market value, Schober's financial status can be evaluated only in comparison with others of the time. Tax lists showed him still trailing Traugott Bagge in taxable assets, although gaining rapidly.[41] Bagge owned much less land but his was more valuable. Schober had clearly surpassed most of his peers in Salem. In 1802, a voluntary subscription was taken to improve the main street of the town. Most of the seventeen contributions were for one or two pounds. Schober gave five pounds, the highest single contribution; only the town doctor approached this generosity, and no other person in Salem gave even three pounds.[42] At forty-six years of age, Schober was approaching the most productive years of his life with two prosperous crafts and a growing profession contributing to the family income. He had business connections in Philadelphia, Petersburg, Charleston, Raleigh, Salisbury, and numerous smaller towns. Stokes county now had a population of 11,026 and neighboring Surry was close behind with 9,505, making Salem the commercial center for more than 20,000 people. The village itself was also growing in the modest manner which Moravians desired. From a 1773 census of 132 persons the village had grown to 222 at the time of Schober's marriage and to 281 in 1802.

Even the nature of Salem's commerce was changing under the pressures of free enterprise. As discussed in Chapter Two, the congregation treasury of early Salem retained the store, tavern, pottery, grist mill, two tanyards, and several large farms, and managers were hired to operate

---

[41]Tax lists of 1799 for Gottlieb Schober and Traugott Bagge, North Carolina Archives, Raleigh, North Carolina.

[42]Board of Overseers, 14 September 1802, Moravian Archives.

them for the community benefit. All enterprises needed subsidies to offset inflation during the Revolution. Soon the farms were engulfed in problems and were leased to private individuals. In 1780, the Brethren agreed to give the deficit-ridden tannery to the operator for an annual ten pounds "recognition fee" to the community account.[43] By 1791 the grist mill fell victim to heavy local competition and the lack of a good miller.[44] At the turn of the century, only the tavern, store, and pottery were financially healthy and blessed with good managers. These communal monopolies were still protected and most private initiative was discouraged. For example, Charles Bagge, disappointed at not succeeding his father as Salem's storekeeper, sought permission to open his own store. When it was denied, he moved to Friedland, a country congregation, to begin his enterprise.[45] Christopher Vogler had to decline a government contract for guns because the Overseers would not approve the necessary non-Moravian workers in that craft.[46] The Moravians did allow enough economic freedom for the separation of the lazy from the efficient, but they believed that the survival of the town would be endangered if no restraints were maintained. It was obvious, however, that private initiative was gradually gaining momentum, and Schober was not the only person whose economic fortunes were turning upward. And prospects for the future appeared even brighter.

In 1802, however, a conflict of major proportions marked the end of easy congeniality and the onset of a strained relationship between Gottlieb and the community. Frustrations were already fermenting by 1800 when Schober wrote a long letter to Johann F. Reichel, a Unity representative in Europe, just prior to the General Synod of 1801.

> We [in Salem] have been school children long enough kept in fear under a school master; instead of that, love should be reigning. . . . Salem is growing rapidly, our children do not have any presumable prospect for the determination of their life; anyone who would gladly offer himself completely to the Lord's service must see himself forgotten by the Unity's Direction because of the distance and anyway the offices are mostly filled from Europe. There is no goal towards which a thoughtful young person can strive. . . . Our

---

[43]Board of Overseers, 4 July 1780, Moravian Archives.

[44]Board of Overseers, 12 July 1791, Moravian Archives.

[45]Salem Diary, 20 August 1801, Fries and others, *Records of Moravians*, 6:2675; Elders' Conference, 29 January 1806, Moravian Archives.

[46]Board of Overseers, 17 July 1798, Fries and others, *Records of Moravians*, 6:2612.

Brothers' House is very much alive in material things and a bad prospect for spiritual up-bringing. But there are more girls than boys here and there the spiritual out-look is even worse; I live near to the Sisters' House and sometimes hear talking how their Helper does not know anything about human misery and depravity and thus is not able to give advice. . . . This congregation could be enlarged and thus many a one who does not feel a call to offer himself for the service of the Lord still would have the prospect of living in the Congregation. For that [to happen] there must be a worthwhile wholesale business through which samples of our manufactured goods could be distributed; I maintain it is possible and also would be profitable for the Unity. In fact, several years ago I wrote out a prospect for that, but like all such things which demand possibilities that look to the future, [so] it was with this. They are too glad to be satisfied with the current stable income and with the hope that "things will go along as long as I am alive or remain here," and so the doors are finally closed. . . .

. . . .
This is then what flowed into a pen out of a full heart. I would not dare to speak in this way to our workers; they would try to drive me out of the Congregation as a scorner. . . . I have often sought an opportunity here to talk things out but have never found one. . . . I beg most sincerely that you will pardon any strong expressions and [be assured] that I mean well with the Savior and with the Brethren's Church, and I hope He holds me close to himself and grants me new life and suitable zeal for service.[47]

This remarkable letter showed that Schober's dissatisfaction was not with the system but with the administrators. No evidence suggested that Schober was critical of Salem itself. In fact, an earlier letter to non-Moravian Evan Alexander in 1793 revealed that Schober both understood and accepted the theocratic nature of the community.[48] All congregations of Moravians, he explained to Alexander, "constitute one Body" because "all have one calling & Aim (viz. propagation of the Gospel) and are bound to one Rule and discipline." Ministers are appointed to superintend the congregation, while occasional "synods consider deliberately whether our doctrine is preached in its purity & try to tie the Bond of love & peace binding us tighter." Schober continued to describe how the synod was constituted, including representatives from each congregation, and pointed out that the Unity Elders' Conference acted as the executive body between synods. Local congregations were governed by "Laws of the Synod (I say Laws, for we value them as such)," implemented by local

---

[47]Gottlieb Schober to [Johann F.] Reichel, Salem, 15 September 1800, Schober Papers, Old Salem Inc. Archives. Translation by Elizabeth Marx.

[48]Gottlieb Schober to Evan Alexander, Salem, 20 January 1793, Schober Papers, Old Salem Inc. Archives.

leaders. "In short, it is the fundamental Maxim among the United Brn. that Principals & Order shall Govern & *not Men*." God's active leadership in the Brethren's affairs was guaranteed, Schober believed, by the lot. Nothing would indicate that Schober's mind had changed by 1802, except that the lot could be used too often in minor matters. The course of events revealed that his quarrel was not with principles of governance, but with men. Schober looked to the General Synod of 1801 to correct the human abuses which he observed in Salem.

The Unity Synod of 1801 was firmly controlled by the more conservative elements of the church who felt that the ideals of the pioneer Brethren were being compromised as the church related to the world.[49] This trend was noted in both Europe and America; church officials in Salem often lamented that their own community was no exception. For example, the annual summary for the year 1794 stated:

> It is true that we entered this year not without concern over various things, and that at its end there remains sadness over the situation here and there in our congregations, yet we must be happy over [the Lord's] government during the year. His thoughts were sometimes not as our thoughts, and on several occasions He required more sternness to prevent impending digressions from the path of righteousness, especially in the congregation of Salem.[50]

Similar expressions were present in the summaries for 1795, and in 1797 it was noted that "among our youth the signs are fewer that they would enter into the true life and a full understanding of their call of grace."[51]

There is little doubt that this assessment was accurate, although in comparison with Christian-professing society at large, Salem remained an enclave of spirituality. Although the local Elders' Conference had the final responsibility for maintaining the spiritual purity of the community, all citizens participated in this task to a degree.[52] In the early years, some local authority was vested in the Congregation Council composed of all

---

[49]Hamilton and Hamilton, *History of the Moravian Church*, p. 177.

[50]Memorabilia of the Congregations in Wachovia for the year 1794, Fries and others, *Records of Moravians*, 6:2495.

[51]Memorabilia of the Congregations in Wachovia, 1797, Fries and others, *Records of Moravians*, 6:2578.

[52]See this author's article "The Role of Dissent in Community Evolution among Moravians in Salem, 1772-1860," *North Carolina Historical Review* 52 (July 1975):235-55.

adult communicants. With the reorganization of 1779, however, *ex officio* members increased, and communicants only elected representatives. By 1790, the council of fifty-seven persons included only twenty-one elected members.[53] The council could not, therefore, be described as the "voice of the people" in a democratic sense, yet it did constitute the point of entry of whatever purely local independence existed. In reality that independence was minimal; the council could discuss local problems and make recommendations to the Elders and Overseers but could enact no regulations on its own. It did elect the Overseers, subject always to the confirmation of the lot. The progressive voices in the General Synod of 1801 advocated a decrease in the use of the lot in the formation of local governing bodies such as the Congregation Council and the Overseers.[54] But the Synod stood firm: the means of sustaining the theocratic government were maintained and even strengthened. A higher ratio of *ex officio* members on the Congregation Council was mandated, thereby effectively reducing the expression of local independence. This was hardly what Schober and other progressive Salem citizens had hoped for.

When the report of the General Synod arrived in Salem in 1802, the community reorganized according to the new mandates. The new Congregation Council included seventy-two members, of whom only twenty-eight were elected by the communicants.[55] One of its important tasks was the selection of the Overseers. During the election a controversy burst forth with Schober as usual squarely in the middle. The records were left unusually ambiguous on this event, forcing inferences when clear detail would be preferred. Such speculation is imperative, however, because the controversy colored Schober's relations with Salem for the remainder of his life. Once again, Gottlieb's temper lighted the fuse.

In early 1802, Schober accused Samuel Stotz, a congregation official, of misusing congregation money—specifically buying coffee for the Lovefeast at two pence per pound but charging the account three pence. Evidently the entire pound was not used so it was prorated at a higher level.[56] The congregation officials supported Stotz, so Schober solicited

---

[53]Elders' Conference, 7 December 1779, Moravian Archives. See also Fries and others, *Records of Moravians*, 3:1330-31.

[54]Hamilton and Hamilton, *History of the Moravian Church*, p. 177.

[55]Congregation Council, 8 November 1802, Moravian Archives.

[56]Gottlieb Schober to [Christain L.] Benzien, Salem, 12 May 1802, Schober Papers, Old Salem Inc. Archives. Translation by Elizabeth Marx.

the support of others—twenty-one married brothers agreed with him. Schober demanded a complete accounting of all monies according to published regulations of the Unity. The accounting was made and all was in order. Schober admitted his mistake and publicly apologized.[57] Soon afterward, the election of Overseers was held. As in the past, the Congregation Council voted for any Brother and the seven highest were to be submitted to confirmation by the lot. Schober received the fourth highest number of votes. When consulted, he stated

> that he really had no desire to be elected to the Aufseher Collegium because he might give offense on account of his temper, but on the other hand he did not have any real joy either in declining in case the Savior would wish to designate him for it. Therefore, he was leaving it up to the [Elders'] Conference to take action in this according to their good judgement. However, since the Conference had no joy in deciding anything alone in this matter, it was unanimous in presenting to the Savior the following question in the lot with *Yes* and *No*: "In view of the declaration of Bro. Gottl. Schober, should he be taken into consideration anyway in the question to the Lot regarding the members to be selected for the Aufseher Collegium?" The answer was No.[58]

No antagonism was evident regarding the election itself or the use of the lot. But something unrecorded in the minutes was said about Schober in the meeting. It could have related to Gottlieb's charges against Stotz. Or, perhaps some members still questioned whether Schober's practice of law was a proper activity for a brother.[59] Whatever the topic, Gottlieb interpreted the conversation as an impeachment of his character and a shadow cast on his previous services to the congregation. But for once he held his tongue. Two weeks later the newly elected Overseers reluctantly agreed to seek an appointment from the state making Schober a justice of the peace for Salem. It was pointed out that he "does not agree to the community orders entirely" but the officials "did not object generally to the candidacy of Brother Schober for this office, mainly since we do not know anybody else."[60]

By April, Stotz and Schober were once again at odds. And again Schober wrote Johann F. Reichel, this time at the latter's request. The

---

[57]Ibid.

[58]Elders' Conference, 2 November 1802, Moravian Archives.

[59]*Helfer Conferenz*, 22 February 1804, Fries and others, *Records of Moravians*, 6:2777.

[60]Board of Overseers, 16 November 1802, Moravian Archives.

letter revealed the depth of Gottlieb's bitterness. He was upset because Salem citizens had not been given the opportunity to elect a delegate to the 1801 Synod as was their right by Unity regulations.

> We were not even once asked whether we wanted to elect a delegate, and I declared myself at that time publicly and directly against such a procedure. That was the first time at which not only Stotz but presumably the majority of the Elders' Conference were offended and the result will not have failed to follow: to say and to write to Europe that I am a restless trouble-maker; the subsequent events indicate this to me.[61]

Schober continued to say that he wrote a letter to the Synod about the matter, but did not send it because he was quietly informed by a congregation leader that Stotz would likely be moved to another congregation by the Synod. Therefore, Schober wrote, he remained quiet despite "malicious public treatment" by local leaders and Stotz in particular. He decided that nothing could likely be done, but

> I cannot and will not be considered a rebel, nor as the least member of the Brethren's Unity—and as this has been proclaimed, I have resolved to write to the Unity Elders' Conference and ask for an investigation, but want to ask for your kind advice. A discussion here in Salem would be fruitless and I forbid it—Stotz once approved the way I was treated and condemned me and he would be acting very inconsistently if he decided differently now, and so my complete conviction remains that Stotz has not acted as he should have and not until he recognizes that, keeps better accounts and shows himself inclined to reconciliation . . . can one have confidence. But since this cannot be decided here, it may be only decided in eternity who acted faithfully.[62]

In May, it was reported that Schober "is still very bitter against Brother Stotz" and has resigned as host for visitors and director of community music. "At this occasion, it was declared once more clearly that all accusations he brings out against Brother Stotz are not true at all."[63] For another month the controversy continued and only the *Helfer Conferenz* succeeded "in removing all the difficulties between [Schober] and the community with the great help of the Lord, mainly the quarrel between him and the community direction of Brother Stotz."[64] Ostensibly satisfied, Schober's resentment lingered and was only thinly veiled. He

---

[61]Gottlieb Schober to [Johann F.] Reichel, 12 April 1803, Schober Papers, Old Salem Inc. Archives. Translation by Elizabeth Marx.

[62]Ibid.

[63]Board of Overseers, 17 May 1803, Moravian Archives.

[64]Board of Overseers, 18 July 1803, Moravian Archives.

persisted in resigning from the responsibilities he held and at the next election of Overseers removed himself from consideration saying that he wished "to refrain from such offices."[65]

While many details of this matter were not clearly recorded, perhaps intentionally to protect the innocent, the ultimate effect on Schober was clear. Never again was his confidence placed in the Salem leadership without inner reservation. Certainly he was no innocent victim in the affair. His accusations against people were frequently unjust or totally exaggerated. Moreover, he consistently pushed congregational regulations to the edge of legitimacy and sometimes beyond. But he believed that Salem was ruled by principles, not by men. He believed that Salem could adjust itself to the changing demands of time while maintaining the dynamism of the Christian ideal. For this man, service to God sprang from immediate personal convictions rather than from the ideas expressed by the previous generation. He never claimed perfection, but was determined to serve aggressively to the best of his abilities and trust that God would forgive his mistakes. The battle of 1802-1803 was the most serious conflict which ever erupted between Schober and his native church. Despite the reconciliation, the trend which developed in Schober's subsequent years bespoke his true feeling. More and more his attention and energies were drawn to matters outside the community. He later served Salem in important legal matters, but only, in language that Schober would not have disdained, at the request of God and not simply the request of congregation officials.

---

[65]Congregation Council, 18 December 1803, Moravian Archives.

CHAPTER 7

From Lawyer to State Senator

It would be incorrect to interpret the controversy discussed in the previous chapter as precipitating a decisive break between Schober and Salem. By the middle of 1803 both sides professed reconciliation. It was decided that the appointment of Schober as justice of the peace would be submitted to the lot. When the answer was "Yes," Gottlieb felt somewhat vindicated or at least believed that God had shown His satisfaction.[1] Schober assumed the office in March 1803 with some hesitation since it would prohibit his practicing law before the county court, and he would also lose the office of postmaster.[2] But the new legal position conveyed increased local prestige and may have offered a reasonable financial incentive from fees. Moreover, he had just secured a license to practice law in the Superior Court of North Carolina.[3] On balance, the judicial position was a positive step with enough social responsibility to pacify his need to serve the community, yet one in which he could avoid tangles with community officials.

[1] Elders' Conference, 12 January 1803, Fries and others, *Records of Moravians*, 6:2734.

[2] Elders' Conference, 19 January 1803, Fries and others, *Records of Moravians*, 6:2734.

[3] Receipt for payment of ten pounds for license for Superior Court, 1803, Schober Papers, Old Salem Inc. Archives; Board of Overseers, 18 July 1803, Moravian Archives.

The North Carolina judicial system had changed very little since colonial days. At the bottom of the system was the justice of the peace, who exercised limited civil and criminal jurisdiction. He, along with the sheriff, was the most visible symbol of justice in the backcountry.

> To these magistrates, the general police of the counties is chiefly committed, as they have authority to cause criminals, and other disturbers of the peace to be arrested; and if the offense is small, to fix the penalty; but if the offense is too great to be brought within their jurisdiction, they commit the offenders to prison to be reserved for trial before the proper tribunal.[4]

Schober and other justices of the county together held the court of pleas and quarter sessions, hearing cases involving taxes, roads, licensing taverns, and general law and order. Moravian records mentioned only a few of Schober's activities in this regard. A non-Moravian arrived in his wagon at the Easter service in 1803 to hawk "gingerbread and brandy" to the worshipers; Schober was requested to prohibit such peddling.[5] In 1804 he was "asked to lend us his help as he did last year. We wish that no cake and ale is offered in the streets."[6] Schober aided the Overseers in securing the appointment of an acceptable supervisor of the local roads. He helped several poor people of the county secure financial help to relieve their worst problems. For as long as Gottlieb was active in the legal profession he administered the duties of this office, gaining respect of individuals both within and outside the community.

The year 1804 brought other significant events to Schober's life. Professionally, the most important of these was the renewal of the Mulberry Fields suit. Judicial processes had, since 1795, moved slowly but inexorably toward the supreme tribunal of North Carolina. Early in 1804 the Moravians were advised that the case would come to a final decision either that year or the next. As the attorney who knew more than anybody else on the case, Schober was asked to resume this legal battle on behalf of the Brethren. With wounds still fresh from comments concerning his profession, Schober declined to become involved. In 1803 he had been passed over in favor of General James Welborn as the Moravian's representative in the suit[7] and now, convinced that his services were not

---

[4]Hazen, *Panarama of Professions and Trades*, p. 125.

[5]Congregation Council, 14 April 1803, Fries and others, *Records of Moravians*, 6:2741.

[6]Congregation Council, 19 January, 22 March 1804, Moravian Archives.

[7]*Helfer Conferenz*, 21 March 1803, Fries and others, *Records of Moravians*, 6:2739.

appreciated, he became stubborn. Duncan Cameron, a prominent Hillsborough attorney, was retained, but Christian L. Benzien, the Unity administrator for Wachovia since the death of Frederic W. Marshall in 1802, again "expressed his earnest wish that Br. Gottlieb Schober would again take part in this case . . . which is so important to the Unity."[8] Benzien even wrote personally to Schober asking that he reconsider. Gottlieb's response to Benzien and the conference revealed the depth of his hurt:

> remarks made by various Conferenz members have been to the effect that because of [my] legal work they [do] not consider [me] a Brother, and [I have] determined never to serve the congregation or the Unity in that way again unless expressly directed by the Lord.[9]

It is impossible to separate the "sour grapes" from sincere conviction. That some Brethren had these opinions of Schober was not denied; to him they challenged the very essence of his religious convictions. He had wished fervently to serve God in the ministry, and, that desire being thwarted by church officials, he had determined to serve the Brethren as legal advisor. For any important church leader in Salem to spurn what Schober considered his religious service to God was not an easily forgotten matter. Now he could in good conscience say "no" to the church's request, but he would not say "no" to God. The lot was taken: "The Saviour approves that Br. Gottlieb Schober shall be asked to serve as our attorney in the cases in court."[10] With enthusiasm replacing reticence, he plunged headlong into the case. Within ten days he was on his way to Superior Court at Morganton in company with Duncan Cameron.[11] Despite a flurry of activity in late 1804 and frequent exchange of letters by Schober and Cameron in 1805, substantial progress in the suit was slow. Only in 1808 would the case again be heard by the Supreme Court, and by that time Gottlieb's stature in the legal profession had been considerably enhanced both in Salem and across the state. Perhaps the most important result of these trips to Morganton was the suggestion by several friends that he should become a candidate for the Senate of North Carolina.[12]

---

[8]*Helfer Conferenz*, 22 February 1804, Fries and others, *Records of Moravians*, 6:2777.

[9]Ibid.

[10]Ibid.

[11]Salem Diary, 2 March 1804, Fries and others, *Records of Moravians*, 6:2763.

[12]Elders' Conference, 30 May 1804, Moravian Archives.

Before considering such a momentous development in Schober's career, other events in Salem involving the Schober household in 1804 demand a brief review. The most joyous occasion in Salem since the dedication of the new church was the opening of the Girls Boarding School.

The education of young people in Salem dated back to the beginning of the town. At that time schools were designed exclusively for the children of citizens of the community. Occasionally during the 1790s, Moravians received requests to board and educate the children of outsiders in these schools, but the Brethren feared the consequences of such an endeavor. About 1800, community officials began to discuss the possibilities more favorably, and in 1803 the lot was affirmative.[13] A building to house sixty female students with their teachers was designed to stand on the square, immediately south of the congregation house. Word spread rapidly through North and South Carolina, whereupon "prominent gentlemen" encouraged the Moravians to hasten the completion of the project.[14] In July 1804 the institution accepted ten students; two of them were from Salem and included Anna Paulina Schober.[15]

> The two children of the congregation in the Boarding School, and the rest of the little school girls, were urged to pray that the Saviour might give them grace to set a good example in all respects to the girls from elsewhere.[16]

By 1805 the enrollment rose to forty-one, again with only two from Salem. The institution charged thirty dollars per quarter for board, lodging, and tuition. Pupils studied grammar and syntax, history, geography, and ciphering in the morning hours while aesthetic arts, such as drawing, painting, sewing, and music, occupied the afternoons.[17] Gottlieb Schober had still another reason to be proud. His eldest daughter, Johanna, became one of the six teachers in the school.[18] Overall, the

---

[13]Frances Griffin, *Less Time for Meddling: A History of Salem Academy and College* (Winston-Salem: John F. Blair, 1979), p. 34.

[14]Salem Diary, 31 May 1803, Fries and others, *Records of Moravians*, 6:2728-29.

[15]Memorabilia of the Congregations of the Brethren in Wachovia for the Year 1804, Fries and others, *Records of Moravians*, 6:2761.

[16]Salem Diary, 30 June 1804, Fries and others, *Records of Moravians*, 6:2767.

[17]Lucy Leinback Wenhold, "The Salem Boarding School between 1802 and 1822," *North Carolina Historical Review* 27 (January 1950): 34.

[18]Memorabilia of the Congregations of the Brethren in Wachovia for the year 1805, Fries and others, *Records of Moravians*, 6:2802.

success of the Girls Boarding School exceeded the Brethren's most optimistic hopes and it soon became an established part of the life of the town. Ultimately, the school increased the Moravians' social interaction with the outside world and was a definite factor in the gradual demise of cultural isolationism. For Gottlieb Schober, this development could not come too soon.

Other members of the Schober household seemed to be doing equally well. After a children's epidemic sweeping through Salem in 1797 almost claimed the life of three-year-old Hedwig, family sickness was minimal. The household was vaccinated against smallpox when the serum arrived in town in 1802.[19] Twelve-year-old Anna Paulina gave the family a scare in 1803 when she fell into the mill pond and almost drowned.[20] Nathaniel seemed about to realize his dream of service to the church in 1804 when he accompanied Adam Steiner to the territory of the Creek Indians to prepare for the opening of a new Indian mission. The two men left Salem on 4 June and returned on 22 August, having covered 1,290 miles in "great heat and scarcity of food, and other unfavorable circumstances."[21] Nathaniel's frail constitution withstood the journey well, but subsequent trips proved too arduous for him. On one of them he was fording the swollen Catawba River when "the rapid Stream took him with his horse to within a few yards of unavoidable destruction, and only the presence of mind given to him in the moment of danger preserved him from drowning."[22] Ultimately, the Schobers and church officials became convinced that the young man could not long withstand the rigors of missionary activity. Emmanuel, the younger son, completed his education in the community and was accepted into the single brothers' choir in 1805.[23] It was thus with personal affairs in order, the family well and happy, and the dispute with community officials behind him that Gottlieb entered the political arena.

Early Moravians in Wachovia voted regularly in all elections. Their impact was maximized on several occasions when community leaders

[19]Board of Overseers, 15 June 1802, Moravian Archives.

[20]Memoir of Anna Paulina Herman, Moravian Archives.

[21]Memorabilia of the Congregations of the Brethren in Wachovia for the Year 1804, Fries and others, *Records of Moravians*, 6:2758.

[22]Memoir of Nathaniel Schober, Moravian Archives.

[23]Board of Overseers, 6 April 1802, 5 November 1805, Moravian Archives.

would strongly recommend certain candidates.[24] Some individual Moravians ran successfully for the office of constable, and Frederick Müller of Friedland was a representative in the North Carolina General Assembly in 1778.[25] The Assembly even met in Salem in 1781, although the Brethren were hesitant when the request was first received. It ended as a good experience for both the assemblymen, who were able to see the Moravian way of life firsthand, and for the Brethren, whose cultural isolationism thawed to some degree. The following year, again meeting in Salem, the Assembly guaranteed the Moravian title to Wachovia and encouraged them to enter more fully into the life of the state.[26] Traugott Bagge represented Stokes County in the 1782 session but was defeated for reelection the following year. George Hauser of Bethania served in the North Carolina House of Commons most of the years between 1788 and 1796. Political activity among the Brethren declined around 1800, even though Salem was an official voting place after 1801. Political arguments and fights around the polls in 1803 caused Overseers to prohibit Brethren from attending rallies.[27]

Schober certainly observed these events and attitudes and used his legal profession to make acquaintance with political leaders. He corresponded with the North Carolina representative in Washington, Robert Williams, inquiring about federal statutes on naturalization and citizenship. Williams' request through Schober that his sister be allowed to live in Salem and receive "instruction in music and the womanly arts" helped provide the impetus for the Girls Boarding School.[28] Other acquaintances had been made in the Assembly when Schober secured the loan to build his paper mill. In early 1805 Schober wrote Gideon Granger, postmaster general, and Joseph Winston, congressional representative, to request that a proposed new post road from Washington to New Orleans pass directly through Salem instead of passing a few miles away. Schober was

---

[24]Elders' Conference, 7 March 1781, Moravian Archives; Board of Overseers, 6 July 1790, Moravian Archives.

[25]Salem Diary, 18 March 1778, Fries and others, *Records of Moravians*, 3:1224.

[26]Congregation Council, 26 July, 12, 30 October 1781, Moravian Archives; Elders' Conference 8 May 1782, Moravian Archives.

[27]Board of Overseers, 3 August 1802, 15 August 1803, Moravian Archives.

[28]Elders' Conference, 10 November 1801, Fries and others, *Records of Moravians*, 6:2682; Board of Overseers, 15 September 1801, Fries and others, *Records of Moravians*, 6:2681.

to mention "the profit to the post through the many passengers which would come to our Boarding School."[29] This suggested that the proposal involved a coach rather than the usual postal rider.

Because of his acquaintances and activities on behalf of the community, it was no surprise when Schober notified the Elders that

> he has been encouraged by several friends to announce himself as a candidate for the next assembly and [asked] whether the Elders' Conference would have anything against his doing so.[30]

The Elders were not pleased. They preferred that "no Brother hold such an office" but agreed to an exception "because of our land affairs" and especially since Schober's activity as a justice of the peace and attorney had been previously approved. Whether Gottlieb ran unsuccessfully in 1804 is unknown. The records contain no information so it is probable that he waited until the following year, when he stood for the North Carolina Senate seat from Stokes County and won.[31] While there are no records of the campaign, some aspects of Schober's political perspective can be ascertained from a letter he received in 1802 from Benjamin Rineham, fellow attorney in South Carolina. Although the political philosophy is actually Rineham's, the manner of writing reflects prior, agreeable conversation between the two men.

> Our elections are just over, and have in general terminated in favor of Republicanism. In the City of Charleston where the bulk of the Electors are Foreigners—Engaged in Foreign Commerce—possessed of Foreign habits and politics—in short being his *Majesty's Liege Subjects*—they have returned *Federal* representation. This circumstance in my opinion affords a strong proof of the comparative correctness and propriety of republican principles—principles calculated to promote and extend the happiness and prosperity of the great Mass of the American people, independent of British or Gallic influence. It is a well known fact that Itinerant Merchants (if I may call them so) whose principal object is to amass a fortune and return to their favorite Monarchy to enjoy it, have too long poisoned and influenced the politics of this Country. But the Spirit of 76 is revived. It has created a good administration, of a Good Government—and may you and I long live in the enjoyment of its beneficent influence.[32]

---

[29]Board of Overseers, 26 March 1805, Fries and others, *Records of Moravians*, 6:2818.

[30]Elders' Conference, 30 May 1804, Moravian Archives.

[31]Salem Diary, 8 August 1805, Fries and others, *Records of Moravians*, 6:2810.

[32]Benjamin Rineham to Gottlieb Shober, Camden, South Carolina, 18 October 1802, Schober Papers, Old Salem Inc. Archives.

Schober would not likely have kept this letter had he not agreed with its content.

As reflected in Rineham's letter, national politics of the period were dominated by two parties. The Federal party, inspired by Alexander Hamilton, favored a strong national government controlled by the wealthy and intelligent minority: the federal government should exercise all needful power not expressly delegated to the states by the Constitution. The Republican party, looking to Thomas Jefferson as its leader, advocated a democratic self-government by the masses of people: while mistakes might be made, they could be corrected more easily and a periodic revolution was not necessarily evil. Republicans sought to protect individual and state's rights from falling under an evolving oligarchy. The central government should exercise only those powers specifically given it and deal primarily with war and peace, foreign policy, and matters affecting the nation as a whole. While several prominent North Carolinians who served in the Congress were Federalist, the trend in the state in the 1790s was toward Republicanism. The General Assembly opposed the Federalist policies of assumption of the revolutionary debts of the states, the creation of a national bank, and John Jay's treaty with England in 1795. The leading North Carolina Congressman was Nathaniel Macon, a staunch Federalist; consequently the North Carolina delegation in Washington did not always vote according to their instructions from home. The General Assembly of the 1790s was clearly Republican and, with two exceptions, elected Republican governors from 1789 to 1815. After the election of Thomas Jefferson in 1800, Republicanism triumphed to such a degree that North Carolina became a one-party state, despite the continuing Federalist influence of Nathaniel Macon.[33]

That Schober was a Republican is almost certain. He held two positions, postmaster and justice of the peace, which were subject to the politics of the day. He had been treated well in the past by a General Assembly dominated by Republicans. Therefore it seems safe to conclude that he sought election on Republican principles with promises to be concerned with local issues.

While remaining quiet, the Elders were pleased with Schober's victory. Christian L. Benzien wrote to church leaders in Europe:

---

[33]Hugh T. Lefler and Albert R. Newsome, *North Carolina: History of a Southern State*, third edition, (Chapel Hill: University of North Carolina Press, 1973), pp. 300, 302.

Very likely [Schober's election] will be very useful for us just now, for petitions are being circulated in various neighborhoods asking the next session of the assembly to take away the freedom from drill and other militia service from us, from the Quakers, etc.[34]

On 1 December 1805 Schober became the first Moravian to take the oath of allegiance in the North Carolina Senate.

Much of the work of the Assembly was done in committees; as a freshman member, Schober could expect a large amount of undesirable work. Early in the session, however, he collected a plum. He made the motion that a joint committee of the Senate and House be appointed "to enquire into the propriety of establishing a State Bank."[35] When the motion passed, Schober was named to the committee, chaired by James Wellborn.

North Carolina was the last of the original thirteen states to charter banks. Private banks were finally established in 1804 in Wilmington and New Bern amid considerable hostility from Republicans. These businesses lacked adequate management and immediately flooded the state with paper currency, which rapidly depreciated.[36] Although banks were considered Federalist projects, Schober's motion did not necessarily reflect that philosophy. On a national basis, two hundred banks were chartered by Republicans between 1800 and 1815.[37] North Carolina was already behind other states, and many assemblymen believed that only a state bank could halt the flow of worthless currency from private establishments. On 3 December the committee reported a bill creating a state bank with capital stock not to exceed $400,000 to be sold at $50 per share. The state was to take a significant portion while the remainder was offered to the public. The bill contained careful restrictions to avoid a proliferation of currency and provisions to establish an orderly financial business. A third reading passed 43-12 on 13 December with Schober voting affirmatively. The House also approved the bill, and it became law.

---

[34]Christian L. Benzien to Unity Elders' Conference, Salem, 28 October 1805, Fries and others, *Records of Moravians*, 6:2826.

[35]*Journals of the Senate and the House of Commons of the General Assembly of North Carolina, 1790-1860*, (Raleigh: State of North Carolina, 1861), 1805, p. 4. Hereinafter cited as Senate Journal, 1805.

[36]Lefler and Newsome, *North Carolina*, p. 304.

[37]Bray Hammond, *Banks and Politics in America from the Revolution to the Civil War* (Princeton: Princeton University Press, 1957), p. 145.

The prominence of Schober's role in such salutary legislation was surprising; even as a freshman he had stepped boldly into the maelstrom of politics. He presented the bank committee's reports to the Senate and must have had a considerable voice in the bill's preparation. There is no concrete evidence that he arrived in Raleigh with a proposal in hand, but the Moravians had often expressed concern about the unstable currency. Certainly Schober's motion showed prior consideration of the matter and insight into the state's needs at the time. Perhaps he had been burned by some of the depreciating currency!

In any case, chartering a bank was one thing; obtaining investors was quite another. The fifty-dollar shares did not sell. In 1806, Salem's community treasury decided to purchase "at least sixteen shares" in the bank, but when they inquired, it was learned that "for lack of enough subscribers, the Bank could not be organized, for our North Carolinians have little conception of such things."[38] When the capital stock remained unsold, the Assembly of 1806 was forced to repeal the charter. Five more years would pass before the State Bank of North Carolina began business in Raleigh, Edenton, New Bern, Wilmington, Fayetteville, Tarboro, and Salisbury. The 1810 bill was not significantly different from its predecessor, but by that time North Carolinians were ready for stability in banking.[39]

Gottlieb's other committee assignment was more drudgery than excitement. He chaired the Committee on Divorce and Alimony. The General Assembly retained to itself the power to grant or deny any divorce in the state. Every year petitions came by the dozens; Schober alone brought two with him to Raleigh. Every year after 1799 the Assembly rejected a bill transferring the power to grant divorces to the judges of the Superior Court.[40] An enormous amount of the Senate's time was consumed in reviewing the petitions. Of the thirty-three considered by Schober's committee in 1805, eighteen were granted, including the two which Schober presented. For each case a bill of divorcement was passed by the Senate on the committee's recommendation. It was indeed a cumbersome procedure and a task in which Gottlieb took no pleasure. At

---

[38]Christian Ludwig Benzien to Unity Elders' Conference, 21 October 1806, Fries and others, *Records of Moravians*, 6:2869.

[39]Lefler and Newsome, *North Carolina*, p. 305.

[40]Guion G. Johnson, *Ante-Bellum North Carolina: A Social History*, (Chapel Hill: University of North Carolina Press, 1937), p. 217.

times of leisure, he began to consider how the antiquated practice could be changed. He knew that North Carolinians were being forced to circumvent the law when family ties ruptured. In some cases where adultery was confirmed in the mind of a spouse, he or she simply left the household. These individuals sometimes "left for the West" or cohabited with another person without bonds of matrimony.[41] The situation was rapidly becoming intolerable, and Schober determined to turn his energies to its solution.

In addition to chartering a bank and hearing divorce petitions, the Assembly of 1805 considered other important legislation, not the least of which involved the University of North Carolina.[42] Since that institution's opening in 1795, the majority of the faculty and trustees had been Federalists. The school received no state money, but laws passed in 1789 and 1794 granted it the benefit of all land escheated to the state, including property belonging to Tories. The Republican Assembly disliked some trends at the university and repealed the land acts in 1800. Succeeding sessions debated the issues further, and in 1805 a compromise was reached: the escheated lands were restored to the university, in return for which the Governor became chairman of the board of trustees and the General Assembly was given power to fill board vacancies and to elect fifteen additional trustees. Schober voted affirmatively on this compromise.

As a justice of the peace and an attorney involved in a major land suit, Schober was well aware of the shortcomings of the North Carolina judicial system. The biggest problem was the lack of a Supreme Court. The Assembly of 1801 created a Court of Conference, composed of Superior Court justices meeting in Raleigh to review any decisions on which they disagreed. Three years later the Court of Conference was made permanent, and in 1805 its name was changed to the Supreme Court, Schober voting in the affirmative. He also introduced a bill to prevent "dilatory pleas in courts of law."[43] The latter bill passed its first Senate reading but was rejected by the House of Commons.[44]

---

[41]Johnson, *Ante-Bellum North Carolina*, pp. 220-21.

[42]Lefler and Newsome, *North Carolina*, p. 304.

[43]*Senate Journal*, 1805, p. 23.

[44]*Journal of the House of Commons*, 1805, p. 89.

Altogether, Schober's first legislative session was an exciting experience for him. For a freshman senator, he had certainly participated more than expected. But he did not return to Raleigh for the General Assemblies of 1806 or 1807. Was he beaten in the election, or did the press of affairs prevent him from running? Was he so disappointed at the failure of the state bank to gain capitalization that he considered the results of lawmaking a poor compensation for the effort expended? The records only mention that the election occurred.[45] Given the Moravian tendency to record almost everything locally which involved Moravians, it would seem probable that Schober did not run for reelection. Perhaps the clearest answer was contained in the events of the spring of 1806.

In May, Br. Charles Reichel related to the Overseers a letter in which Gottlieb Schober accused a young sister of illicit sexual relationships. The girl had been in Salem at least three years, probably coming from one of the country congregations. She resided in the sisters' house and had already been approved by the lot for service in the Girls Boarding School. The Elders' Conference investigated the matter "with impartiality" but "did not find anything that would justify such an indictment against a person presumably innocent, an indictment that would probably ruin her character completely."[46] The confidential matter leaked to the girl's family, and Schober was threatened with a lawsuit for defamation of character. He declared that he was ready to prove his contention in court if necessary, but preferred that the matter be handled internally. He did not necessarily want her excluded, "because it is always possible that a Magdalene can become a good Sister,"[47] but he did not think she should be appointed to the Girls' School. The Elders felt that Schober was too harsh, but he would not moderate his charges. Instead he set about gathering evidence for a possible court case. He convinced a young non-Moravian named Geiger to confess

> that he had not only known and used her [sexually], not only once but many times, in which connection details made it believable.

Then under pressure from the Elders and the girl's brother, and with the possibility of a lawsuit, Geiger denied his statements to Schober.

---

[45]Salem Diary, 14 August 1806, Fries and others, *Records of Moravians*, 6:2852.

[46]Board of Overseers, 6 May 1806, Moravian Archives.

[47]Gottlieb Schober to Charles G. Reichel, 1 May 1806, Schober Papers, Old Salem Inc. Archives. Translation by Elizabeth Marx.

So I went to [Geiger] and with difficulty brought him to an interrogation and with serious and judicial demands to know only the truth, I was convinced by his words that he had used her as a prostitute as often as he wanted to. From other details which I had not known which came to light [it was evident] that she had fornicated not only with him but with various [ones].[48]

But the young woman would admit nothing. And to Schober's amazement, the Elders refused to act against her without a confession. This procedure disturbed Gottlieb almost as much as the misdeeds of the young lady.

The wench is supported by her supervisors in her meaningless lies, strengthened in her most impudent manner of life when she strolls everywhere in the town, talks about the accusations impudently and relates her trespasses to others, is acknowledged as gallant and as evidence of her innocence, and although her impudence and lewdness flashes from her eyes and she runs around the town always like a shameless wench, they say of her that she is the only one who has an exemplary manner of life and these are the real reasons for the discord in the Sisters' House. The Congregation leadership declares her guiltless.[49]

As expected, the gossip in Salem was heavy. Now Schober's own honor and character came into question. It was reported that he "declared that if the girl was not sent from the community within five weeks, he would denounce her publicly as a whore and indict her at court."[50] Still community leaders were adamant and prepared to defend the girl at community expense. Schober and others were officially admonished because their talk in the village "has done a lot of damage among our youngsters who will lose all respect and obedience toward their elders and teachers." Realizing that the girl would always be the subject of whispers in Salem, the Elders decided to send her to a Pennsylvania community "through which we are going to prove her innocence."[51] The implication of this action and statement was that the girl's subsequent life would prove her innocence or guilt. Schober continued to growl about the damage to his honor and character, but after the girl left Salem in September, the matter gradually died. In subsequent letters, Gottlieb indicated that he was wrong in the manner of his accusation; he never

---

[48]Ibid.

[49]Ibid.

[50]Board of Overseers, 13 May 1806, Moravian Archives.

[51]Ibid.

admitted that the substance of his charge was incorrect. There was no further mention of the girl's character in Pennsylvania.

This incident illustrated an unhappy trend occurring in Salem: moral values were deteriorating among the younger generation. When early Salem had occasional violations of community moral codes, quick and final exclusions of the guilty provided a tight moral control on the community. Just after the turn of the century, however, moral offenses began to increase. Addiction to drink led to three exclusions around 1797. Some others resisted the marriage procedures, preferring to select their own mates. The community tightened regulations in 1803 in order to avoid unnecessary association between single brothers and sisters on daily business occasions.[52] The year 1806 was an especially bad year in this regard. Several young brothers were caught stealing, and a total of five persons were expelled for moral offenses. On 3 June church authorities noted that

> For some time we have regretted the free way of behavior of [two young single sisters]. There have been some rumors lately against them and this caused Br. & Sr. Reichel, together with Sr. Benzien to talk to them. It was found that some of the items of these rumors were not true. On the whole, however, they were guilty. They were warned in a serious but cordial way to change their way of life or leave the community. Both of them promised to improve in the future.[53]

One week later a sign-out system was installed in the single sisters' house.

While this context of moral problems gave Schober's accusation against the young single sister more credence, his failure to substantiate the charges to authorities who would have believed reasonable evidence left an unsavory aftertaste. Once again he had not controlled his reactions and his vitriolic language left permanent scars. Still he did not learn. In October Gottlieb accused Rudolph Christ of misusing donations given to purchase new musical articles.[54] His abusive language and behavior led to his suspension from Holy Communion with a stern lecture from the Elders recalling his propensity to point an accusative finger too quickly. At first Schober resisted but conversation with Christ established that the

---

[52]Congregation Council, 24 March 1803, Fries and others, *Records of Moravians*, 6:2740.

[53]Board of Overseers, 3 June 1806, Moravian Archives.

[54]Elders' Conference, 1 October 1806; Board of Overseers, 7 October 1806, Moravian Archives.

latter was guilty only of not consulting other organists before he made purchases with the donated money.

The cumulation of successive errors on his part began to affect Schober. His lingering bitterness was impairing his judgement; he considered resigning from his community responsibilities. He asked that the lot again confirm his call to service. It appears that he realized his errors and sincerely wondered whether he should continue. But the Elders commended his faithful service in local and real estate matters. In the words of Christian Benzien:

> I deeply wish that everything which hinders Br. Schober in the performance of such services with a happy heart could be eliminated. His desire to let Christ be the judge [in the lot] does not please me. To the best of my knowledge Br. Schober failed greatly during the last sad occurrences since April or May. But after all, a poor human being can fail even with the best of intentions. Oh how often do I have cause to beg Jesus not to enter into judgement against this poor sinner.
>
> Br. Schober can imagine that I am steadily before Christ about him, for I should think he is completely sure of my love. The sinner's rod ought not to be considered a disgrace among us, but should bind troubled hearts that much tighter within the love of the sinner's friend.[55]

Through the mediation of this dedicated man, the community and Gottlieb Schober were reunited with "a new spirit" in Holy Communion.[56] The following week he was once again at the organ for the worshiping congregation.

---

[55]Letter of Christian L. Benzien; the addressee is uncertain but probably either the Elders' Conference or Schober himself. Salem, 6 October 1806, Schober Papers, Old Salem Inc. Archives. Translation by Grace F. Dollitz and the author.

[56]Elders' Conference, 12 November 1806, Moravian Archives.

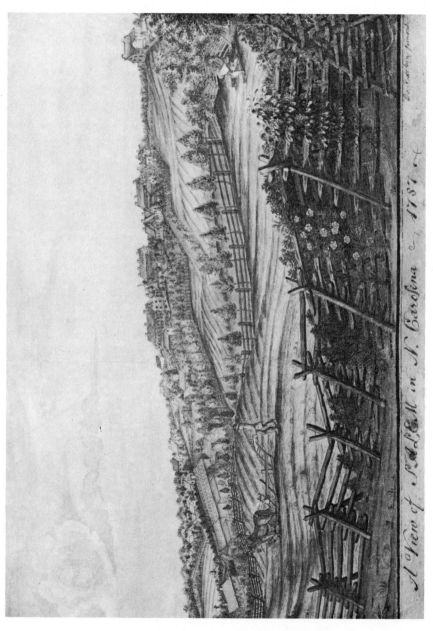

View of Salem from the West, 1787
(painted by Ludwig Gottfried Redeken)

CHAPTER **8**

The Frustrations of Law and Politics

IN COMPARISON TO the busy times of the past, the year 1807 was a quiet one in the Schober household. Gottlieb realized that his uncontrollable temper and tongue must be disciplined. His time was occupied by the usual kinds of tasks of a tinsmith, mill owner, attorney, and justice of the peace. He worked on the document for the indenture of apprentices to close loopholes.[1] He negotiated with the Overseers concerning the building of a new westward road around the paper-mill pond.[2] Despite sensitive issues in both areas, the "new spirit" of cooperation was evident. The most important activity of the year was the acceleration of preparations for what the Brethren hoped would be the conclusion of the Mulberry Fields suit.

The litigation had dragged interminably for both Moravians and Schober. Prospects for final settlement had looked good on several occasions, only to have the courts dash Moravian hopes.[3] Schober had taken several depositions in 1799 to perpetuate testimony since the case was stretching so long. In 1801 the lawyers argued before the Court of

---

[1]Board of Overseers, 27 January, 7 April 1807, *Moravian Archives.*

[2]Board of Overseers, 23 June, 7 July, 22 September 1807, Moravian Archives.

[3]The Wilkes County Land Suit, Fries and others, *Records of Moravians*, 3:1416-17.

Conference in Raleigh where judges agreed that the land did not escheat to the state. They declared, however, that the original suit of Hugh Montgomery against the inhabitants of the land should have included the Moravians as complainants. Schober worked hard on the case during this period, but Duncan Cameron presented the Moravian arguments before the Raleigh Court. With victory appearing close, Salem authorities in 1802 decided to follow the court's directive and prepare a new suit for the District Court at Morganton. Evidently Cameron and James Welborn prepared the new bill; since Schober was at this time embroiled in heated controversy, his participation, if any, was minimal. He returned to the case in 1804 determined to see the matter to conclusion. Correspondence between the attorneys increased substantially as the new bill was amended several times by court direction. Since other individuals had by this time purchased parts of the disputed land from the original defendants, Cameron and Schober had to make sure that everybody received copies:

> this is a labor which might if our adversaries had the spirit of accommodation in them be dispensed with but as we have no favors to ask or to expect, we must do everything which the ordinary course of business points out as necessary to be done.[4]

With this kind of thoroughness, the preparation proceeded. Cameron promised:

> I am much afraid that your interest may suffer from the weakness of my talents and want of knowledge, but while I make this declaration, permit me also to assure you that nothing shall be omitted on my part which can in the smallest degree hasten the decision of the suit and bring it to a termination favorable to your interest.[5]

A few days later Schober acknowledged receipt of the amended bill and Cameron's letter, responding that

> It only cost one hundred and eighty cents [postage], but the confessions in your letter which resemble Christian meekness very much and which convey an idea as if you were doubtful of your talents to do justice to our cause is alone worth that cost.[6]

A friendship was beginning which would increase considerably over the following years.

---

[4]Duncan Cameron to Gottlieb Schober, Hillsboro, 28 June 1804, Moravian Archives.

[5]Ibid.

[6]Gottlieb Schober to Duncan Cameron, Salem, 7 July 1804, Moravian Archives.

The correspondence resumed in 1805 with Cameron directing his less experienced colleague in the needful steps of preparation. While perhaps seeming tedious to a layman, the letters reveal the complexities of the case and give a basis to judge the legal skill of Schober. The letters also contained a succinct summary of the Moravian argument. Cameron wrote:

> After having perused and considered the Copies of Lenoir's & others' Answers to the last amended Bill I think a "general replication" may with safety be put in to them—of this you can give Notice to Mr. Henderson, and then proceed to take Testimony in support of the material Allegations in the Bill—I am of the opinion that the fact of the Land being granted to Cossart as Agent and Trustee of the Unitas Fratrum may be safely rested on the intrinsic evidence furnished by the Grant and the Survey attached to it—the Grant evidently appears to have been made by Earl Granville by way of *gratuity* & it is equally clear that Cossart in his *individual* capacity had no claim on his Bounty or Justice; the Unitas Fratrum however had a very strong demand on both, of this Earl Granville seems to have been sensible, and endeavored by executing the Grant to fulfill that demand, and to make retribution for the loss they had sustained by purchasing a vast tract of his poor & unsaleable Land—It will be important to prove the notariety of the Moravian title or claim to the land, and the partial possession which I am informed they had of both Tracts—it is however unnecessary for me to direct what proof should be sought after and obtained as your knowledge of the Subject is more ample than my own.[7]

Schober spent a large part of May in Wilkes County and upon his return wrote:

> Yesterday, I returned from Wilkes where the whole last week was taken up in taking our depositions, my aim was to prove general Notice of the Moravian claim before the War, confessions of the defendants that they knew of our claim, before they entered the land or purchased, and that we were in possession before Montgomery purchased, and since, of part of each Tract, all of which I think is sufficiently proven and when at leisure, shall send you an extract of each proven point—When we had concluded, I had some nocturnal conversation with Lenoir on the Subject of the dispute, in which by some ambigious [sic] expressions I found that something was hanging over our heads, which for want of sufficient foresight would be fatal to us. I could not divine what that was, but, in conversation I had with one of the possessors of the Land on my way going home, I found that by a conversation he has had with Allfred More since he is Judge that the Judge told him that we could never recover as we had never been in legal possession "and that the Deeds under which we claimed were not registered in due Time, that we could not prove the Trust except by Moravians who are interested & c." all the points he had mentioned we had sufficiently consi-

---

[7]Dun' Cameron to Gottlieb Shober, Hillsboro, 14 April 1805, Moravian Archives.

dered, but about the Deeds nothing had been considered—As soon as I came home I examined the Deeds, and they are registered March 23, 1772. Mr. Bagge swears that the Deeds had arived from Europe at the end of the Year 1770 or in the beginning of the year 1771, that he delivered those deeds to the Registerer of Rowan to be registered in March, 1771—by all which it however appears that they were not registered in one Year after their arrival in this County as the Law requires—

This Sir is the cause of sending the bearer to you express, to know your opinion, whether we can nevertheless proceed or stop short—or how the defect can now be remedied if at all. . . . if this is incurable, by evidence or court, can a legislative sanction do any thing to cure it, and would they do it during a depending Suit?

. . . .

Just now another thing strikes me, perhaps that if proven would show an impossibility of the Deeds being proven in Time—in 1771 the regulation were in town, & perhaps the papers were all taken to a safe place for preservation.[8]

Two days later the messenger returned with Cameron's response which "eased me of three quarters of my pain respecting the registration of our Deed." Schober too had been searching; he discovered

an act of Assembly 1770 Ch. IX which I believe governed our People at the Time, as this Act does not say it shall be registered, but "tendered or delivered to be registered" But . . . there still remains a quibble to combat. Lenoir was in the Assembly in 1787 and if you read the XXIII Chapt, sect II you will see, I trust, a none efficacious cloven foot [a loophole favoring Lenoir's position].[9]

Another tangle Schober uncovered was whether the deed registration in Rowan County was valid when the land actually lay in newly created Surry County. While these were minor points, Schober knew full well that the ultimate decision might swing on such a point. Lenoir was determined to explore every possible legal maneuver to validate his own claims so that Cameron and Schober could afford to leave no possibility untouched. It could probably be proved, Schober mused, that

in 1771 April & May the Regulation was at its highth [sic], so that perhaps Surry County did not begin to act as a created being before the regulation ceased to exist, if you think this will be necessary I will collect proof to that point.[10]

---

[8]G. Shober to Duncan Cameron, Salem, 21 May 1805, Moravian Archives. The "regulation" refers to a local rebellion against crown authorities in England. The Regulator Movement centered in Alamance County, but touched many places in central and eastern North Carolina in 1771 and 1772.

[9]G. Shober to Duncan Cameron, Salem, 23 May 1805, Moravian Archives.

[10]Ibid.

After this flurry of letters, Schober turned to the time-consuming task of gathering his evidence. He carried the major burden of preparation in this regard, corresponding with Cameron only when the latter's experienced counsel might help. Lenoir and the other defendants dragged matters as slowly as possible—or so it seemed to Schober—so that in 1806 depositions were still being taken. In that hectic year of Schober's life, he spent a total of twenty-one days in Wilkes County gathering evidence. Costs of traveling in those days were shown in vouchers which Schober submitted, such as one for 27 August 1806, covering eight days and totalling $16.81. This included board for two men and their horses, one pipe and tobacco, two glasses of whiskey, one pint of wiskey, one quart of rum, and two extra meals.[11] A shorter trip cost $12.12 for "Yadkin Ferry, Huntersville, Catawba Ferry Crossing, Oats at Mattaffey's, Lawrence's overnight expenses in Morganton, a tavern bill of $5.37, returning at Cockron's Feeding, Mattaffey's overnight, and Mr. Lane for a Horse."[12]

Schober described his activities on these trips in a letter to Benzien:

> When Lenoir's days [of examination of witnesses] began, I expected to hear a great deal of fine swearing—On the first day he only began after two o'clock and in three days only examined five witnesses, the first four were only examined to discredit one of our witnesses and if possible to accuse G. Welborne of subornation of perjury, it therefore became me to cross examine them sharply and have in my opinion succeeded to destroy the effect of their testimony by their own words. On Wednesday he had summoned the same witness which we had examined on Saturday before and he and I belabored him until midnight but it turned out nothing to his purpose.[13]

Schober was satisfied that the evidence proved

> everything we alleged in the bill in support of our title excepting the power of attorney from F. Wm. Marshall to J. M. Graff. Judge McCoy swears that there was one in existence, that he proffered it in Wilkes County to be seconded, that after some referrals it was done & c. But on record nothing is found.[14]

In 1807 the judicial system of North Carolina was reorganized so that the case was shifted to the Court of Equity in Iredell County. It was finally

---

[11]Document dated 27 August 1806, in Schober Papers, Old Salem Inc. Archives.

[12]Document dated 16 March 1805, Schober Papers, Old Salem Inc. Archives.

[13]G. Schober to Reverend C. L. Benzien, Salem, 22 June 1806, Moravian Archives.

[14]Gottlieb Shober to Duncan Cameron, Salem, 28 February 1806, Moravian Archives.

heard in 1808. Schober was well prepared, but the defense was also able to spring some surprises. Defense counsel Henderson pointed to the lack of proper registration of the deed in Wilkes County, and, while Schober countered this with precedents from similar cases, the court referred the matter to the North Carolina Supreme Court. Defense as expected also attacked the power of attorney granted from Marshall to Graff.

> I was . . . prepared to prove . . . it was lost but unfortunately a few days before we went to Statesville the original was found in an old pigeon hole and . . . on the back are endorsements by Judge Spencer that it was in the year 1779 proven before him by the subscribing witness, that with an order for registration. I deemed it, together with Judge McCoy's deposition proving that he had presented it for registration in Wilkes where it was rejected sufficient, but the Judge decided against me and the case now goes to the Supreme Court.[15]

Several other points worried Schober; Cameron, who was prevented from attending the Iredell hearing because of illness, nevertheless continued to believe that the main points were strongly in the Moravians' favor. Schober followed the suit to Raleigh and was successful in sustaining the points of contention, allowing the hearing in Iredell to continue. It would appear that Cameron left the case after this victory probably because of his health; from this point Schober worked with Archibald D. Murphey, another prominent Hillsboro attorney who was destined to become a leader in the growth and development of the state. Murphey visited Salem in July, 1808, where "all attention was shown to him, especially by the Brn. Benzien and Schober, who had a number of conversations with him, informing him as to our constitution and institutions."[16]

Schober also likely shared with Murphey his intention to run again for the General Assembly. Eleven days later "our Br. Gottlieb Schober was elected senator from Stokes County."[17] A note of pride was inherent in the diary entry; he had redeemed his personal failures of 1806 and regained stature in the community by his hard labor on the Mulberry Fields case. His only quarrel during the year was more humorous than serious. He traded a mare with filly and $50 to a fellow Moravian for another horse, only to discover afterward that the animal "is blind in one

[15]Gottlieb Shober to Duncan Cameron, Salem, 2 May 1808, Moravian Archives.

[16]Salem Diary, 31 July 1808, Fries and others, *Records of Moravians*, 6:2921.

[17]Salem Diary, 11 August 1808, Fries and others, *Records of Moravians*, 6:2921.

eye and hardly sees in the other."[18] The previous owner knew the problem but did not tell his buyer; when an undoubtedly angry Schober confronted the brother, the $50 was already spent. Obviously the Overseers supported Gottlieb but probably laughed privately that the shrewd Schober had finally been temporarily outwitted.

On 21 November the senator from Stokes County answered the initial roll call in Raleigh, and fireworks started immediately. A petition from Stokes County resident Johnson Clement alledged that Schober's election was improper. Such challenges were frequent at every Assembly, but it must have irritated Gottlieb to appear before the committee on elections. No improprieties were found in Schober's case and his seat was confirmed.[19] His appointment to the Finance Committee, probably the most important regular committee, indicated his enhanced stature among his fellow senators. He also came prepared with a barrage of bills to present to the body. The first of these was entitled "A Bill Concerning Divorce and Alimony."

Divorce legislation had been presented in previous years, and therefore Schober's presentation was probably not entirely his own composition. For several years bills had regularly been killed at the second Senate reading. Schober's activity on the 1805 Committee on Divorce and Alimony, however, had convinced him that legislation was needed. Undoubtedly he had worked on the bill to make it more acceptable to the bodies of the Assembly. The bill provided

> That when a marriage hath been heretofore, or shall be hereafter contracted and celebrated between any two persons, and it shall be adjudged in the manner hereinafter mentioned, that either party at the time of the contract, was, and still is, naturally impotent, or that either party lives in adultery, in every such case it shall and may be lawful for the innocent and injured party to obtain a divorce, not only from bed and board, but from the bond of matrimony itself.[20]

It further provided relief from bed and board for wives who were physically abused by a husband or abandoned by him, in which case the wife was entitled to alimony not to exceed one-third of the husband's estate. Jurisdiction in divorce cases was to be given to the superior courts

---

[18]Board of Overseers, 19 February 1808, Moravian Archives.

[19]*Senate Journal*, 1808, pp. 4, 14.

[20]*Senate Journal*, 1808, section entitled, "Bills ordered by the General Assembly to be printed and stitched up with the Acts, for Public Information."

with jury trial available but not required. The bill therefore proposed to remove divorce completely from the General Assembly. First readings in both chambers passed. The Senate approved a second reading 30-22; the House voted negatively 56-59, then reconsidered and referred it to a joint committee. The House later approved the second reading, and the Senate its third 26-25. It was finally defeated in the House 55-57. Recognizing the close vote, both bodies agreed to print the bill for public information. Only after six more years of handling petitions would the Assembly enact a law on divorce; the act passed in 1814 was almost exactly Schober's bill of 1808, even to the wording. The only significant change was to reserve to the Assembly the right to confirm the court's decision, without which the divorce was void.[21] Even this law was not long unchanged, but Schober had left his mark on the social life of North Carolinians.

The Stokes Senator was also still disturbed by the banking and currency situation in North Carolina. He presented a bill designed to help strengthen the "present paper currency of the State."[22] First readings were passed, but it failed on the second in the Senate by a vote of 18 to 33. His next bill dealt with internal improvements in the state, providing for developing and maintaining public roads and highways. It was immediately rejected by the House.[23] At the request of Salem officials, Schober presented a bill "to lay a tax on such citizens who, on account of religious scruples, have hitherto been exempted from doing military duty in time of peace."[24] This was a circuitous method to perpetuate military exemptions for Moravians and Quakers; it was rejected by motion at its second Senate reading.

Schober's voting on other bills reflected his concern for strengthening the state judicial system, good fiscal management and equitable taxation, and internal improvements. On taxation, Schober entered a vigorous protest on the Revenue Bill for 1809 presented by the Finance Committee. He believed that since owners of town lots were not represented in the Senate, taxation without their consent violated the North Carolina Constitution. He further stated that

---

[21]Johnson, *Ante-Bellum North Carolina*, pp. 218-19.

[22]*Senate Journal*, 1808, p. 21; *House Journal*, 1808, p. 26.

[23]*House Journal*, 1808, p. 27.

[24]*Senate Journal*, 1808, p. 25.

it is in the highest degree unjust, that a poor man possessing a house in a town, worth one hundred pounds, should pay as much tax as three hundred acres of land, which, with their improvements, may be, and often is worth five thousand pounds.

. . . .

Taxation ought, in every well regulated government, to be in the proportion to the property protected by the State, otherwise it protects the rich at the expense of the poor of the community and which in [the first section of the Revenue Bill] as it stands, is the case.[25]

This speech essentially attacked the strong, vested interests of North Carolina politics of the time. Since only men owning fifty acres of land were eligible to cast votes in Senate elections, and the poorer man with only a town lot was excluded, the Senate did in fact tax without representation. Election laws of the time placed government in the hands of the wealthy; it was precisely the wealthy to whom Schober spoke—men who had to own at least three hundred acres of land to qualify as a Senator. In short, North Carolina government was at this time essentially an oligarchy. "The General Assembly, which made the laws and elected the governor and other state officials as well as United States senators, was virtually all-powerful in the state government."[26] Moreover, the Assembly itself was politically dominated by delegates from the eastern part of the state, who tenaciously maintained the status quo at every turn. When a new western county was created, easterners tried to match it by subdividing an eastern county. The eastern bloc consistently opposed internal improvements such as roads, since the wealthier East would bear the major portion of the cost while the West would reap the most benefit. It was probably this attitude which so quickly and resoundingly killed Schober's road bill. This perspective also passed the revenue bill which Schober correctly labelled undemocratic. Still, he would not be silent. He violently attacked the Assembly's authorization of the state treasurer to invest money at six percent out of state when it could earn eight percent in local bank stock which would have

profited this State the annual sum of four thousand dollars and upwards, relieved our citizens in distress, created a necessary fund for the sinking of our present paper money, and enabled this State to improve inland Navigation and roads without taxation.[27]

---

[25]*Senate Journal*, 1808, p. 51.

[26]Lefler and Newsome, North Carolina, p. 323.

[27]*Senate Journal*, 1808, p. 57.

Still the authorization was given. With these positions, Schober aligned his voice and vote against the conservative, wealthy majority in the Senate. This power bloc was not able to defeat every bill threatening the status quo, but it carefully protected the interests of the wealthy.

Schober did vote more conservatively than the majority of the Senate on two occasions. One was a resolution of support of national policies. America was having difficulty relating to the European powers who were themselves locked in a power struggle. On the continent, Napoleon was seeking to enforce French dominance and trying to break English commercial power and cripple English control of the seas. England responded with a naval blockade of continental ports. America was officially neutral, but tried to continue her foreign trade with both. The English navy occasionally stopped American ships to search for contraband and ever more frequently took sailors to serve on the British war ships. This impressment of sailors, under a guise that the men were English deserters, infuriated Americans and the government. The American navy, however, was far too weak to uphold American integrity before the powerful British.

In June 1807 the American *Chesapeake* refused to submit to search by the British *Leopard* and was fired upon. President Jefferson then used the only weapon available—an embargo act prohibiting all exports from America. The measure was devastating to American shipping, but the president hoped to hurt England and France even more and force them to respect American neutrality. Most citizens disliked the embargo act, yet the *Chesapeake* incident called for drastic action. Even though the measure hurt North Carolina commerce, the power bloc of wealthy landowners presented a strong resolution in support of the national policies early in the session. Some members, including Schober, felt that the expression was too strong and moved to substitute a softer version which condemned "the repeated violations of the rights of the United States" and pledged

> to support [the federal government's] just measures with unanimity and zeal, and in the cause of their country to submit to all privations, to encounter all the inconveniences, and make all the exertions which a resistance to foreign insolence and injustice shall demand of freemen and Americans.[28]

This more moderate statement, although itself a firm commitment to the federal government, was rejected by the Senate 16-37, with Schober

---

[28]*Senate Journal*, 1808, p. 11.

voting yes. The Senate returned to the stronger resolutions, but the minority, led by Richard Williams and Schober, moved to strike one of the seven resolutions and amend another. The part which Schober and others disliked was the specific statement of approval of the embargo acts: "The Legislature of North Carolina consider them as the best means which could have been devised to preserve our citizens and property from the devouring grasp of the belligerent powers." They wished to substitute that North Carolinians "will cheerfully aquiesce in their continuance, until a repeal can be obtained of the unjust regulations which occasioned them."[29] Other than this point, the tone of the two sets of resolutions was similar; the latter was more specific in naming the *Chesapeake-Leopard* incident and making the willingness even to go to war, implicit in the softer version, more explicit by stating

> we value peace as one of the greatest blessings which any nation can enjoy; yet, rather than surrender our liberty and independence, we will surround the standard of our country, and risk our lives and fortunes in her defence.[30]

The stronger resolutions carried 37-15, Schober voting no.

Although the ambiguity of party labels makes analysis difficult, Schober seems to have voted with more conservative Republicans, perhaps even with the Federalists. But his position was crystal clear, thanks to the amendments which he seconded. He supported American foreign policy of the time but did not like the embargo act nor consider it a satisfactory answer to the problems confronting the state and the nation. Most historians conclude that the embargo act was a mistake. America should have either endured the affronts for the sake of profits to be made or built a navy that would command respect. Instead, the burden fell unduly on one segment of the economy and population—especially New Englanders. Smuggling was thereby encouraged, and, after unsuccessful attempts at enforcement, the law was quietly disregarded. It certainly was not, as Schober and the minority maintained, the best alternative for America at this time.

The other conservative vote by Schober involved the issue of slavery. North Carolina in 1794 had prohibited the importation of slaves into the state. The 1808 Assembly considered a bill to repeal the act of 1794, and Schober consistently voted in the affirmative. A federal law, passed in

---

[29]*Senate Journal*, 1805, p. 12.

[30]Ibid.

1807, prohibited further importation of slaves but allowed a grace period during which the states had time to conform. The North Carolina bill was probably designed to take advantage of the grace period, with full knowledge that it would soon be superceded by the federal statute. The bill reflected an eastern plantation perspective, and, on this issue, Schober followed. The bill was ultimately killed but not without a struggle. Lest Schober be judged too harshly, this vote must be paired with another affirmative vote on a slave issue. He consistently favored a bill to allow persons who were against slavery on grounds of conscience to free any slaves they might come to possess. This bill was ultimately withdrawn—on threat of defeat—by the Quakers who presented it, but Schober's affirmation was registered on the roll call.[31]

Altogether Schober acquitted himself well in his second Senate term. He was active in committee and very vocal on the floor. His bills showed foresight, and, given the nature of North Carolina politics, even their defeat stood to his credit. Subsequent events and legislation confirmed that in areas in which Schober was interested and informed, his judgments were sound. When he left Raleigh on 20 December 1808, he never reentered political office at the state level. In all likelihood, he could have returned to the Senate in 1809 had he chosen to do so. Other men, such as Archibald D. Murphey, used a successful law practice and a career in the State Senate as a platform from which to become influential state leaders. Murphey served in the Senate from 1812 to 1818 where he led an aggressive program of reform.[32] He fought the general backwardness of the state, advocating true democratic government as the best agency of self-development. He worked for internal improvements in transportation and public schools to educate the young. Had Schober been in the Senate during these years he would have added his support to Murphey's ideas. But Schober served his fellowman only when he could interpret that effort as his service to God. Ultimately he found a purer expression of that desire, and when Murphey entered the Senate in 1812, Schober had begun a new career, that, by virtue of Article 31 of the North Carolina Constitution made him ineligible for service in the General Assembly.

From the bustle of the state capital, Gottlieb returned to the quietness of Salem and his beloved family. All were healthy, and the children were

---

[31]*Senate Journal*, 1808, pp. 27-28.

[32]Lefler and Newsome, North Carolina, pp. 328-38.

growing up. Nathaniel served as Salem's postmaster and helped his father on legal matters. He was a careful secretary and scribe, so that he was seriously considered when the Overseers searched for a person to keep their minutes. Emmanuel was also serving the congregation but began to follow the footsteps of his father in the study of law, much to the disapproval of Salem officials. But the big news was Johanna. Excitement must have seized the household when in 1809 she quietly declared her intention to marry Vaniman Zevely.[33] For Gottlieb and Maria, however, elation was tempered by apprehension; they knew that marriage in Salem was not by personal preference. Only the Elders could approve a match, and even then, the union had to be confirmed by the lot. That two single people in Salem should know each other well enough to request marriage was sufficient to cause questions. The timing was especially bad because in June two young people of the community had become involved sexually so that a necessary marriage had to be performed by the resident justice of the peace, Johanna's father.[34] While there was no suggestion of a similar relationship between Johanna and Vaniman, Gottlieb knew that the Elders would firmly hold to Moravian practice. That supposition proved correct. Schober reported to the Elders' Conference that the two young people

> do not wish to give up each other. Much as he regrets the situation he wishes that they may be allowed to marry in orderly fashion. They have said that they did not wish to leave the congregation, and he wishes that they might be considered as auswärtige members.[35]

An *austwärtige* member belonged to the congregation but lived outside Salem; he had privileges of worship and fellowship but no voice in the management of community affairs. This status had developed as a compromise in the 1780s for those who lived on farms near Salem but did not come under the lease system and moral control of the congregation.

---

[33]Vaniman Zevely, sometimes also referred to as Van Neiman, was born 13 November 1780 at Ninety-Six, South Carolina, of Swiss immigrant parents. After their deaths, he moved to Salem in 1798 to join the Moravians. He was apprenticed to the cabinet maker and later pursued this craft in the single brothers' house. After Johanna's death in 1821, Vaniman remarried and later became a missionary in Virginia. Salem Diary, 11 May 1836, Fries and others, *Records of Moravians*, 8:4216.

[34]Board of Overseers, 13 June 1809, Moravian Archives.

[35]Elders' Conference, 12 August 1809, Fries and others, *Records of Moravians*, 7:3094-95. Auswärtige means "outside-dwelling."

Schober hoped that his daughter could in this manner remain connected with the congregation.

The Elders reluctantly agreed at first, but when the Overseers raised questions of the example this might set for others, the Elders agreed. Schober was informed that the boards could not approve the marriage nor the status as *auswärtige* members; if Johanna and Vaniman were married "it will be understood that they have left our fellowship."[36] The couple was nevertheless married, the bride's father officiating, and moved from the immediate community. Seven months later they were readmitted to the Salem congregation as *auswärtige* members.[37]

Other than Johanna's marriage, the year 1809 was quiet for Schober. Legal work occupied most of his time, especially the Mulberry Fields case. In April, he and Archibald Murphey traveled to Iredell court, but Schober again had to report that "the case was not finished at this court, but was referred to the next Supreme Court in Raleigh."[38] In June another point was settled in Raleigh, enabling the Iredell hearing to continue. All of these dilatory tactics by the defense and the delays in the judicial process began to take their toll on Schober's patience. Was he really accomplishing anything? Was he truly serving God or merely participating in an all-too-human enterprise? Such questions plagued his mind during the fall of 1809. All of his activities in the legal sphere were becoming burdensome. Suddenly, on 9 January 1810, Schober announced his resignation as justice of the peace.[39] No specific reasons were made public, and probably only Gottlieb's close friends knew the extent of his frustrations with legal matters. Community officials wondered at the meaning of this resignation; soon the reasons became disturbingly clear. In April Schober again went to the Iredell Court, probably hoping at last to conclude the matter. When another postponement became inevitable, he wrote a letter to Br. Benzien in Salem. Benzien immediately shared with the Elders that Schober "feels an inner urge to accompany Pastor [Carl] Storch on a trip to South Carolina, to preach to the Germans there and seek out awakened souls."[40] The Brethren registered surprise and

---

[36]Elders' Conference, 31 August 1809, Fries and others, *Records of Moravians*, 7:3095.

[37]Salem Diary, 13 May 1810, Fries and others, *Records of Moravians*, 7:3110.

[38]Salem Diary, 27 April 1809, Fries and others, *Records of Moravians*, 7:3075.

[39]Board of Overseers, 9 January 1810, Fries and others, *Records of Moravians*, 7:3117.

[40]Elders' Conference, 2 May 1810, Fries and others, *Records of Moravians*, 7:3120.

declared that the preaching trip was "unauthorized." In his letter to Benzien, Schober indicated that an important factor in his decision was his continuing distrust of the community officials. He believed that had he requested permission to work in the Lutheran churches of the area, it would have been denied. Benzien admitted "the adverse opinions against you of the brethren here and there," but regretted Schober's precipitous action—a course which would still have been possible if a request had been refused. He continued:

> even though it is quite unpleasant for me that you entered into your new plan without any connection with us, still your declaration did show that you did not pass by the best Counsellor of all and have acted according to a conviction which I dare not undertake to judge.[41]

The man with whom Schober traveled to South Carolina was Carl Storch, a well-known Lutheran minister of the area who had been in Salem many times for worship and other business. While relations between Moravians and Lutherans were most cordial, Schober's decision was his own and probably would not have been approved beforehand. He preached his first sermon on 29 April and, upon his return to Salem, indicated his intention to continue to speak to Lutherans in the area when requested. When the Elders discussed this development they asked Schober "not to preach in the neighborhood of our congregations." It was agreed that he would play the organ at communion, since then "he will not be so much in the eye of the congregation."[42] In short, Salem officials were displeased with this new development, and somewhat perplexed as to how it should be handled. It was not unusual for a Moravian to preach in a Lutheran church, but never without prior permission.[43] To censure him would question his inner conviction to preach; but to disregard it would be a dangerous precedent.

While the Brethren awaited directions on the matter from the Unity Elders' Conference in Europe, Schober continued to preach. Even the distress of Maria Schober would not change his mind. She "wishes nothing more longingly than that you might give up your plan." She did not want to stand in her husband's way but was concerned

---

[41]Chr. Ludw. Benzien to Gottlieb Schober, Salem, 31 May 1801, Schober Papers, Old Salem Inc. Archives, Translation: Elizabeth Marx.

[42]Elders' Conference, 9 June 1810, Fries and others, *Records of Moravians*, 7:3120.

[43]Salem Diary, 17 September 1785, Fries and others, *Records of Moravians*, 5:2086; 25 September 1808, Fries and others, *Records of Moravians*, 7:3123.

in regard to material things, in regard to the children, and in regard to the opinions that are to be feared and such like, and she is frightened to think that in the future she shall be so little with you and be able to serve you.[44]

Schober seemed determined to follow his conscience, but quietly, hoping not to alienate congregational authorities. His expressed desire to serve God in the ministry had long remained only a frustrated dream. He tried to substitute service to the congregation in legal matters but that too lacked the fulfillment for which Schober yearned. By midsummer he made a decision: he would resign from his responsibilities related to the practice of law and devote himself to pastoral work. On 1 August he relinquished his position in the Mulberry Fields suit, offering future advice, but leaving that thorny matter for others to complete.[45] Benzien wished him well. Personally and on behalf of the community leaders, he expressed appreciation for Gottlieb's efforts in the land suit. Furthermore, Benzien added,

be assured that even if we have no share in your mission, I will accompany you in your pilgrim way from the bottom of my heart, indeed daily and constantly with prayer and pleading. I do not doubt in the least that you will lift up Jesus and his redeeming death . . . from every pulpit and in every home, where you have opportunity. . . . I shall be deeply happy when you can inform me that you are finding people who are looking for a Savior or who are our brothers, for you are long acquainted with the fact that in the case of the latter I do not inquire about [church] constitutions or private opinions.[46]

Gottlieb's friends were quietly curious and even more supportive than officials might have wished. In Bethania, on 19 August,

---

[44]Benzien to Schober, 31 May 1810, Schober Papers, Old Salem Inc. Archives, Translation: Elizabeth Marx.

[45]*Helfer Conferenz*, 1 August 1810, Fries and others, *Records of Moravians*, 7:3122. Even if Schober had continued, he would never have witnessed the final solution. In 1814 the Supreme Court of North Carolina ruled in favor of the Moravians. The following year the executors of the estate of Montgomery offered the tracts at public sale, and James Wellborn purchased the land. But Lenoir persisted in the fight and secured a rehearing in Iredell county which was referred to the Supreme Court again in 1824. Four years later the court for the final time reaffirmed the Moravian claim. The Brethren still had not received money from the original mortgage which by that time had shifted to other persons. An additional suit was necessary to collect a part of the money and the rest was written off as a loss in 1856. See Fries and others, *Records of Moravians*, 3:1417-19.

[46]Benzien to Schober, 31 May 1810, Schober Papers, Old Salem Inc. Archives. Translation: Elizabeth Marx.

there was no preaching here, as nearly all our members had gone to Shores Town to hear Br. Gottlieb Schober, from Salem, who was recently given permission by the Lutheran Ministerium to preach in this neighborhood.[47]

Early the following month a group of Lutheran and Reformed Christians gathered a new church, elected elders for each group, and "as their pastor Mr. Gottlieb Schober was unanimously called and asked to accept the position, to which he agreed in the name of Jesus."[48] On 21 October 1810, at the Organ Lutheran Church in Rowan County, Schober was ordained by Carl Storch, Philip Henkel, and Robert J. Miller.[49] The Lutheran Synod, meeting at the same time, invited the churches Schober served to request membership in the synod. In the Salem Elders' Conference the report of the event was ominous:

> On October 21, Br. Gottlieb Schober was ordained a Lutheran minister. We believe that by this step he has left our church, but for the sake of his family he will be permitted to continue to live in Salem, so long as no ill results appear.[50]

Gottlieb was undaunted by the possibility of future trouble. As he said in a later sermon, the ministerial office "is more reverential than any office men give; as holy as honorable, but also as dangerous as it can possibly be."[51] It was no easy yoke: to be responsible for the spiritual welfare and eternal destiny of human beings humbled even Gottlieb Schober.

---

[47]Bethania Diary, 19 August 1810, Fries and others, *Records of Moravians*, 7:3127.

[48]"Church Book of Shiloh Church," Moravian Archives.

[49]*Kurzer Bericht von den Conferenzen der Vereinigten Evangelisch Lutherischen Predigern und Abgeordnetan in dem Staat Nord-Carolina vom Jahr 1803, bis zum Jahr 1810*, (Neu-Market, Virginia, Ambrostus Henkel, 1811), p. 18.

[50]Elders' Conference, 7 November 1810, Fries and others, *Records of Moravians*, 7:3123.

[51]F. W. E. Peschau, trans., *Minutes of the Evangelical Lutheran Synod and Ministerium of North Carolina, 1803-1826* (Newberry, South Carolina: Aull & Houseal, 1804), p. 25.

CHAPTER 9

A Call
to Preach
and Publish

GERMAN IMMIGRANTS OF the Lutheran religious persuasion arrived in America in force in the early eighteenth century, attracted primarily to Pennsylvania. As the best farm lands of eastern Pennsylvania filled, settlers filtered southward, first into Maryland and Virginia and slowly into North Carolina. A separate group of German colonists built New Bern in 1710, but they were almost completely destroyed by Indian attacks. By the 1750s Lutherans were becoming more numerous in North Carolina, although ministers were very scarce.

In Pennsylvania, the lack of ministers was also acute, causing European Lutherans to dispatch a number of missionaries. Among the more prominent of these was Nicholaus Ludwig, Count von Zinzendorf, who arrived in 1741. This was the same Count Zinzendorf who had allowed the *Unitas Fratrum* to settle on his European estate in 1722. At that time, neither Zinzendorf nor the Brethren considered the *Unitas Fratrum* a separate denomination; rather they were an *ecclesiola in ecclesia*, a little society within the church. Therefore Zinzendorf remained a Lutheran and when Pennsylvanians wrote to the University of Halle appealing for preachers, Zinzendorf was among those sent. He labored among the congregations in Pennsylvania for several years, appearing intent on establishing a cross-confessional unity of all Protestant Christians which he called a "Congregation of God in the Spirit." He believed that every church possessed some "jewel" of truth which would benefit other bodies, and no group could claim to embody the complete truth in themselves.[1] No person should disturb the "Diversity of religious Denominations," but "all these Ideas betray their human origin."[2] Zinzendorf therefore did not wish the distinctive emphasis of a particular group to disappear, but that all groups should unite around the central affirmations of Protestantism. He was happy if Lutherans, Moravians, German Reformed, and any other Christians could join together to form a church. Preaching of this sort confused the Lutherans in Pennsylvania, and when Henry Melchoir Muhlenberg arrived as a pastor in 1742, he found the congregations disspirited and disorganized. He labored mightily to combat Zinzendorf's ideas and to define the distinctive Lutheran congregation.

As other ministers of similar persuasion arrived, the tide turned against the ecumenical efforts of Zinzendorf, and in 1748 a synod of the Lutheran ministers in Pennsylvania was formed. It rapidly encompassed the majority of Lutherans in that state, changing its composition in 1761 to include lay delegates at the meetings. By 1779 Lutherans in America had broken their bonds to Europe and emerged as an independent spiritual entity. Primarily through the work of Muhlenberg, the Pennsylvania synod continued to grow stronger and became the model for similar organizations in other states after the Revolution.

The Lutheran synod in North Carolina was formed in 1803, the third such body in America. Its purpose was to recruit, train, and ordain ministers for the region and to further the work of the churches in the area in whatever way possible. When the synod was established there were already a number of strong Lutheran churches in the Carolinas. In the eighteenth century, German colonists had settled in Charleston, Purysburg, Orangeburg, Barnwell, Edgefield, Abbeville, and other places in South Carolina.[3] In North Carolina, most Germans came originally from Pennsylvania. A large group of Lutherans and German Reformed settled in Rowan and Cabarrus counties, south and west of the Moravians

---

[1] N. L. Count von Zinzendorf, *Maxims, Theological Ideas and Sentences*, extracted by J. Gambold (London: J. Beecroft, 1751), pp. 332-33. See also A. J. Lewis, *Zinzendorf: Ecumenical Pioneer* (London: Westminister Press, 1962), pp. 141-50.

[2] N. L. Count von Zinzendorf, *Nine Publick Discourses Upon Important Subjects in Religion* (London: 1748), p. 125.

[3] See G. D. Bernheim, *History of the German Settlements and of the Lutheran Church in North and South Carolina* (Philadelphia: The Lutheran Book Store, 1872), pp. 175ff.

in Wachovia. Small struggling congregations received a great impetus by the arrival in 1773 of Adolph Nussman and J. G. Arndt. Both labored in the Rowan County churches until after the Revolution, bringing stability and vigor to the small Lutheran beginnings in the state. Soon other pastors arrived: Christian E. Bernhardt in 1786 and Carl Charles A. G. Storch and Arnold Roschen in 1788. Storch assumed direction of Organ Church near Salisbury, a congregation of eighty-seven families.[4] Robert J. Miller, an Englishman, was ordained a Lutheran minister in 1791 for work in Lincoln county to the west. Philip Henkel took over a Lutheran pastorate in Guilford County in 1801. Still the number of ministers was woefully inadequate, and those who labored in the field became convinced that North Carolina Lutherans must provide for their own needs. In May 1803, ministers and lay delegates met near Salisbury to form the North Carolina Synod. The early minutes expressed to the churches their hopes:

> Ye yourselves will know, that it is necessary, if the Christian Church is to be perpetuated, that order must be preserved both among the ministers and in the congregations. Dear brethren, we look to you to assist us in this noble undertaking. God's work calls for help; the condition of our church and people calls for help; the condition of thousands, both of old and young, calls for help; and shall this call of God and the cry of so many immortal souls not be heard at all, or heard in vain?[5]

Besides setting up the usual mechanics of organization, such as time of meeting, officers, and the role of elected deputies of the congregation, the first synod attacked directly the major problem in North Carolina. For congregations that had no regular pastor, the synod made provisions for periodical visitation for preaching and Holy Communion. For areas where German settlers were scattered and no churches existed, the synod commissioned missionary trips to preach and explore possibilities for new churches. To increase the number of ministers, the synod began to license promising young men as catechists while they received private instruction from some of the older ministers. In this manner a student became a candidate for the ministry and was "ordained as soon as he had received a call as pastor of a church, without having to pass through a

---

[4]Bernheim, *History of the German Settlements*, p. 330.

[5]Quoted in Bernheim, *History of the German Settlements*, p. 357. The last part of this paragraph beginning with "Dear Brethren" was written by Schober in 1810 as part of a circular letter endorsed by the same men who wrote the first part in 1803. It is included here because, as Bernheim also felt, it summarized the reasons for the organization of a synod most eloquently.

state of licensed probation."[6] Candidates for the ministry had to understand Latin and be able to read the Greek New Testament. As the synod waxed in vitality, contacts between Lutheran ministers and the Moravians in Salem became more frequent.

Carl Storch worshiped with his German compatriots in Wachovia as early as 1795.[7] When the new church in Salem was dedicated in 1800, Storch and Paul Henkel, another Lutheran pastor, were invited. Two years later Storch was characterized as "a true friend of the Unity" when his visit to worship was recorded in the congregation diary.[8] And the friendship was reciprocal. Moravian ministers had for a long time preached in Lutheran and German Reformed churches, usually when the church had no pastor. Beginning in 1776, Brethren traveled to Haw River to preach, baptize children, and visit in Lutheran homes.[9] Since these congregations were also founded on the Augsburg Confession, Moravians could gladly join them in worship, exhorting them to make their knowledge and conviction a matter of the heart as well as the head.[10] There was only one point of friction. The Lutherans about 1802 were involved in the religious revivals known in American religious history as the "Second Great Awakening." The camp meeting, especially popular among Methodists and Baptists, caught the Lutheran imagination, much to the concern of Moravians who feared emotional excesses. They liked the preaching but,

> some things happened which were very offensive and running contrary to the teachings of the Gospel, for example, people fell down and lay for a long time in a kind of swoon, experiencing the pangs of the new birth, they said, not only for themselves but also for others.[11]

This report was brought to Salem by Gottlieb Schober who attended a revival meeting at the request of Salem authorities. They learned that a similar gathering was to be held near Salem and asked Schober to investigate. Ultimately the Brethren convinced the Lutheran Paul Hen-

---

[6]Bernheim, *History of the German Settlements*, p. 372.

[7]Salem Diary, 23 August 1795, Fries and others, *Records of Moravians*, 6:2535.

[8]Salem Diary, 27 May 1802, Fries and others, *Records of Moravians*, 6:2698.

[9]Salem Diary, 5 June 1777, Fries and others, *Records of Moravians*, 3:1152.

[10]Friedberg Diary, 27 May 1776, Fries and others, *Records of Moravians*, 3:1115.

[11]Salem Diary, 4 October 1802, Fries and others, *Records of Moravians*, 6:2702.

kel to move the meeting from Salem to Guilford County, about thirty miles away.

Despite the cordial relations between Moravians and Lutherans, Schober's decision to associate with them came as an unpleasant surprise. Moravians had long ago abandoned their early status as a society within the Lutheran Chruch and conceived themselves as a separate denomination. They preached among Lutherans, as they also did among Baptists and Methodists, only until a minister of that group arrived on the scene. They did not encourage conversion to the Moravian Church because they believed that most people would not prefer the highly disciplined life of the *Unitas Fratrum*. When Schober accepted ordination, Moravians believed that he had given up membership in the Salem congregation. The Unity Elders agreed that

> so long as [Schober] merely worked among awakened souls in this neighborhood he should be counted as belonging to us, but if he became an ordained minister it would be understood that he had left our denomination.[12]

The decision was not surprising. Moravians in Pennsylvania experienced a similar incident when Ernst L. Hazelius united with the Lutherans in Philadelphia.[13] Hazelius was the first professor in the newly organized Moravian Theological Seminary in Nazareth. In 1809 he and several other Brethren became disenchanted with conservative Moravian leaders who insisted on maintaining the use of the lot in marriage. This opposition was aired publicly and to the Unity Elders. When the Unity supported the status quo, Hazelius departed. He expressed his dissatisfaction in a letter to each of the Pennsylvania and North Carolina congregations, so Salem officials knew of the episode.[14]

Their reaction to Schober, therefore, was to be expected. Although Schober likely anticipated the consequences of his ordination, the reality must have hurt. His participation in the local mission society was reduced to an honorary status without vote, and even that only at his personal request.[15] His wish "to play the organ now and then for Communion" was

---

[12]Elders' Conference, 30 January 1811, Fries and others, *Records of Moravians*, 7:3144.

[13]Amos A. Ettinger, ed., *Two Centuries of Nazareth, 1740-1940* (Nazareth, Pennsylvania, Nazareth Bi-centennial Inc., 1940), p. 74.

[14]Joseph M. Levering, *The History of Bethlehem, Pennsylvania, 1741-1892* (Bethlehem, Pennsylvania: Times Publishing Co., 1903), pp. 589-90.

[15]*Helfer Conferenz*, 14 August 1811, Fries and others, *Records of Moravians*, 7:3151.

at first denied, but two months later the Elders noted that "Pastor Schober often attends our public services, and usually goes to the organ gallery. The Organist is at liberty to invite him to play."[16] Public services were, of course, open to all; several years passed before Gottlieb again partook of Holy Communion with the Salem congregation. That Schober was allowed to maintain his household in Salem was an exception. Moravians still held the man and his family in high regard; perhaps also they recognized the courage of his convictions. Most persons at fifty-four years of age would not casually sever the relations of a lifetime and enter a new career. At a time when most people were mellowing with the passing of years, Schober was launching into the most influential period of his life. Moravians respected this dedication:

> We remember with gratitude his many years of service of this congregation in music and in other lines. We wish for him the blessing of the Lord, and commend him to the Lord and the Holy Spirit in his present work.[17]

When Schober was ordained in 1810, he was already the pastor of two German congregations in Stokes County near Wachovia. Beginning in 1810, he accepted small congregations at Shiloh, also called Muddy Creek, and Nazareth, near Germanton. Before long he added two others, Hopewell and Bethlehem. Schober reported to the synod of 1811 that, in the two years of his ministry, he had given religious instruction to 113 persons, confirmed seventy-five and baptized six adults.[18] At his first

---

[16]Elders' Conference, 11 December 1811, Fries and others, *Records of Moravians,* 7:3153; Elders' Conference, 22 January 1812, Fries and others, *Records of Moravians,* 7:3172.

[17]Memorabilia of the Congregations of the Brethren in Wachovia for the Year 1810, Fries and others, *Records of Moravians,* 7:3106.

[18]*Proceedings of the Lutheran Synod of North Carolina* for the Year 1811, p. 6. The proceedings of the Synod of the Lutheran Church in North Carolina exist in several forms. In 1811, the synod collected its minutes from previous years and published them in the *Kurzer Bericht von den Conferenzen der Vereinigton Evangelisch Lutherischen Predigern und Abgeordneten in dem Staat Nord-Carolina vom Jahr 1803, bis zum Jahr 1810* (Neu-Market, Virginia: Ambrostius Henkel, 1811). Beginning in 1811 the proceedings were printed annually in both German and English, but English copies survived only for the years 1811, 1812, and 1819 and from 1827 forward. F. W. E. Peschau translated the most important parts in his *Minutes of the Evangelical Lutheran Synod and Ministerium of North Carolina 1803-1826* (Newberry, South Carolina: Aull and Houseal, 1894). References in this study taken from Peschau's translation will be identified. Other citations were taken directly from the original printing of the proceedings and translated by this author. The wording of the title of the minutes varied from year to year but was usually *Succinct Information of the Transactions of the German and English Lutheran*

synod as a Lutheran minister, Schober was elected secretary. The new member, along with Synod President Storch, soon sounded a note which was to characterize Schober's Lutheran career:

> Revs. Storch and Shober introduced and advocated the opening of a correspondence with the Pennsylvania Synod, in accordance with the warmly expressed wishes for a closer union with these brethren of our common faith.[19]

The synod also decided to encourage the foundation of Sunday schools among the congregations, to adopt Luther's Smaller Catechism as the standard of instruction, and to commission the preparation of a liturgy by President Storch. Nine congregations from Tennessee were added to the four from South Carolina which were admitted in 1810 so that the synod was truly "of North Carolina and adjacent states," encompassing a total of twenty-six congregations.

In the 1812 synod Schober reported forty-eight confirmations and sixty-four baptisms, four of which were adults in his four churches. He preached twice before his fellow ministers and the lay delegates, the first based on Psalm 126: "They that sow in tears shall reap in joy." A second address in preparation for Holy Communion was paraphrased in the minutes and revealed a strong Lutheran stance on this sacrament. He sought to convey an immediacy of Christ's presence in the service: "Our dear Saviour on this day [burns] with desire to keep the holy communion with his disciples, as much as he did on the night in which he was betrayed."[20] He lamented that only "thirty-three out of such a large congregation" came forward to partake of the sacrament causing concern regarding the faithfulness of others. Are these unhappy with Jesus' yoke? Have they been conquered by the lusts of sin? Are they ashamed of their Lord? Are they unreconciled with their neighbors?

> In short, it is incontrovertible evidence that the nature of Esau, viz. carnal, worldly and voluptuous enjoyments, and even angry passions, are preferred

---

Synod for North Carolina and Adjacent States, hereinafter shortened to "Lutheran Synod Minutes." All of the minutes are available in the archives of the North Carolina Lutheran Synod, Salisbury, North Carolina, hereinafter cited as "Lutheran Archives."

[19]Lutheran Synod Minutes, 1811, p. 5.

[20]Lutheran Synod Minutes, 1812, Peschau translation, p. 5. Summaries of Schober's sermons were reported in the past tense. Where the meaning is clear, verb tenses in quotations are changed from past to present to portray Schober's thoughts more faithfully. Such changes are enclosed in brackets.

to the heavenly, happy and inexpressible perception of the peace of God in the soul.

True believers, he said, can this day partake of the "Body and Blood of the Saviour, to approach with confidence to the Throne of Grace . . ." even if weak in sin, provided they love only God. Then in graphic language Schober recreated for his hearers the suffering of Jesus.

> Come, then, proclaim his death; let his Holy Spirit place him before your eyes in all his sufferings; go with him to Gethsemane—see [the] sweat, bloody sweat, trembling for the anguish of his soul—hear the bitter cries in his agony, all this to save you from the power of Satan—See him . . . mocked, derided, striken and spit in the face. . . . Contemplate him in the crown of thorns. . . . Listen how the crowd of his enemies demand the murderer to be set at liberty, and him, the best of men, to be crucified. Desire . . . to assist him to carry the cross up to Golgotha. . . . Rejoice that the word, sounding through all eternity for all repenting sinners, is yet efficacious for you. "Father, forgive them, for they know not what they do."

All of this, Schober concluded, was for man's salvation. Such reflections, particularly during the Holy Sacrament, bring life eternal. Through Jesus' resurrection and his Spirit dwelling in us, and "because we [are] made true partakers of his body and blood," he will raise us up on the last day. Therefore, "renew your covenant this day with your gracious Lord, that you will by his grace remain faithful to him. . . ."[21]

Those who read Schober's sermon could readily recognize a strong sacramental presence joined with Schober's Moravian heritage of vivid pictorialization of Christ's suffering and presented with a revivalistic tenor characteristic of preaching on the American frontier. The publication of the sermon attested to its acceptance by the ministers in attendance, and Schober's position as synod secretary, with responsibility for publication of the proceedings, guaranteed that the printed word faithfully reflected the meaning of the speaker. Therefore, this and other sermons revealed the theological principles uppermost in Schober's preaching in this period. One other source gave Gottlieb's contemporaries an insight into his thinking. In 1811 he made arrangements for reprinting a small pamphlet which "I found in an old bookcase: It contains an inestimable treasure, which you will find, if you employ it well." Its title was *A Choice Drop of Honey from the Rock Christ or A Short Word of Advice to all Saints and Sinners.*[22]

---

[21]Lutheran Synod Minutes, 1812, Peschau translation, p. 7.

[22](New-Market, Shenandoah County, Virginia: Ambrose Henkel and Co., 1811).

Gottlieb made it very clear that he was not the author of the pamphlet; since the title page did not name an author it is likely that he did not know who wrote it. In all of his other publications authors or sources were clearly credited. The book was the work of Thomas Wilcocks (or Wilcox), a rather obscure Calvinist Baptist of England. Wilcocks (1622-?) published the book during the height of Puritan activity in England and it immediately gained popularity among Puritans. By 1807 the book was in its fiftieth English edition. In 1667 the first American edition was printed by Samuel Green in Cambridge, Massachusetts. Later American editions were printed in Boston, New York, Newport, Wilmington, and Philadelphia.[23] Schober used a London edition printed in 1788 which probably had no indication of the author. Wilcocks' adherence to the particular or Calvinist Baptists of the period would have damaged circulation even among Puritans, probably accounting for the lack of recognition of authorship in later editions.[24]

Schober's attraction to this Puritan pamphlet was natural. It explored themes very dear to Gottlieb's thinking even though its Calvinistic foundation differed from Schober's grounding in the Augsburg Confession.

A Choice Drop of Honey was addressed to professing Christians, especially those for whom faith was more social than religious and who perfunctorily relied on nominal church membership as a guarantee of salvation. Ideas were repeated frequently, almost hammered into the reader, yet a simplicity of thought, motive, and action gave the book a quiet strength. It was a meditative composition, short enough to encourage frequent readings. Its message, Schober believed, was badly needed in North Carolina.

First and foremost, this small book was Christocentric. The sole source of man's redemption was Jesus Christ. Man cannot contribute

---

[23]Joseph Sabin, *Bibliotheca Americana* (New York: J. Sabin and other publishers, 29 vol., 1868-1936), p. 28, p. 354.

[24]*The British Museum General Catalogue of Printed Books,* [Photolithograph edition to 1955] (London: Trustees of the British Museum, 1965), p. 560, refers to Wilcocks as a particular Baptist. Some Baptists of the period followed the theology of John Calvin on the question of predestination and were called Particular Baptists. Others adhered to Jacob Arminius' doctrine of free will and were called General Baptists. Both groups were transplanted to America, but the latter died out. Particular Baptists, although softening their stance on predestination somewhat, became the ancestors of the modern denomination by that name.

anything except his own sin; "bring nothing but thy wants and miseries, else Christ is not fit for thee, nor thou for Christ."[25] By coming to Him "thou standest upon the Rock of Ages," for He has drunk the bitter from the cup and left for mankind the sweet salvation of the Father. "To accept Christ's righteousness alone, his blood alone for salvation, that is the sum of the gospel."

> Prepare for the cross, welcome it, bear it triumphantly like Christ's cross, whether scoffs, mockings, jeers, contempt, imprisonments, & c. but see it be Christ's cross, not thine own.[26]

Second, the pamphlet assumed the absolute depravity of man. Nothing that he was, could do, or ever would be counted toward his salvation. Even his ability to have faith was a gift of God. Man's salvation was God's choosing: "there must be a divine nature first put into the soul, to make it lay hold on [Christ]." "If thou findest thou canst not believe; remember it's Christ's work to make thee believe. . . ."[27] Man's greatest enemy is his own nature which rebels at being so dependent on God. Nature would have made salvation something that the human being could have earned or purchased, but "not a penny of nature's highest improvements will pass in Heaven."

> Let nature but make a gospel, and it would make it quite contrary to Christ. It would be to the just, the innocent, the holy, & c. Christ made the gospel for thee, that is for needy sinners, the ungodly, the righteous, the accursed. Nature cannot endure to think gospel is only for sinners; it would rather chuse to despair than to go to Christ upon such terrible terms.[28]

Third, the professing Christian must beware lest his performance of churchly duties and responsibilities lull him into comfort. A church member may pass the church tests of man while failing Christ's test. "Thou may'st come to baptism and never come to Jesus, and the blood of sprinkling." "*Judas* may have the sop, the outward privilege of baptism, supper, church fellowship, & c. but John leaned on Christ's bosom." Many people may call Christ their Saviour; few really know him to be so.

---

[25]Wilcocks, *A Choice Drop of Honey*, Schober reprint, p. 8.

[26]Wilcocks, *A Choice Drop of Honey*, Schober reprint, p. 24.

[27]Wilcocks, *A Choice Drop of Honey*, Schober reprint, p. 12.

[28]Wilcocks, *A Choice Drop of Honey*, Schober reprint, p. 19.

> The honey that you suck from your own righteousness will turn into perfect
> gall, and the light that you take from that to walk in will turn into black night
> upon the soul.[29]

The work was concluded with detailed admonitions for the true
Christian. He should

> search the Scriptures daily. . . . Judge not Christ's love by providences, but by
> promises. . . . Be serious exact in duty . . . but be much afraid of taking comfort
> from duties as from sins. . . . Be much in prayer. . . . Be true to truth . . . restore
> such as are fallen . . . with the grace of the gospel. . . . Be faithful to others
> infirmities, but sensible of thy own. Visit sick beds and deserted souls much. .
> . . Abide in your calling. . . . Be content with little of the world. . . . Think much
> of Heaven. . . . Think everyone better than thyself. . . . Mourn to see so little of
> Christ in the world, so few needing him. . . . Remember Christ's time of love
> when thou wast naked.[30]

The little book of thirty pages was laced throughout with Biblical
references. Major ideas were backed with specific citations, communicat-
ing the author's intention to provide a true scriptural interpretation. He
cited the Old Testament books twenty-three times, mostly the prophets.
The New Testament books appeared sixty-eight times, almost half of
which were the writings of Paul.

Schober may not have advocated every principle of this pamphlet
with as much force as the author, but he certainly liked most of it.
Nothing, he believed, should ever compromise the centrality of Christ. It
was probably that motif which initially attracted his attention, because he
felt it was sadly neglected in the backcountry areas in which he preached.
And without that understanding, all was lost. This pamphlet, therefore,
when taken with other writings, can reveal the ideas which gripped
Schober's mind and inspired his messages as a Lutheran minister.

Two ideas implicit in the pamphlet, however, were foreign to Schober's thinking: the nature of the church and predestination. As a particular Baptist, Wilcocks affirmed a true church composed only of
regenerated believers who have made a conscious confession of Christ. It
would not include infants or allow for infant baptism. Indeed, Wilcocks
saw infant baptism as a source of undedicated Christians—those for
whom baptism and confirmation had been only ritual with little real
meaning. Schober, on the other hand, strongly advocated the baptism of

---

[29]Wilcocks, *A Choice Drop of Honey*, Schober reprint, p. 29.

[30]Wilcocks, *A Choice Drop of Honey*, Schober reprint, pp. 21-25.

infants, although he too deplored empty ceremony. In 1813 he preached a sermon entitled only "Child's Funeral—Smith, 1813;" fourteen years later he used the same text for a similar occasion in Germanton.[31] Both sermons dealt with children in the career of Jesus and in general defended the right of children to membership in the church. His notes began:

> Whoever denys that Children are fit to be partakers of experimental knowl-
> edge of their Creator & Saviour is either ignorant himself—wilfully blind to
> the power of Omnipotence or an Enemy to Jesus—as they in their self
> conceited Wisdom refuse his request—suffer little children to come unto me,
> for of such is the kingdom of heaven.

These reflections perhaps inspired his more comprehensive writing on the subject entitled "The Validity of Infant Baptism." The composition was left only in manuscript form[32] although its length of forty-eight closely written pages and its manner of organization would suggest that Schober intended publication. The manuscript is undated and inclusion at this point is purely circumstantial. In the early years of his ministry Schober confronted the most aggressive religious group on the frontier: the Baptists. Most Baptist ministers in the backcountry had little or no education to enable them to understand the Scriptures in the original languages. Therefore they tended, Schober believed, to construct a rather weak religious foundation for their members, more emotional than substantial. This composition was written against the Baptist position of believer's baptism of adults by immersion, but it was more explanatory in character than argumentative. Schober wanted to enlighten his readers, not just condemn another interpretation. Some of the material seemed to be Schober's own composition. He did acknowledge his indebtedness to several authors, particularly William Wall's *History of Infant-Baptism* written in 1705. Wall's work

> was regarded as one of the greatest on the subject, even by Baptists, who
> accepted the accuracy of much of his research while rejecting the conclusions
> he drew from it. Well into the nineteenth century it was regarded by many
> Paedo-Baptists as the most erudite apologia for their point of view.[33]

---

[31]The 1813 sermon is among the Schober Papers, Moravian Archives. The second, entitled "Funeral, Germantown, 4 August 1827 is in the Schober Papers, Old Salem Inc. Archives.

[32]Schober Papers, Old Salem Inc. Archives. Hereinafter cited as "Infant Baptism Manuscript."

[33]D. M. Hembury, "Baptismal Controversies, 1640-1900," *Christian Baptism*, A. Gilmore, ed. (Philadelphia: Judson Press, 1959), p. 295.

Schober's arguments were very similar to other advocates of the baptism of children, but he did show clarity of expression and ability to present a convincing case. But most important, the composition provided an important corrective to the assumptions of *A Drop of Honey.*

At the outset, Schober admitted that the proofs for or against the baptism of children were disputable and inconclusive. One who would learn the truth must first have an open mind on the question and consult the scriptures, the practice of the apostles, the writings of those close to the New Testament period, and the practice of the church in history. Many, however, "are fond of party, unwilling to put themselves to the trouble of inquiring—listing themselves under a particular sect shelter under disguise of Religion, zealous in defending their private opinion—and degrading all others."[34] Baptists, he said, are most industrious in denying infant baptism as an "unscriptural absurd practice;" but as far as can be gathered from

> reason, Scripture and writing of ancient fathers, the Church has every where & at all Times till lately admitted infants, & that no church ever refused such when grown up into its communion nor presumptuously rebaptised them [until] abt. 250 years ago.

Schober proceeded to develop his arguments under six major points, providing extensive documentation for each important idea.

First, Schober tried to show a continuity of the spiritual nature of the church beginning with the covenant of Abraham and Moses and continuing through the New Testament. The church was not based on natural generation under the Jews and changed to spiritual generation under the Christians. In the former, non-Jews could become a part of the Jewish faith through spiritual regeneration and became heirs to the promises of Abraham,

> therefore the spiritual constitution of the church under the Gospel is no more argument against infant church membership than the like constitution of the Church under the Mo. dispensation was an argument ag. church membership at that Time.[35]

Second, Schober argued that church members are to be admitted on the same terms under the gospel as they had been under the Law. Baptism and circumcision were both rites of admission to the respective cove-

---

[34]Schober, Infant Baptism Manuscript, p. 2.

[35]Infant Baptism Manuscript, p. 6.

nants, each carrying the rights and responsibilities of membership. Christians should not change the character of the rite unless Christ himself directed a change. The first preaching of the Apostles included children with their parents as the heirs of Christ's promises. Since Christ

> never made an alteration as to persons to be admitted into the church, so as to exclude infants, it must remain (being no where forbidden) that children of Christian parents have the same right to church membership now as Jewish children formerly.[36]

While the Christian dispensation substituted baptism for circumcision, there was no apparent change in the persons to be admitted. Baptism came "not as an anti-type in the place of a type, but as one positive institution in place of another." Both rites required the explanation of adults when the child could understand the meaning of the event.

Third, Schober contended, Jews not only baptized adults proselytes but also their children. Both circumcision and baptism were necessary to complete the conversion. He quoted extensively from Maimonides, a Jewish historian, and the Talmud to substantiate this claim. Infant baptism was well known in Jesus' time, but neither the prophets nor Jesus ever condemned the practice of the ancient Jews in this regard. In the absence of any condemnation and without directions to change, it was entirely proper for the young church to continue the institution and, according to Christ's instructions, to baptize all nations.

> Is it not probable that he who came not to destroy the Law and the prophets but to fulfill them, departed as little as possible from this their Ancient custom of adm[itting] Ch[urch] members. Circumcision, which was a stumbling block to gentiles, it was necessary to lay aside and as the Chr. Rel. was to be universal, to be pres[ented] all Nations; all characters that kept up enmity between Jews and Gentiles, must of necessity be abolished in order to further the Gospel . . . and the easy rite of bap[tism] succeeded to cir[cumcision].[37]

Fourth, infant baptism was practiced by the apostles as far as can be determined by reason. The apostles baptised entire households which, in some cases if not all, would have included children. Jesus specifically prohibited the apostles from keeping little children from coming to him "for of such are the kingdom of heaven." From Jesus they received a blessing, and if he could accept them in heaven, surely we should accept them in the church.

---

[36]Infant Baptism Manuscript, p. 9.

[37]Infant Baptism Manuscript, p. 19.

Fifth, the current arguments against infant baptism drawn from particular texts are superficial. Opponents argue that children can not fulfill the requirements of a Christian and therefore only adults should be baptised. For example, opponents contend children cannot "teach" as required by Matthew 28:19. Schober explored the Greek meaning of the passage to show that children can become disciples and are so called in various places; this, he said, was the true meaning of the passage. Opponents also argue that belief before baptism could only occur in adults. Schober was content to assert that the faith of parents, godfathers, or the congregation enabled children to be called believers. After all, he countered, it is ultimately the faith of the heart and not the baptism of the flesh which leads to salvation, therefore,

> both Jews and Christians should not be taught *that their children were unprofitably cir[cumscized] or bap[tized]* but that there was no resting in external performance, & that the respective cov'ts. were of no effect without conformable action.[38]

Finally, Schober asserted that infant baptism was the practice of all national churches from apostolic times to the present. The church fathers, writing just after the New Testament, supported the baptism of children. Hermas, Justin Martyr, Clement of Alexandria, Irenaeus, Origen, and Cyprian gave clear indications of early Christian practice. Early councils ratified its continuance so that

> from that Time to the reformation by Calvin we have no certain acct. of any church or people that denied inft. bap ... & it is well known that all national churches in Europe and Asia practiced it. .... It is hard to suppose that God would suffer it to have succeeded for sixteen hundred years if it was so dangerous to his kingdom as is proclaimed by some.[39]

Schober concluded his composition by considering briefly the manner of baptism. Since it is the washing by Christ's blood that is ultimately important, the manner of water baptism was insignificant. Immersion, sprinkling, or pouring were all acceptable. Certainly, the quantity of water had little to do with the event. He freely admitted the New Testament meaning of the word "to baptize," but he also pointed out places where the same word was used in connection with the washing of

---

[38]Infant Baptism Manuscript, p. 34.

[39]Infant Baptism Manuscript, p. 41.

hands. He concluded that the adoption of one mode, to the exclusion of all others, was not justified by the scriptural usage.

A second theological idea in which Schober disagreed with the assumptions of Wilcocks was on the question of predestination and free will. In a synod sermon preached in 1813, Schober earnestly recommended continual prayer to his listeners. God does listen to man's prayer, and his plan of the ages is not unchangeable. The prayers of the righteous man, if motivated by the Holy Spirit, do change things through God's power. "In prayer, all are united with God, they love him, and if they remain in Jesus and his words in them, they can do the will of the Father. . . ."[40] Schober quoted the Apostle Paul extensively, how "the Lord answered him on his prayer" to be released from Satan's temptation, and how he counseled all Christians to be much in prayer in order to avoid the error of false teaching.

> If then, so much depended on prayer in his time—if this highly enlightened apostle was so desirous to be assisted by prayer—how much more must his example in our days be applicable, when so many lose the good narrow way.

Even ministers need to pray because of the weight of responsibility on their hands. They must lead eternal souls to God and if they fail or are lax, God will require an answer for their efforts or lack therof; "how easy, then can they err, when instead of supporting the weak in faith, they afflict them; instead of comforting . . . they oppress them . . . and on the other hand, cry peace where there is none." In this great responsibility, the minister's need is prayer "that the Spirit of the Lord will guide us and lead us into all truth." Schober especially admonished the younger preachers to seek God's help.

> But many of them who are propelled by the first fire of love to serve the Lord, begin to study in order to enable themselves to address their hearers worthily in the great cause: after some time the love waxes cold, family cares too soon encumber them, and instead of becoming vivifying speakers, endowed by unction from above, as was expected, a machine is brought forth which is contented with the forms, without innate life.

Others, he continued, choose the ministry as a life of ease or soon became tired. Some study eloquent delivery to secure the praise of men. But remember, he said, "God . . . [uses] men and their words . . . to effect His purposes with the human race . . ." whatever their age or station.

---

[40]Lutheran Synod Minutes, 1813, Peschau translation, p. 21.

Encourage the young who feel God's call to service and let all who hear that call continually seek the will of God in prayer. If God would grant his grace "we should very soon behold living fruit and the revival of true religion in all our congregations."[41]

This sermon of Schober revealed a balanced view of God's providence. The hard predestination of Calvinism was softened in a manner consistent with the Augsburg Confession but clearly avoided the other extreme of total human free-will. God is accomplishing his purpose through men, and they must constantly seek the guidance of his will.

Another emphasis of Schober emerged from this sermon: the need for an educated ministry. The previous year the synod discussed this problem, and Schober's sermon in 1813 helped crystallize planning for an "institution for the education of young men for the ministry."[42] With limited funds, however, the problem was not easily solved. Several years passed before the synod founded an educational institution. Until that time, young men continued to study with established ministers and some moved to ordination with less than perfect preparation.

Equally important for the development of vital Christianity was the provision for religious instruction of the people, particularly children. Lutherans in 1810 circulated a letter to the congregations recognizing the dearth of opportunities for children to learn religious ideas. Schober drafted this letter, although it was issued by the whole synod.[43] The letter entreated Lutherans

> to furnish your Families with Catechisms; and have your Children instructed in them. . . . If our Children are neglected to be instructed in the fundamentals of our holy faith; if we do not inform them intelligibly according to their capacity of their lost situation without a Saviour; what will become of the next generation? it will be a generation of Infidels; a generation which as they know nothing of the Patience of the Redeemer can not be kept or preserved from the hour of Temptation which shall come and is now come upon all the Earth to try them that dwell thereon. . . . We would also recommend (especially in places where there is no regular ministry) the appointment of Sunday meetings for the people to sing and pray together; to read the holy Scriptures and other approved Books on religious Subjects; . . . at such places Children might also be catachised.

---

[41]Lutheran Synod Minutes, 1813, Peschau translation, p. 28.

[42]Lutheran Synod Minutes, 1813, Peschau translation, p. 19.

[43]Lutheran Synod Minutes, 1810, in *Kurzer Bericht von den Conferenzen . . .*, pp. 30-34. English draft in Schober's handwriting and with marginal corrections and rewrite, Schober Papers, Old Salem Inc. Archives.

These few measures could revive the churches, provide young men for the ministry, and "gather thousands of those who are now wandering on the dark Mountains of Error" Schober believed.[44]

But three years later the situation was little improved. Schober served five churches, and despite a great effort he, like his fellow ministers, could not meet the need. Since he could only preach in each congregation once every four weeks, he turned to his Moravian friends for help. At Schober's request and with permission of the Elders, Br. Gotthold Reichel preached several times at the Lutheran churches a few miles north of Salem.[45] Moreover, just prior to leaving for the Lutheran Synod of 1813, Schober talked with the *Helfer Conferenz* in Salem concerning the problem, arousing "in us a desire to renew the visits to nearer and farther neighborhoods which were formerly attended with so much blessing."[46] This cooperative response of the Moravians was probably reported to the Lutheran synod. The synod then passed a resolution that Storch and Schober should request the Moravians to provide "several capable Christian men to teach our children, according to our custom, Luther's Catechism."[47] In a letter to Jacob van Vleck, Storch and Schober requested preachers for adult Lutherans "who . . . have fallen into the hands of ignorant leaders of various denominations, and have either built upon the sand, or have built with hay and stubble upon good ground."[48] They expressed great distress to "see how the youth of the land are neglected," but rejoiced that about 250 Lutheran young people had asked for religious instruction.

With few ministers Lutherans realized the need could not be met unless the Moravian Church, which "we know . . . from its beginning has purposed to win souls for Jesus without regard to denominations [and has honored] the Little Catechism of Luther . . . as containing the principles of the Christian faith," will agree to "commission one or more of your efficient deacons to give instruction to such as may apply for it, using the

---

[44]Ibid.

[45]Salem Diary, 7 February 1813, Fries and others, *Records of Moravians*, 7:3194.

[46]*Helfer Conferenz* 18 October 1813, Fries and others, *Records of Moravians*, 7:3207.

[47]Lutheran Synod Minutes, 1813, Peschau translation, p. 20.

[48]Carl Storch and G. Shober to the Rev'd Jacob V. Vleck, no date but received in Salem, 13 December 1813. Fries and others, *Records of Moravians*, 7:3542.

Lutheran Catechism according to our custom."[49] The Moravians considered the matter, but felt compelled to decline, at least for the present, because "in our own country congregations, there is great lack of opportunity to give the young people the needed instruction in Christian doctrine . . ." and not sufficient workers to accomplish even this task. But, the Moravians continued, "you may be assured that we prize this letter from your Synod . . . and we hope that in future . . . we may show our willingness . . . to aid in the vineyard of the Lord."[50] While the Lutherans gained no tangible relief for their problem, the fraternal relation between the two Christian groups was strengthened. To a large degree, Schober was responsible for this growing relationship. Simultaneously, the tension caused in Salem by Schober's ordination was gradually relaxing.

---

[49]Ibid.

[50]Reply to letter of Pastors Storch and Shober, Salem, 26 February 1814, Fries and others, *Records of Moravians*, 7:3544.

CHAPTER 10

Leadership among Lutherans

Aᴛᴛᴇʀ ʜɪs ᴏʀᴅɪɴᴀᴛɪᴏɴ, Gottlieb Schober and his family continued to live in Salem. He was not, however, considered a Moravian. It was a most unusual arrangement for that period, made possible only by Schober's long attachment to the community and the promise of behavior consistent with Moravian ideals. After 1810, the appearance of Schober's name in community records diminished significantly; when he was mentioned, it was always "Pastor Schober," "Schober," but never "Br. Schober." Not until 1819 does this practice change, and even then the use of the term "Brother" was infrequent. Both Gottlieb and community authorities viewed his denominational attachment as Lutheran, not Moravian.

Many years later, Gottlieb's daughter, Anna Paulina Herman, told a Lutheran historian that her father always considered himself a Moravian; "he lived and died as a member of that Church."[1] Information from the period 1810 to 1819 does not support that interpretation. It reflected a judgement made a generation after the events and after a reconciliation between Schober and his native church. It is true that Gottlieb was far more concerned with Christian principles than denominational distinc-

---

[1]Bernheim, *History of German Settlements*, p. 442.

tives; he believed both groups were together on the Augsburg Confession. His daughter could, therefore, argue that no important change had been made. But neither Moravians nor Lutherans of that period would have agreed with that interpretation.

Schober's activities in Salem during this time are difficult to document. Scattered references would indicate that most of his law practice was dropped. He continued as the village tinsmith and paper maker but spent a great deal of time studying and writing in connection with his new calling. He was still interested in land, although more in development than speculation, leading to the publication in 1812 of a handbill addressed to the citizens of Surry County:

> I have the right by virtue of a resolution of the last general assembly to obtain 5,000 acres of land in 200 acre tracts. Now as I wish to use this privilege for the benefit of the citizens, I do hereby offer to any person who wishes to enter and secure 200 acres of land to deliver the location to me or to my son Immanuel together with a note for the entry money payable in twelve months in any saleable country produce, and I will give my note to such person to convey to him or his order as soon as possible after the surveyor has made the return of his works and I receive my grant. . . .[2]

Response was disappointing but as late as 1826 Gottlieb and one man were still negotiating a deal stemming from this grant.[3] Schober again tried to buy the land on which the paper mill stood, offering $500 for it in 1813, but the Overseers considered the offer too low for land so close to the community. Part of the land was considered for the establishment of a "machine for the carding of wool" by Vaniman Zevely, Schober's son-in-law, but the matter was dropped because "Pastor Schober has changed his mind."[4]

Nathaniel's situation in Salem was a matter of some concern. He was the community postmaster and elected member of the Congregation Council, but his future prospects were not bright. Although he was considered for several positions in Salem, nothing materialized. His health prevented the realization of his dream to serve the church, causing him increasing distress. Finally in 1810, Nathaniel decided to leave Salem

---

[2]Document in Schober Papers, Old Salem Inc. Archives.

[3]Thomas A. Ward to Gottlieb Schober, Clarksville, GA, 4 September 1826. Schober Papers, Old Salem Inc. Archives.

[4]Board of Overseers, 18 January 1814, Moravian Archives. Also undated entry immediately prior to above reference.

for his father's farm which was eleven miles south of Salem in Rowan County. There he intended "to establish himself a store" but asked to maintain his connection with the Salem congregation. Permission was at first denied "because of the unpleasant circumstances that might arise for the community." When Nathaniel persisted, the Board of Overseers reversed its decision "so long as he remains single and keeps the character of a brother."[5] The Overseers hoped he would ultimately return to Salem but knew of no position at that time which would satisfy him. While no evidence of a father's guidance survived, Gottlieb knew the potential of a storekeeper's occupation and likely gave his son encouragement.

By early 1811 Nathaniel indicated a desire to marry according to regulations of the community, but the lot disapproved his suggestion of Susannah Elizabeth Peter. Ultimately he married a single sister from the Hope congregation, Rebecca Höhns, in a ceremony performed by the groom's father.[6] In October 1813, Gottlieb purchased another farm of 1,032 acres a few miles east of Salem from William Dobson. The tract contained an important crossroads, the north-south road running from Danville, VA, to Charleston, SC, with a branch running through Salem, and the east-west road coming from Wilmington and Cross Creek (Fayetteville) toward the mountains to the northwest.

Dobson operated an inn to accommodate stagecoach passengers along with a store for local convenience.[7] After Schober's purchase, Nathaniel and Rebecca moved to the crossroads to take over the business there. Nathaniel's store made him a reasonable living, although the war between the United States and England created difficulties. In 1815 he wrote to his father:

> Goods will now sell slow, people already begin to say "we will wait a while, they are dear yet,"—and they buy only what they cannot do without, but we must paddle along as fast as we can, the loss can not be very great, but the profits for the next year may be small. . . .
> . . . .

[5]Board of Overseers, 30 January, 20 February 1810, Moravian Archives. For an indication of the location of the farm, see Salem Diary, 5 December 1810, Fries and others, *Records of Moravians*, 7:3114.

[6]Elders' Conference, 6 February 1811, Fries and others, *Records of Moravians*, 7:3144-45; Salem Diary, 14 May 1812, Fries and others, *Records of Moravians*, 7:3168.

[7]Jules G. Körner, Jr., *Joseph of Kernersville* (Durham, North Carolina: Seeman Printery, 1958), pp. 33-34, pp. 98-99; Fries and others, *Records of Moravians*, 7:3134n; Stokes County Deed Books 5:121, 7:151, 10:352.

> Plague on the cotton! I must try and sell it for cost and charges,—in the country here I don't think it will sell, though spinning about here is paid higher for than in Salem, from what you state,—I have none finer than what I sent you, but plenty coarser.[8]

Health continued to be a problem for Nathaniel. He was constantly bothered by a cough which became severe in bad weather. He wrote to his brother Emmanuel:

> I have used the horehound pills Daddy sent but cannot say that I perceived any particular effect produced by them. . . . Am now taking a raw egg every morning before breakfast, which has been often and highly recommended to me, it tastes well and feels healing to the throat and breast as it passes down. . . .[9]

He remained thin, although

> my appetite is good, and [I am] at liberty to eat as much as I please, so that in this respect I am better off than Van [Zevely], who it seems is as hard put to reduce himself, as I am to get fat.[10]

His letter contained one reference to preparation around Salem for possible conflict with the English: "I heard several of your great guns today, and shall be glad if some of the boys dont get worse wounded by peace, than they would by War."

Emmanuel continued to study law with his father and with Archibald Murphey. When he tried to set up practice in Salem in 1811, permission was first denied, then reluctantly approved with the hope that he "would give up his plan completely."[11] The young man persisted in spite of the Elders' displeasure and hassle. In 1812 the Elders were "disturbed by the length of time which Br. Emmanuel Schober is spending with Mr. Murphy to prosecute his studies."[12] He was considered in 1814 for the office of justice of the peace, but the Overseers felt that a single brother should not hold such a position. Likewise, when the county court named

---

[8]N. Shober to The Rev'd G. Shober, Crossroads, 1 March 1815, Schober Papers, Old Salem Inc. Archives.

[9]N. Shober to Immanuel Shober, Crossroads, 23 January 1815, Schober Papers, Old Salem Inc. Archives.

[10]N. Shober to the Rev'd G. Shober, Crossroads, 1 March 1815, Schober Papers, Old Salem Inc. Archives.

[11]Board of Overseers, 25 June 1811, Moravian Archives.

[12]Elders' Conference, 25 March 1812, Fries and others, *Records of Moravians*, 7:3175.

him to "take the patrol over the Negro slaves," the Brethren expressed preference for a more experienced person.[13]

Anna Paulina had become a young woman. Early in 1811 John Vogler requested permission to make her his wife; the Elders "had no hesitation in submitting the proposal to the Lord. The answer was 'No.' "[14] She soon left Salem for a visit of several months in Pennsylvania, where she must have met John Rice, a Philadelphia confectioner. The following year he wrote the Salem Elders, asking permission to marry Anna. Salem officials referred the matter to Bethlehem who received an affirmative lot. Rice then wrote Gottlieb to request his daughter in marriage. The parents were agreeable, but by this time Anna was back in Salem, and she refused the proposal.[15]

Gottlieb remained busy with his secular affairs and his pastoral work. He generally stayed out of trouble with congregation officials, although old conflicts were stirred again between Schober and Conrad Kreuser. The latter purchased a quantity of sheet iron for Schober in Savannah, charging a commission for the purchase. The freight was more than expected, but Schober paid everything without objection. Upon opening the boxes, "Pastor Schober found that all the sheet metal was rusty and spoiled, which meant a considerable loss for him." He wanted to return the goods to Kreuser, since the latter charged a commission for purchasing and should have inspected the goods he bought. But the Overseers supported Kreuser, although advising him to refund the commission. Schober was far from satisfied, but saw no other way to recover his loss.[16]

Throughout 1814 Gottlieb was immersed in an ambitious writing project which culminated the following year with the publication of his translation of *Scenes in the World of Spirits*,[17] written by the German author, Johann Heinrich Jung, better known by his assumed name, Heinrich Stilling.

Heinrich Jung-Stilling (1740-1817), early in life a tailor and school-master, studied medicine in Strasbourg to become a surgeon. He met and

---

[13]Board of Overseers, 20 December 1814, Moravian Archives.

[14]Elders' Conference, 23 January, Fries and others, *Records of Moravians*, 7:3143.

[15]Elders' Conference, 1 April, 13, 27 May 1812, Fries and others, *Records of Moravians*, 7:3175-76.

[16]Board of Overseers, 5, 28 March 1815, Moravian Archives.

[17](New Market, Virginia: Ambrose Henkel and Co., 1815).

became close friends of Wolfgang Goethe and Johann Herder, two poet/philosophers of the period. In his own autobiography, Goethe characterized Jung-Stilling as a man of

> sound common sense, which rested on feeling and therefore was determined by the affections and passions; and from this very feeling sprang an enthusiasm for what was good, true and just in the greatest possible purity.[18]

He had an indestructible faith in God and in the assistance immediately flowing from him. He could express himself eloquently among friends, speaking, Goethe said, as if in a dream so that listeners seldom wished to interrupt his train of thought. He tended toward mystical expressions and was, therefore, somewhat narrow, but that characteristic

> was accompanied by so much goodwill and his eagerness with so much gentleness and earnestness, that a man of intelligence could certainly not be severe towards him, and a benevolent man could not scoff at him or turn him into ridicule.[19]

From 1787 to 1803 Jung-Stilling taught at the University of Marburg as professor of economics, during which time he wrote *Scenen ans dem Geisterreiche*, one of his many fictional works with a mystical theme. Jung-Stilling was a Presbyterian, but first and foremost he was committed to "the doctrine of *Jesus* and his apostles . . . ."[20] Late in life he came to know the Moravians in Europe and found in them spiritual compatriots. It was probably through this association that Schober became acquainted with the book and decided to translate it for English readers.

Scenen was written in two volumes, but Schober translated only the first. He promised "to express the sense contained in the original with fidelity . . ." and "did not permit himself to change, cover or alter the opinion of the Author." Schober admitted that parts of the book were very difficult to translate—especially a section of poetry written in Hexameter metre, which Schober struggled to retain in translation. He believed that the book would

> dish up some new well seasoned and agreeable sauce, or views in religious conceptions, in order to induce immortal souls to reflect on the *manner* of

---

[18]Wolfgang Goethe, *My Life*, Book 9 quoted in R. O. Moon (trans.) *Jung-Stilling: His Biography* (London: G. T. Foulis and Co. [1938]), p. 9.

[19]Goethe, *My Life*, Book 10, quoted in Moon, *Jung-Stilling*, p. 11.

[20]*Scenes in the World of Spirits,* Preface to second edition, p. vii.

their future existence, and in good earnest to prepare to meet their Lord and Redeemer with fruits of faith and love.[21]

The book was a work of religious speculation about life after death. Jung-Stilling assumed that the concepts of reward and punishment after death were necessary for human society, consistent with divine justice, and assured in divine revelation. He set about to depict in "reasonable and scriptural manner," scenes from the next world, based on "essential and external truths."

> I believe that by lively expositions of the destinies, which men have to expect after death, to effect much good, to support and strengthen some in their way to perfection and to deter many from the commission of vice.[22]

Writing in the manner reminiscent of a Socratic dialogue, and of John Bunyan's *Pilgrim's Progress*, Jung-Stilling created fifteen "scenes" from the next world. A complete exposition of the work is unnecessary at this point, and a few examples will suffice to reveal the character of the work to which Schober was attracted.

The first scene, entitled "The Great Awakening," depicts a man coming to consciousness immediately following death:

> Nowhere life and breath, no stirring, no motion. Everything appears to me only a shade; I move on as upon a cloud, below me the earth is no more, above me no stars, no sweet rays of the moon. I alone in this chilly void. How do I feel? I float along easy, as fog on the wings of the wind, easy I float, I rise, I sink according to the slightest wink of my will. If this is dreaming I have never dream'd thus with such clear and manifest knowledge. Almighty God! No! I don't dream—it is awakening to eternal life.[23]

He meets another spirit who, it turns out, was a skeptic in life and does not know what to expect in this new existence. They meet Satan, but both recoil when evil is truly exposed:

> see, what a bloody roll developes itself in emptiness. See what flaming writing blazes above it, as if written by phosphorus. Lord! what abominations painted in living colours. . . . O if men on earth would once behold such a spectacle!

They also meet the Prince of Light, traveling on a carriage of clouds, "dazling bluish white, like high polished silver . . . his raiment, quiet

---

[21]Translator's Preface entitled, "To the Indulgent Reader," p. iv.

[22]*Scenes in the World of Spirits*, Preface to the first German edition, p. vi.

[23]*Scenes in the World of Spirits*, pp. 1-2.

lightening; his hair, evening clouds, after the sun had brightly descended." To the first man, the Prince of Light says: "You believed much, but loved less, you will see the Lord and rejoice, yet you will serve the lowest of his friends." To the skeptic, he says

> You must begin to learn your ABC as children, and then it will be seen if your poor tenebrity can be enlightened by the tender rays of wisdoms—follow me to the place of your destination.[24]

In the second scene, the bewilderment of several scientists is revealed; "I believed," one said, "it to be the duty of man to study the works of the Creator and thereby to learn to know *him*. . . ." No, comes the answer, "this is the case when secondary objects are taken for primary ones." One should study man and creation "out of *love to* God" and not as a means to increase human happiness. These scientists are sent "in the region of shades (Hades) until your souls are entirely purified from all attachment to the corporeal nature. . . ."[25]

The third scene describes "The Joyful Meeting" as a soul beholds the city of God, carried there on the eagle wings of faith and love. In the fourth, another soul discovers the realities of hell, described first in tones of disorder, darkness, corruption, and finally in vivid pictures of fire, brimstone, and catastrophe.

In subsequent scenes, other kinds of men arrive in eternity—the poor man, the determinist, the greedy merchant, the antiquarian, and the Christian who seeks salvation in churches and forms—each finding himself assigned to appropriate experiences of purification, enjoyment, or suffering. Jung-Stilling makes his point in each case: man's salvation is by faith in the righteousness of Jesus Christ. Through him only is access to the city of God obtained and eternity enjoyed. No human enterprise or effort can accomplish this task; most serve only to delude man as to the real source of his redemption.

Beginning in the tenth scene, Jung-Stilling depicts the experience of the blessed:

> O, in what glory am I clothed: my radiance encreases in brightness and beauty; it appears to me, as if I was encircled with a rainbow, consisting of

---

[24]*Scenes in the World of Spirits*, p. 12.

[25]*Scenes in the World of Spirits*, p. 22.

blending colours of light, and inwardly such a source of peace openeth as surpasses all understanding.[26]

Advancing into the heavenly world, the soul exclaims:

> What an incomprehensible beauty of all nature!—An atmosphere like silver gauze over light lazuli blue; an earth like bright gold in fusion; all the miriads of objects as if made out of jewels by the greatest artist.
>
> . . . .
>
> Every where glowing colours of light; and nothing but ideals of original beauty! Teach me the language of the blessed, that I may worthily sing the praises of joy's creator! What an innumerable multitude of radiant heavenly princes with high flowing palm-branches are moving hither! Great and exalted God! what majesty! how glorious then wilt thou be![27]

Then a holy man of an Eastern religion comes to eternity where he is shown the "great mysteries" of the true faith. Jung-Stilling is thereby able to incorporate the leading ideas of the Christian faith. Man was created good, and with perfect freedom to choose between good and evil. Original man allowed himself to be seduced by evil. To reconcile man, God created "a being out of himself . . . called the *Eternal Word* or the *Son of God*."[28] God revealed himself to a particular people under the name of Jehovah, but they rejected him. Finally, God's Son came in the flesh to earth:

> he revealed the law of morality pure and clear, and lived up thereto in the highest degree, so that he was the highest pattern of humanity; he [performed] extraordinary deeds . . . [so that] the most common human understanding was absolutely convinced that he was the ambassador of God to men.

But again he was rejected, and this time the Jews executed him. This suffering of the innocent satisfied divine justice and made possible the reconciliation of sinful man with God. Death could not finally control the Son of God; on the third day he was raised to reign forever. Through this mystery, the corrupted man is saved when he approaches the throne of God through the sufferings of the Son of God.

In a final scene, Jung-Stilling speaks of the nature of the church. True Christians are very scarce, he says. Most do not really understand the corruption of sin; some even consider Jesus only a good man and a large

---

[26]*Scenes in the World of Spirits*, p. 158.

[27]*Scenes in the World of Spirits*, p. 162, p. 164.

[28]*Scenes in the World of Spirits*, p. 184.

number of humans actually hate all religion. But all must finally come under the just judgement of God.

Altogether, *Scenes in the World of Spirits* was a book designed to fit its own time. European Christianity was caught between a formalized state religion and a rapidly rising concept of "heart religion" called Pietism. Literary works were rejecting the coldness of rationalistic thought and embracing a warmer and more human Romanticism. Jung-Stilling was caught up in both Pietistic theology and Romantic literary expression. The result was a book which was mystical in character almost to a point of losing contact with reality. Schober liked this book, but even he drew back at times from the fantastic depictions, shown by his footnotes signed "Translator" at places he considered overdrawn.[29]

The important thing about this book for the study of Schober is the very fact that he chose it to translate for American readers. It was a prodigious project; the handwritten manuscript of tremendous proportions among the Schober papers testifies to the effort expended. The book was not typical of native American writing of the time and certainly was not produced for the average reader of the North Carolina backcountry. Schober perhaps sensed that more enlightened Americans could appreciate the kernels of religious truth and the deep feeling of the Romantic writer. He was not wrong—just ahead of his time. A leading interpreter of American religion sees the Romantic writings as very important in the development of religious expression of the nineteenth century. The Romantics, he says,

> proclaimed the coming of a new age in which the full potentialities of human life would find release from the bondage of legalism and conventionality.... They saw artistic expression in all genres as a way to truth and a ground for hope.... Revelation was not bound by doctrinaire tradition but was plenary; it could be drawn from dreams, from folk tales, from the depths of consciousness, and from nature itself.[30]

He sees the influence of Romanticism in Jonathan Edwards and Ralph Waldo Emerson and concludes that the development of Romanticism in the nineteenth century may in fact mark the beginning of the modern era in the Western world.[31] To be sure the wisdom of Schober's choice could

---

[29]*Scenes in the World of Spirits*, p. 42.

[30]Sydney E. Ahlstrom, "The Romantic Religious Revolution and the Dilemmas of Religious History," *Church History* 46:2 (June 1977), p. 155.

[31]Ahlstrom, "The Romantic Religious Revolution. . . ." p. 170.

be questioned; Jung-Stilling was only on the fringe of European Romanticism. The enduring value of his writings cannot begin to compare with those of Goethe, Schiller, Wordsworth, Coleridge, Schleiermacher, or Fichte. Schober's own pietism would have blinded him to the values of these authors. But Jung-Stilling spoke his language and Schober wanted to share that vision of truth with his fellow Americans.

Despite the immense amount of time consumed by the translation, Schober found time to maintain his responsibilities as a Lutheran pastor. At the Lutheran Synod of 1814 he reported sixty-one baptisms in his congregations. The following year he was ready to report another thirty-eight, but as he traveled to the meeting he became ill and was forced to return home. Much influenza was reported in Salem that year, and the fifty-nine year old pastor was beginning to feel his age. The illness lingered until the warm days of spring erased the chill from the air. During the summer Gottlieb resumed many of his duties although still bothered by occasional weakness. He even made a trip to South Carolina with Carl Storch and Robert J. Miller to counsel some churches regarding the baptism of children of inactive Christians. He was present at the October 1816 synod in nearby Guilford County and appeared well recovered.

That synod was one of the most creative meetings of the body to date. Schober preached the opening sermon in fine style and in later discussions agreed to take on two additional small congregations in Rowan County, Beck's and Pilgrim, whose pastor had moved to Indiana. He reported forty-nine baptisms for the year and

> that a short time ago a Sunday School was begun in one of his congregations. Girls of all ages and boys up to 12 years old were given free instruction in reading German by teachers from Salem.[32]

Members of the synod were very pleased and immediately recommended Sunday schools "not only for the children, but for all who wish to learn to read German." It was felt that pastors should maintain oversight, using the catechism of Luther in order to increase religious knowledge as well as developing skills in German.

Actually Schober's initiative in regular religious training on Sunday began in 1813—the first such effort in North Carolina. Schober organized in his churches a "free school . . . [where] young people are instructed

---

[32]Lutheran Synod Minutes, 1816, p. 4.

in reading and singing . . ." on the Sundays when he was preaching at other congregations.[33] Three years later several teachers at the Girls Boarding School indicated their desire "to begin a Sunday school for children who otherwise had no religious instruction."[34] Schober immediately offered his church near Salem close to the home of Henry Rippel, a lay leader. In early September, twenty-five children gathered to learn to read English and German. The response was exciting, and the Moravians in Salem were so pleased with the idea that they started a similar school in Salem to teach poor children from the surrounding country.[35] The movement grew slowly but steadily in the congregations of various denominations. Before many years passed, Sunday schools became an important part of rural congregations in North Carolina. Long before free schools were available, many young people learned to read and write in the sessions which lasted from early morning to late afternoon.

The synod also struggled with two problems whose theological implications caused concern. Churches in South Carolina were unsure of a proper response when parents who were inactive Lutherans requested baptism for their children. Storch, Schober, and Miller visited with the churches and gave a report of the situation to the synod: could "unawakened souls" answer the baptismal questions properly? How could true faith be imputed to the child when the parents seemed not to possess it? The synod discussed the problem, finally agreeing that pastors could baptize children "provided honorable Christians will act as sponsors and assume and answer the questions . . ."[36]

The other problem related to ordination of a young man named David Henkel. He was an authorized catechist, but asked for ordination in order to administer the sacraments. There was much debate on the request; evidently Henkel had not been actually called to a church or else he had not met the educational requirements of the synod. Debate was quite heated, and, to avoid an impasse, Schober suggested a compromise of giving Henkel authority by the laying on of hands to administer the sacraments for one year. Storch hotly opposed the compromise, but it

---

[33]Salem Diary, 7 February 1813, Fries and others, *Records of Moravians*, 7:3194.

[34]Elders' Conference, 28 August 1816, Moravian Archives.

[35]Salem Diary, 20 April 1817, Fries and others, *Records of Moravians*, 7:3327.

[36]Lutheran Synod Minutes, 1816, Peschau translation, p. 27.

passed and Henkel was given a "temporary ordination."[37] Schober hoped that by 1817 all necessary requirements for full and permanent ordination would be met. The resolution of the conflict portended ill for the future.

One other action of the synod seemed innocent enough and constructive but led to momentous consequences in years to come. Several ministers recognized that the Lutheran church in North Carolina was little known and poorly understood because of the churches' use of German in an English speaking environment. Philip Henkel suggested that an extract of the minutes of the synod and its rules be prepared in English so that the ideas and operations of Lutherans could become known. The secretary, Gottlieb Schober, was instructed to prepare a document of "our Orders and Rules" as soon as possible.

Schober left the synod very tired; the strain of the meeting had taken a toll on his physical strength. Within a week, Schober was again ill, and he wrote to Emmanuel who was in Baltimore on business that "I had several hard fainty or staggering attacks called vertigo, but as yet there appears no dangerous symptoms."[38] By mid November the relapse became so serious that he began to prepare his memoir.

> My life has now extended sixty years and will, judging by many signs, probably soon be at an end. Certainly it was long enough and the utmost goal that I prayed for in my twentieth year when everyone expected in an illness I had, that I would take my departure then. If it last longer it depends on the Lord, and he will know why. For, that he should find me useful in his service is not believable to me now. Since I began to preach, little visible good has come out, wherefore I must recognize myself as a very useless servant. He has thousands of means and ways to attain his purpose and does not need such a poor creature as I am.[39]

Gottlieb was obviously despondent. Although he "had in the studying, preaching and administering of the sacraments many an undeserved joy of my soul," he was now ready only to serve God in the eternal kingdom.

> How beautiful the thought! Here I was useful for nothing. From youth there was an ever enduring compulsion to serve, but the will was lacking. There it will be otherwise in the kingdom where one is always sound and well. Here

---

[37]Lutheran Synod Minutes, 1816, pp. 10-12.

[38]G. Shober to Emanuel Shober, Salem, 5 November 1816, Schober Papers, Old Salem Inc. Archives.

[39]Memoir of Gottlieb Schober, Moravian Archives.

the best intention was often of no endurance, the dependence on visible things often confused faith, love and hope. . . .

The crisis passed and gradually Schober regained his strength and his resolve. He soon was convinced that the illness was God's way of awakening a new sense of humility. It is amazing, he wrote,

how the great merciful God and Saviour let himself down so far and leads, consecrates, protects and keeps such a poor wretched human being, and how his patience and mercy never becomes cold nor old until he finally achieves his purpose.[40]

The physical recovery meant that God was not through with him! As his spirit revived, the sense of mission was rekindled, and Schober returned to his tasks with vigor.

He turned immediately to the task assigned by the synod. It occurred to him that a more ambitious composition was in order. The year 1817 would mark the 300th anniversary of the beginning of Martin Luther's reformation. What better way to commemorate that event than a history of the Reformation that would continuously narrow in scope until it focused on North Carolina Lutherans and their work! During early 1817 Schober worked feverishly. It was a major undertaking to be completed in so short a time. He used Joseph Milner's *History of the Christian Church*, Viet Seckendorf's *History of the Reformation*, abridged by John F. Roos in 1781, Charles Buck's *Theological Dictionary*, David Hume's *History of England*, and Frederick William Young's volume on the doctrine of Martin Luther.[41] When the synod opened in October 1817, Schober asked that his manuscript be examined. Its lengthy title suggested the contents:

A Comprehensive Account of the Rise and Progress of the Reformation of the Christian Church, by Doctor *Martin Luther,* actually begun on the 31st day of October, A.D. 1517; together with interspersed views of his character and doctrine, extracted from his books; and how the Church established by him arrived and progressed in North America; as also, the Constitution and Rules of that church

The Synod appointed Robert J. Miller, Philip Henkel, and Joseph E. Bell to review the manuscript. They

---

[40]Ibid.

[41]Gottlieb Schober, *A Comprehensive Account of the Blessed Reformation of the Christian Church by Doctor Martin Luther* (Baltimore: Schaeffer and Maund, 1818) Preface, p. ix. The book title was quickly shortened in Schober's time to *Luther.* That designation will be used for subsequent citations herein.

considered it a very useful and much needed work and calculated to make our Church known better and they also recommend that it be published at the Synod's expense.[42]

The report was adopted and the treasurer (Schober) was directed to proceed with publication of 1500 copies with synod funds.

The books shall be sold and the receipts from the sale of books shall flow into the Treasury, and after paying off the incurred indebtedness, all is to go towards helping to forward the kingdom of our Lord.[43]

Schober's purpose for the book was clearly stated in the preface. He hoped to show, first, the power of God in the life of Martin Luther which enlightened him concerning the nature of the true church. Second, he promised to examine the character of the reformer, his weaknesses and strengths and his devotion to the pure truth in the Word of God. Third, Schober planned to recount the success which God gave to this enterprise and how it spread over the world. By this

It is humbly hoped, that all Protestant churches, and the individuals of them, will, by reading this short sketch of the almost miraculous escape of their forefathers from intolerable oppression, be awakened to unceasing thanks and praises, combined with humble thanks to God on high, that he would preserve them, and the Lutheran Church in particular, in the enjoyment of pure evangelical doctrine, and all the means of grace; and to raise the spirit of love and union, among all the believers in the divinity of Jesus Christ, the only mediator between God and man; so that we may arrive to that happy period foretold, of living blissfully, as one flock, under one Shepherd.[44]

In the historical sections of *Luther*, Schober made no claims to originality. Using published sources, he reviewed the "oppression of Christendom" by the "Roman Pope and his Church," the events of Luther's career including the ninety-five theses, opposition from Rome, the Diets of Worms, Nuremberg, Speyer, and Augsburg, the reformation in Switzerland, Scotland, and England. Schober used 143 pages of octavo size to reach this point in his narrative. He then detailed the transplanting of the Lutheran Church to America and its arrival in North Carolina. The constitution of the synod was reproduced along with a summary of Lutheran practices. The latter section treated the nature of the sacraments, rules for observance of baptism and the Lord's Supper, guidelines

---

[42]Lutheran Synod Minutes, 1817, Peschau translation, p. 34.

[43]Schober, *Luther*, Preface, p. viii.

[44]Ibid.

for the organization and governance of congregations, the treatment of slaves, and a summary of the actions of the synod of 1817.

The book was well written for the audience to which it was addressed. Initially it stirred no opposition and the synod as a whole praised Schober's efforts. Tucked in the middle of the book, however, was a summary of the Augsburg Confession, including interpretative notes by Schober. In years to come these notes, conveying Schober's interpretation of the Confession in an ecumenical fashion, made him famous or infamous, according to the perspective of those making the judgment. For that reason, a brief review of Schober's ideas on the Confession is necessary.

The Confession of Augsburg was developed in 1530 in an attempt to heal the breach between the followers of Martin Luther and the Roman Catholic church without compromising the essence of Luther's ideas. It was written by Philip Melanchthon, Luther's close associate, "to show that the Lutherans had departed in no vital and essential respect from the Catholic Church, or even from the Roman Church, as revealed in its earlier writers."[45] It took pains to separate Lutherans from the more radical reformers such as Zwingli and the Anabaptists. The idea of justification by faith was prominently set forth, while the concepts of the mass, denial of the cup to the laity, monastic vows, and prescribed fasting were firmly rejected. But the confession affirmed neither the idea of Scripture as the sole source of authority nor the priesthood of the believer, both very important ideas in Lutheran theology.

Schober's publication of the Confession was designed to enhance the understanding of Lutheranism by North Carolinians unfamiliar with the group. Consequently, he concentrated on the essentials of each article, omitting the commentary in the Confession which showed Lutheran differences from the radical reformers. In two or three places, however, his translations did result in a slight change of meaning, almost always in a manner more acceptable to other denominations. In Article VII on the Christian church, the accepted translation is "and to the true unity of the church, it is enough to agree concerning the doctrine of the Gospel and the administration of the Sacraments."[46] Schober translated, "For it is sufficient for the true unity of the Christian church, that the preaching be

[45]Williston W. Walker, *A History of the Christian Church*. Rev. Edition (New York: Charles Scribner's Sons, 1959), p. 334.

[46]Quotations of the Confessions are taken from Henry E. Jacobs, *Book of Concord*, (Philadelphia: United Lutheran Publication House, 1882), p. 37ff.

pure, according to the true understanding of the gospel, and the sacraments administered according to Divine scripture." In Article IX on baptism, the confession says baptism "is necessary to salvation and that through Baptism is offered the grace of God." Schober did not include the words "to salvation," softening the statement slightly but not materially. On the Lord's Supper, the Confession stated that "the Body and Blood of Christ are truly present and are distributed to those who eat...." Schober said "the body and blood of Christ are really present, and are given and administered under the external signs of bread and wine." In addition, Schober added a footnote:

> As Christ has promised unto his disciples and true followers, that he will be with them to the end of the world ... and as he has been pleased to give us the gracious assurance to be present with us whenever we assemble in his name, how firmly may we not rely on his promises, especially when we celebrate the Lord's Supper according to his holy institution, in solemn commemoration of his sufferings and death, and appropriate his merits to our own heart.[47]

While it could be argued that Schober's use of the term "really" for "truly" constituted a change of meaning, such fine distinction would be unconvincing. But the footnote speaks of the kind of presence of Christ usually described as spiritual and the word "commemoration" is more Calvinistic than Lutheran. It seems clear that Schober, while clearly affirming a real presence, was interpreting it in more of a spiritual sense than Luther or Melanchthon. Finally, on the article concerning confession and absolution, Schober clearly felt that it was no longer binding.

> This article was inserted at the time of the delivery of this confession, chiefly to shew a conciliatory spirit to the other party, but the practice of private confession and absolution is entirely discontinued in our Lutheran Churches.[48]

Schober did in fact interpret the Confession in a manner more congenial to the beliefs of other Christian denominations, especially the Reformed and Presbyterian groups. Lutherans have differed in their evaluation of his effort. It was clear that his peers in the North Carolina synod agreed with his ideas. Even those who later accused him of forsaking historic Lutheran distinctives admitted that he was in the mainstream of American Lutheran interpretation at the time. Two of his later detrac-

---

[47]Schober, *Luther*, p. 106.

[48]Schober, *Luther*, p. 107.

tors were members of the investigating committee which reviewed the book initially and recommended wholeheartedly that it be published by the synod! Samuel S. Schmucker, an early historian who favored an ecumenical interpretation, commended Schober as consistent with current Lutheranism. Schmucker was confident that American Lutherans accepted the fundamentals of the Augsburg Confession "together with acknowledged dissent on nonessential aspects of doctrine."[49] He went to great lengths to show how both Schober and Storch, and indeed most prominent American Lutherans of the time, would not demand a literal and absolutely binding interpretation of the Confession. Later Lutheran historians, however, have taken a less complimentary view of Schober's efforts. G. D. Bernheim considered some of *Luther* "compromising and unionistic."[50] The latest study of North Carolina Lutheranism seemed to accept Bernheim's judgment rather uncritically: Schober

> was not in favor of Lutheran distinctiveness in confessions and preferred cooperation with other Lutherans and other denominations even at the risk of compromising historic Lutheran doctrine. He desired a united Lutheran church and indeed a united Protestantism in America.[51]

While Bernheim, writing in 1862, may be forgiven his zeal for denominational exclusiveness, the same trait advocated in 1953 is less admirable. Schober did not hide his belief that the fundamentals of the Christian faith were more important than denominational distinctives. In the conclusion to *Luther*, Schober pointed out that the important doctrines of most Protestant denominations were not significantly different from those of Luther. Why is the one Church of Christ split into so many forms? "MY FRIENDS, *at a proper season*, the Lord will unite us all...." In the meantime, we should concentrate on the converting of souls to Jesus, not proselyting among ourselves.

> But thank God, we see the morning star rising, union is approaching, in Europe by Bible Societies, in America likewise, in which are united all persuasions for propagating the everlasting gospel . . . By Missionary Societies united and separate, sending out hundreds . . . By the exertions of rich and poor to send out sound religious tracts . . . By the hundred thousand

---

[49]Samuel S. Schmucker, *The American Lutheran Church*, (Philadelphia: E. W. Miller, 1852), p. 200.

[50]Bernheim, *History of the German Settlements and of the Lutheran Church*, p. 433.

[51]Jacob L. Morgan, Bachman S. Brown and John Hall eds., *History of the Lutheran Church in North Carolina 1803-1953*, (N. P., 1953), p. 43.

children now by Sunday schools taught to know their God and Saviour . . . By frequent revivals of religion in our country. . . .[52]

After having studied the ideas of the several groups, Schober could see nothing of importance to prevent a cordial union.

> And how happy would it be if all the churches could unite, and send deputies to a general meeting of all denominations, and there sink down upon the rock, Jesus, at the same time, leaving to each their peculiar mode and form; this would influence all the Christians to love one another when and wheresoever they met, and they would commune together.[53]

It is difficult to believe that this idea was stated so clearly and forcefully in 1817! Here was indeed a significant link in the history of the ecumenical movement;[54] it was a vision 100 years before its time. With unerring intuition, however, Schober realized that the hope he envisioned would be severely questioned.

> I think my sentiments and experiences are as orthodox and calvinistical as need be, and yet I am a sort of speckled bird among my calvinist brethren. I am a mighty good church man, but pass among such as a dissenter *in prunello*. On the other hand, the dissenters, think me defective either in understanding or conscience for staying where I am.—Well, there is a middle party called methodists, but neither do my dimensions exactly fit them; I am some how disqualified for claiming a full brotherhood with any party; but there are a few among all parties who bear with me, and love me, and with this I must be content at present; and so far as they love the Lord Jesus, I desire and by his grace, I determine, with or without their leave, *to love them all!*
>
> It is impossible I should be of one entire color, when I have been indebted to all sorts, and like the jay in the fable, have been beholden to most birds in the air for a feather or two. . . . why could I not be content with [one] color, without going amongst other flocks and coveys to make myself such a motley figure? *Let them be angry;* if I have culled the best feathers from all, then *surely I am the finest bird.* . . .
>
> Let us rejoice in our individual beauty, never however, so as to stick to colors, but all of us expect to put on the unspotted and uncolored white raiment, wherein at some period we may all find one another in the innumerable armies surrounding and praising the Lamb slain.[55]

---

[52]Schober, *Luther*, p. 209.

[53]Schober, *Luther*, p. 210.

[54]The best one-volume history of the ecumenical movement recognized Schober's contribution in his preaching among Lutherans, but did not show awareness of the book *Luther* or his important role in the formation of the General Synod. See Ruth Rouse and Stephen C. Neill, *A History of the Ecumenical Movement, 1517-1948*, (Philadelphia: Westminster Press, 1954), pp. 242-43.

[55]Schober, *Luther*, pp. 211-13.

This was a vision of the Church of Christ. In a real sense, the mind of Gottlieb Schober transcended the sectarianism of American denominationalism. But he was no mere visionary; each man must do his part to translate ideals into reality. For Schober, the first step was unity among Lutherans in a General Synod. That effort would consume the remaining energies of his life.

Besides approving Schober's composition, the synod of 1817 made positive steps toward an institution for theological education. The matter had been under discussion for several years, but financial support was lacking. Just before the meeting, a letter arrived from John Bachman, pastor of St. John's Church in Charleston, South Carolina, proposing a cooperative effort for a theological school. His church was connected with the New York synod from which, Bachman wrote, missionary Lutheran teachers might be available in the future. The synod considered this possibility, deciding to await Bachman's personal visit the following year. Philip Henkel and Joseph E. Bell then reported that they had made a beginning of a small institution in Greene County, Tennessee, which they hoped would be adopted by the North Carolina synod.[56] According to Bell, the chief teacher, students would study theology along with Greek, Latin, German, and English languages. The synod praised the efforts of these ministers and voted enthusiastically to lend their support to this new seminary. The ministers announced a special collection for May 1818 and appealed to the churches to give generously.

The synod was closed with a sermon by Schober commemorating the anniversary of the Reformation. He spoke from Revelation 3:15 "O that you were cold or hot."[57] His remarks were not preserved, but without doubt, he was inspired by the work of this synod. What better way to remember the work of Luther than to pour oneself into the enlightenment of Christians and the preparation of ministers to preach the gospel of Jesus Christ. Schober would have warned, however, that neither Jesus or Martin Luther tolerated lukewarm believers. God has a purpose for every Christian and only a life of total dedication was an instrument worthy of God's use.

As Gottlieb rode from Pilgrim's Church in Rowan County back toward Salem, he must have wondered what God had in store for him.

---

[56]Lutheran Synod Minutes, 1817, p. 11.

[57]Lutheran Synod Minutes, 1817, p. 12.

Only a year ago he faced death, despairing on the failures of his life. But God had chosen not to take him. How would God use him in the days to come? Could it be that God would call him to sound the beginning of true church unity in America?

Model of Salem
as it appeared about 1830

CHAPTER 11

An Ecumenical Vision

Contributing to the sense of failure and depression which Gottlieb experienced during his illness in 1815 was the renewal of problems relating to his land speculation of previous years. The claim on Maryland Indian lands was still unsettled and Schober still hoped for a favorable verdict. It was the North Carolina claims of the 1790's, however, which now arose to haunt him and to deepen his despondency.

A large part of the Surry County land which Schober entered in 1795 was sold to Timothy Pickering of Philadelphia. Some years later it was determined that parts of the land were subject to an older title. Gottlieb wrote to Pickering that, "I allways am ready to make you satisfaction according *to our original contract* for the *quantity* of Land found covered by older Titles."[1] This offer, however, was not accepted by Pickering, who employed legal counsel to sue Schober in court. Gottlieb retained Thomas Ruffin of Hillsboro to represent him and personally acquainted the attorney with the specifics of the case when Ruffin visited Salem in early 1815. While no record of that conversation remains, subsequent correspondence indicated that both parties agreed to arbitration outside of court.

---

[1]Quoted in Gottlieb Schober to Thomas Ruffin, Salem, 12 February 1816, Schober Papers, Old Salem Inc. Archives.

Schober became concerned in early 1816, however, when he learned that Pickering wanted arbitrators to consider not only the issue of land covered under older titles, but also the quality of all of the land and the original purchase price. This, Schober believed, was unfair. Although Pickering had not seen the land prior to purchase in 1795, he had accepted the word of his own agent regarding quality and price. Schober offered through Ruffin to settle the whole matter out of court for $1,000 in North Carolina currency. "I am willing to do so to be done with it, but I am confident that amount could not be recovered."[2] The offer was rejected. Arbitration was set for 15 November 1817, in Raleigh and continued the following summer. The decision went against Schober. In May and December 1819, Gottlieb paid a total of $3,000 to Pickering's agent.[3] The matter of quality and price was not mentioned in the settlement, so the award must have related to older titles. Still it was severe disappointment to Gottlieb; he could only hope to recoup part of his loss from his partners in the enterprise.

Although carefully not mentioned in 1795, Schober shared the risks and rewards of land speculations with several friends, including Johann Heinrich Herbst and Samuel Stotz of Salem and Jacob Van Vleck of Bethlehem.[4] Letters were written to all partners or their descendants to the effect that as each had shared in the profits of 1795, "it is nothing but justice that every honest and able partner should refund to me the proportion [of the loss now sustained]."[5] The response of at least some of the partners angered Schober far more than the arbitrators' negative decision. And by late 1819 the explosion of his wrath was so interwoven with other matters as to once again raise the question of his continuing presence in Salem. The Pickering case was but one of the complicated strands that made up Schober's life of this period. Another distressing element of the time related to Gottlieb's oldest son Nathaniel.

---

[2]Ibid.

[3]Receipts dated 14 May and 26 December 1819 signed by William Gaston, attorney for Timothy Pickering, Schober Papers, Old Salem Inc. Archives.

[4]Receipt dated 17 July 1795 showing disbursements to partners by name of money received from Timothy Pickering. Schober Papers, Old Salem Inc. Archives.

[5]G. Schober to Messers Joshua Bowman, Henry Senseman and Pete Transou, Salem, 2 September 1819. Schober Papers, Old Salem Inc. Archives.

From birth Nathaniel possessed a weak physical constitution. He was constantly troubled with a bad cough and in winter seemed always to have colds and fever. By 1817, "his lingering complaint turned to a consumption, which gave way to no remedy...."[6] Desiring to spend his last days in Salem, he sold his 1,032 acres at the crossroads east of Salem to Joseph Kerner. There was no good position available for him in Salem except the office of postmaster, and it was soon obvious that his body would not sustain him long. His health continued to deteriorate, but "he appeared to rejoice in his Situation, and enjoyed as long as he could attend public worship...." He

> united in prayer with others to the Lord for assurance of his adoption and obtained full faith according to the Word of God, that his Soul was redeemed. ... Only 14 days before his death he desired to partake of the body and blood of the Saviour in the holy Sacrament, and when this was administered to him and his wife ... those present were deeply impressed with the presence of the Lord; and the humble Joy which glittered thro his feeble Phisognamy, proved beyond contradiction that the Lord had united with him so effectually that all fear of death had vanished and that his Soul longed to see him face to face....[7]

On 14 June 1818, Nathaniel died. The Schober household knew both grief and comfort. The eldest son was gone, leaving a wife and two small children; but at the same time his long suffering was over, and the family was confident in its belief that Nathaniel was eternally safe.

The remainder of the family was blessed with sound health and active lives. Emmanuel was fully engaged in the practice of law and was involved in the opening of a branch of the Bank of Cape Fear in Salem. He further followed his father's footsteps by winning in 1819 the first of several terms in the North Carolina Senate.[8] Anna Paulina was still teaching in the Girls' Boarding School. The entire family shared her delight in receiving an invitation to accompany Salem's representatives to the Unity Synod meeting in Europe in 1818. Although she was away from Salem for more than a year, she returned to delight the family with stories of the travel and the synod. Certainly the $1,734.13 which the trip

---

[6]Memoir of Nathaniel Schober, Moravian Archives.

[7]Ibid.

[8]Salem Diary, 12 August 1819, Fries and others, *Records of Moravians*, 17:3403.

cost placed a burden on family resources; but Gottlieb knew that the value of the experience to his daughter could not be measured in dollars.[9] Maria Theresa also taught in the Girls' School until 1819. In that year she was married to Peter Wolle, a Salem single brother who had just been named associate pastor of the Bethania congregation.[10] Johanna and Vaniman Zevely still lived in the neighborhood of the paper mill on a 160 acre tract of land which Gottlieb owned and later transferred to the young couple. On this land in 1815 Vaniman set up the first steam-powered wool-carding machine in the area.[11] They also built a sizable brick dwelling on this plantation between 1815 and 1818.[12] It was the first house to stand on the land where the town of Winston was established several decades later.

Gottlieb himself, despite his advancing years, seemed to flourish in a renewed grasp on life. He still served his Lutheran churches regularly and, as already mentioned, worked extensively on matters of the synod. He did retire from the tinsmith trade in 1818, but his other business affairs were as complicated as ever.

Early in 1819, the actions of the Moravian Unity Synod of 1818 were read in Salem, causing considerable stir and discussion. A significant change was the elimination of the lot from the marriage process except in the case of ministers.[13] Marriage was still within the providence of God's will and the approval of local Elders was necessary, but Moravians recognized that divine guidance in this matter might be found through personal conviction as well as in the lot. While this change of practice did not affect Schober, the alteration of philosophy did. Another action of the synod required a new signing of the community regulations by all members of the congregation. As Salem prepared to meet this requirement, an unidentified brother arose in the Congregation Council to point

---

[9]Schober Papers, Old Salem Inc. Archives.

[10]Peter Wolle came to Salem from Nazareth, Pennsylvania, in 1814 to assume leadership of the boys' school. He was later a leader in the Single Brothers' House. The Wolles served in Bethania from 1819 to 1823 when he was called to Pennsylvania.

[11]Memorabilia of the Congregations of Wachovia, 1815, Fries and others, *Records of Moravians*, 7:3254.

[12]Adelaide Fries, Stuart T. Wright and J. Edwin Hendricks, *Forsyth: The History of a County on the March*. Rev. ed. (Chapel Hill: University of North Carolina Press, 1976), p. 98.

[13]Results of Synod of 1818, Chapter 4, Fries and others, *Records of Moravians*, 7:3565.

out that according to community regulations only members of the Unity of Brethren were allowed to own houses in Salem, yet Pastor Schober was in violation of these rules. The brother did not wish

> to cause any difficulties with Pastor Schober, but [is concerned] simply because he binds himself by his signature of the new principles to the removal of all such disorders. . . . The other members of the Council . . . believe this objection ill-founded because our pledge only refers to the future and not to circumstances of the past.[14]

Nevertheless, the matter was referred to the Elders' Conference and the Board of Overseers. By the time the Elders considered the matter, Schober had advised church leaders on his own accord that "he was entirely willing to sign the congregation rules, and that he greatly wished that he might again be considered as a Brother."[15] After discussion, the Conference decided

> That this is a good opportunity to correct the anomalous situation. The doubt whether a Brother can be at the same time a Lutheran minister is invalid, for in former times this was often the case and it is in harmony with the foundation principles enunciated by our Synod.[16]

The most obvious example of a similar situation was none other than Count Zinzendorf himself. Zinzendorf was an ordained Lutheran minister and served a Germantown, Pennsylvania, congregation in 1741, although he was also a bishop in the Unity of Brethren. Whether this historical fact was considered in 1810 when Schober was ordained cannot be ascertained. The decision in 1810 was made in Europe, not in Salem, by the Unity Elders' Conference. Now, quietly, the Salem Elders' Conference corrected an error of the past. Although Schober's actions and tongue had in the past caused enough rancor so that influence from Salem might have affected the 1810 decision in Europe, the ensuing years had healed the wounds and established the sincerity of Schober's intent. To clear any doubts he immediately sought formal permission of the Overseers to continue operating his bookstore. That establishment had expanded in recent years, but the Overseers had not challenged Gottlieb on the matter. The Board approved Schober's selling of "books and medicine, and

---

[14]Congregation Council, 22 April 1819, Moravian Archives.

[15]Elders' Conference, 5 May 1819, Fries and others, *Records of Moravians*, 7:3413.

[16]Ibid.

certain small wares which are advantageous in his trading for rags [for the paper mill]."[17] Once again he was happily a Moravian Brother.

> He has declared that he sought principally the union of heart and enjoyment of fellowship, and desired no part in the management of the affairs of the congregation, though he did not wish to be entirely excluded from Congregation Council.[18]

Within a few days, Schober was on his way to Baltimore where he attended a synod of Lutheran ministers. The trip and its consequences threw Gottlieb once again into the throes of controversy.

The Lutheran Synod of 1819 met in April of that year instead of October. The change was caused by a letter from the Synod of Pennsylvania expressing a desire for "a more intimate union with all the Synods of our church, in the United States. . . ."[19] The various synods were invited to send delegates to the Pennsylvania synod meeting in June to explore the possibilities. The North Carolina synod was therefore changed in order to consider this idea and to authorize delegates to attend the Pennsylvania meeting. Although the October meeting time had just been changed to Trinity Sunday (usually late May or June) by the Synod of 1817, the president, seeing this as sufficient cause, took the initiative to change the date to April with the consent of several ministers and prior notification of all members. At the April gathering these procedures were explained to the delegates and unanimously agreed to by the body. Attendance was normal with fourteen clerical leaders and fourteen laymen as compared to the 1817 attendance of twelve and nine and the 1820 attendance of thirteen and seventeen.[20]

The synod first considered the question of a union. There seemed to be no question as to its desirability, provided the North Carolina body was not compromised. Schober was elected to attend the Baltimore meeting

---

[17]Board of Overseers, 10 May 1819, Fries and others, *Records of Moravians*, 7:3414.

[18]Elders' Conference, 15 May 1819, Fries and others, *Records of Moravians*, 7:3414. After 1818, the Salem Congregation Council once again consisted of all males of the congregation who had reached the age of majority. Results of Synod, 1818, Fries and others, *Records of Moravians*, 7:3567-68.

[19]Lutheran Synod Minutes, 1819, p. 5.

[20]The latest history of North Carolina Lutherans incorrectly emphasizes that attendance at the 1819 was unusually low, enforcing an interpretation that the called synod was unwise and, by implication, unrepresentative. Morgan, Brown and Hall, eds., *History of the Lutheran Church in North Carolina*, p. 46.

"for the purpose of regulating with them, in the name of the Synod, such a desirable union, and to attempt that such a one be affected." It was resolved

> That if he accedes to a constitution for the purpose of uniting our whole church, and that constitution is according to his instructions, received from this Synod, that such a constitution be adopted by us. But that if such constitution is not consonant with such instructions, the same must first be communicated to our next Synod; and only then, if adopted, can it be binding on us.[21]

A committee for instructions was appointed, its report later approved, and the instructions given to the elected delegate.

The synod proceeded to the business of the new seminary endorsed by the 1817 meeting. A constitution had been requested at that time and again by letter of the secretary in June 1818. Nothing had been received nor were the sponsors present in 1819. The synod decided unanimously to hold the $246 given for the institution until its character was approved by the synod. The absences without explanation of Philip Henkel and Joseph Bell were not excused, and the group expressed regret for "the irritating letters written to individuals of this ministry by the rev'd Mr Ph. Henkel and J. E. Bell." Schober, as secretary, was to write them of the action of the synod regarding available money for the seminary and the need for a constitution, expressing

> our conviction of the necessity of supporting an institution submissive to Christian rules, and subject to the constitution of the Lutheran and Reformed Churches.[22]

The final important action of the 1819 Synod that involved Schober related to David Henkel. He had come to the synod expecting the full ordination that had been postponed by previous synods. Instead, the young man had to fight a possible censure by the body. A letter from Andrew Hoyl of Lincoln County stated that Henkel "had treated him rashly, and made use of improper means to deprive him of his good reputation." After a hearing of both parties, the complaint was found to be well grounded. "During this examination, a good deal was also asserted against the doctrine preached by David Henkel. . . ."[23] In the next session

---

[21]Lutheran Synod Minutes, 1819, p. 6.

[22]Lutheran Synod Minutes, 1819, p. 10.

[23]Lutheran Synod Minutes, 1819, p. 11.

Adam Castner asserted that Henkel and his congregation unjustly excommunicated him. After another hearing, the synod reinstated Castner and examined Henkel on the charge

> that he preached the doctrine of transubstantiation—that whoever is baptised and partakes of the Lord's Supper is saved—that he has the right to forgive sins, and other doctrines leading to superstition. . . .

Henkel declared that he did not believe such, and that he had never and would never preach these doctrines. The synod cleared him of the accusations but declined to renew his license as a candidate. He was made a catechist for six months after which he must

> produce to our president sufficient credentials that peace reigneth in his congregations, and that from without, especially from our reformed, or Presbyterian brethren, no important complaint existed against him. . . .[24]

If these conditions were met, the president, Charles Storch, could renew his candidacy until the next synod. To the printed minutes, Schober attached a pastoral reflection of his own, probably without authorization by the synod. He addressed the reader, apologizing that the synod transactions "had more the appearance of law court business, than business belonging to the ministry of the gospel."[25] But the synod must attend to its members, and problems must not be hidden, "yet I endeavored not to paint any thing in livelier colors than the original picture required. . ." The many differences existing among us are lamentable, he said, especially that

> some teach according to their own spirit and will, and do not permit the spirit of meekness, love, tenderness, mercy and patience to reign; but suffer the spirit of distrust, jealousy, wrangling, disputing, and disposition to domineer. . . .

The solution, Schober stated, was to pray for the guidance of God and,

> setting aside all wisdom from below, know nothing among our congregations but Jesus Christ and him crucified, and to proclaim justification by and through him alone. . . .[26]

No names were mentioned, but in light of the accusations against David Henkel, Schober's feelings were quite clear. The rumblings of trouble ahead were thus faintly heard.

---

[24]Lutheran Synod Minutes, 1819, p. 12.

[25]Lutheran Synod Minutes, 1819, p. 20.

[26]Lutheran Synod MInutes, 1819, p. 21.

Schober attended the Pennsylvania Synod meeting in June 1819 where he discussed the possibilities of union. He spoke forcibly that the union should be founded on the Augsburg Confession but was unable to secure agreement for the inclusion of this Confession among the founding principles.[27] Many Lutherans of this period were increasingly viewing the Confession only as a symbolic statement, rather than binding theological doctrine. Schober's interpretation of the Confession was considered conservative in Lutheran circles in the North, forcing him to return to North Carolina with a proposal to be submitted to his own 1820 synod. The proposal was circulated among the Lutheran pastors and immediately encountered opposition from several of them. The ensuing controversy ended in the creation of the Synod of Tennessee, dedicated to the Augsburg Confession as a binding doctrinal statement and to absolute opposition to the General Synod. The details of this division belong more to a narrative of Lutheran history than to a study of Schober.[28] But, as usual, he was so immersed in the affair as to necessitate a summary of events. The controversy centered on two points: the ordination of David Henkel and the idea of a General Synod of Lutherans in America.

Soon after the April 1819 synod, Philip Henkel in Tennessee received a letter from his brother David relating details of the doctrinal examination to which he had been subjected and the action of the synod withholding ordination. Philip came to North Carolina on Trinity Sunday 1819, insisting that the April meeting had been illegitimate. When no other ordained ministers arrived, and Storch informed him that there was no further business to be conducted, Philip ordained David Henkel and Joseph E. Bell to the full ministry in clear violation of the synod's established procedures and in total disregard of the events of the April meeting concerning David's ministry and preaching. Several congregations of the area were addressed in which the senior ministers of the synod were accused of failing to advance some young men in the ministry.[29]

---

[27]Samuel S. Schmucker, *The American Lutheran Church*, (Philadelphia: E. W. Miller, 1852), p. 214.

[28]The best sources are Jacob L. Morgan, Bachman S. Brown and John Hall, eds. *History of the Lutheran Church in North Carolina* 1803-1953 (n.p.: United Evangelical Lutheran Synod of North Carolina, 1953). Of less value is the older work of G. D. Bernheim, *The History of the Evangelical Lutheran Synod and Ministerium of North Carolina* (Philadelphia Lutheran Publishing House 1872). A revision was made by George H. Cox in 1902.

[29]Lutheran Synod Minutes, 1820, pp. 3-6.

The Synod of 1820 therefore met in a high state of tension at its now established time of Trinity Sunday. It proved to be a climactic meeting for several reasons. President Storch first reviewed, step by step, the events of the preceeding year, including the April 1819 meeting, its consideration of the Pennsylvania request, the actions regarding David Henkel, and the July ordination of Henkel and Joseph Bell. Storch counseled that "as errors had been committed on both sides," the breach could be healed by Philip's reuniting with the body and subjecting himself to the rule of the majority. It was clear that the ordinations of Henkel and Bell were not at this point considered valid. Philip was silent, but the young ministers began to speak of the errors of the synod:

> they accused us of not teaching water baptism to be regeneration, and that we did not accept the elements in the eucharist as the true body and blood of the Lord, corporeally; and therefore, and because the plan for a general union of our church . . . was against the Augsburg Confession . . . they could not unite with us. . . .[30]

Since the synod meeting place was a congregation pastored by David Henkel, the body felt it necessary to adjourn and conduct the remainder of its sessions in a Lincolnton hotel. Later Joseph Bell asked to reunite with the synod and when he agreed to abide by its rules and the will of the majority, his ordination was validated. Several members made the same request on behalf of David Henkel, but he himself did not appear nor agree to the conditions. Therefore he was declared "no minister of the Lutheran Church of North Carolina and adjacent States."

The opposition of the Henkels crystallized around the proposal for a General Synod, even though they voted in favor of the initial exploration. After Schober's trip to Baltimore, he circularized the results of his conversations with the Pennsylvania brethren. He reported to the Synod of 1820 that he had been cordially received and "they immediately appointed a committee, in unison with [myself], to deliberate upon, and form a plan for a general union. . . ."[31] A plan was developed, then debated on the Pennsylvania Synod floor, paragraph by paragraph, and finally passed. The North Carolina group

> was now to deliberate whether the plan can be adopted. The plan was hereupon read paragraph by paragraph, debated and elucidated, and the

---

[30]Lutheran Synod Minutes, 1820, p. 6.

[31]Lutheran Synod Minutes, 1820, p. 15.

expediency of a general union admitted also by such who had their scruples as to the present plan.[32]

The vote was called: fifteen yes and six no—the necessary two-thirds majority was achieved. It was then reported that the Synod of Ohio had also approved the plans. North Carolina was entitled to two clerical and one lay delegate. Robert J. Miller, Peter Schmucker and layman John B. Harry were elected, with alternates available if needed. Schober was one of these alternates. The plan for the General Synod was not published with the 1820 minutes as might have been expected. In light of subsequent events, that omission may have been deliberate.

The plan was fairly simple. It assumed that Christ gave no particular prescription on church government, thereby allowing the church freedom to make regulations according to circumstances. A general synod of churches was therefore possible but not mandatory. The synod would exist

> for the exercise of brotherly love, for the furtherance of christian harmony;
> for the preservation of the unity of the spirit in bond of peace. . . .[33]

It claimed the name "The Evangelical Lutheran General Synod of the United States of America" and defined its members as deputies from regional Lutheran bodies, apportioned according to the number of ordained members in the body. All deputies would have equal rights and votes. The synod was to acquaint itself with local situations and to examine and approve all manuscripts and books such as catechisms, liturgies, compilations of hymns, and confessions of faith designed for use in public worship. The General Synod could recommend new materials of this nature and lower bodies were expected though not mandated to use these them. At the same time the General Synod clearly did not allow itself

> to prescribe uniform ceremonies, to introduce alterations, in things respecting faith, or in things which respect the manner of publishing the gospel of Jesus Christ the Son of God and foundation of our faith which might oppress the conscience of the brethren in Christ.[34]

---

[32]Lutheran Synod Minutes, 1820, p. 16.

[33]Appendix to Minutes of the Lutheran Synod of Tennessee for 1821 entitled "The Objections of the Committee against the Constitution of the General Synod," p. 13.

[34]Appendix to Tennessee Synod Minutes, 1821, p. 25.

The plan provided for orderly expansion of regional bodies by subdivision, while trying to avoid the occurrence of schismatic divisions. Differing grades of the ministry were recognized, along with progression from one to another. The synod did not view itself as an appeals tribunal in regional matters, but did reserve the right to advise synods, congregations, and ministers on matters of doctrine and discipline and to seek to settle disputed matters in a amicable manner. The synod could propose plans for denominational institutions, such as seminaries, homes for widows and orphans and create a treasury for the accomplishment of this aim. Finally, the synod was to promote the interests common to all Christian bodies for the ultimate benefit of the Church of Christ.

Ministers opposed to the idea of a General Synod were quick to locate and exploit flaws in the proposal. In published critiques, no part of the plan was commended; if a particular section elicited no objections, it was simply passed over without comment. Some of the criticisms related to an interpretation of a word or phrase and were easily countered by proponents. In fact, in retrospect, the opponents seemed to weaken their impact by concentrating on minor points. Consequently, the true weaknesses were lost in a tumble of rhetoric. Opponents recognized that while the synod claimed the name "Evangelical Lutheran" it failed to include reference to any documents, such as Luther's Catechism or the Augsburg Confession, long held dear by more conservative Lutherans. This was a legitimate problem because the liberal Lutherans wished to avoid anything more than a broad acceptance of the Confession with acknowledged disagreement in nonessential items. Consequently the plan was purposefully and wrongfully left ambiguous. Similarly, the synod's role regarding approval of materials used by the congregations in worship was left cloudy. It claimed no power to prescribe uniformity in worship, yet insisted that only approved materials be used.

To be sure, these and other weaknesses could be corrected once the basic idea of a General Synod was approved. But conservative ministers would have no part of the idea now or later and even prohibited their congregations from hearing the preaching of a Lutheran "connected with the General Synod."

Later generations of Lutheran historians have described these events as the "drawing away" of the Tennessee Synod. But at the time, it could hardly be faithfully described as anything except a bitter schism. Both sides propagandized wavering congregations and celebrated their victories.

The issue of the synod was unfortunately entangled with the personal and doctrinal problems associated with David Henkel. His preaching on baptism and the Lord's Supper was at variance with most American Lutherans of the time and probably with historic Lutheranism, although enough ambiguity existed so that Henkel could claim to be faithful to the German reformer. The differences were set forth in a letter to the Synod of 1820 from a Methodist minister, James Hill, who asked clarification on the Lutheran position. Some ministers in his area were preaching that "baptism by water effects *regeneration*, and that the body and blood of Christ are corporeally received along with the bread and wine in the Lord's Supper."[35] The synod officially answered that

> baptism is beneficial, and ought to be attended to as a command of God: but we do not believe that all who are baptized with water are regenerated and born again unto God, as to be saved, without the operation of the Holy Ghost; or in other words, without faith in Christ. And, as to the second question, we do not believe, nor teach, that the body and blood of our Lord Jesus Christ is corporeally received along with the bread and wine in the Lord's Supper; but that the true believer does spiritually receive and partake of the same through faith in Jesus Christ, and all the saving benefits of his death and passion.[36]

This letter drew the lines of theological battle between the synods of North Carolina and Tennessee, and, more particularly, between Gottlieb Schober and David Henkel. For the next several years, relations between the two groups were poisoned by this controversy as each leader used his sharp intellect and even sharper pen to establish truth and error. That clash will deserve close attention later, but since events in Salem also contributed to Schober's state of mind, a return to that scene is necessary.

The letters which Gottlieb had written in 1819 to his former partners in the 1795 land speculation loss were only partially effective. The heirs of Philip Transou refused "to participate in the burden of the loss he had suffered now as they had participated in the gain of this speculation."[37] Since these heirs were Maria Schober's family, the matter was rather sensitive. Schober asked the Overseers to determine the correct settlement, but they viewed the whole matter as "rather phony." Nevertheless an investigating committee was appointed to talk to the Transou heirs.

---

[35]Lutheran Synod Minutes, 1820, p. 13.

[36]Lutheran Synod Minutes, 1820, p. 18.

[37]Board of Overseers, 21 February 1820, Moravian Archives.

Schober was satisfied. Two months later the matter was still unsettled and another conversation revealed that the Transous had sought legal advice and found that "according to the laws of this country, they would not have to pay anything to Pastor Schober [and] they have decided to act accordingly."[38] Schober's wrath was vented in a biting letter attacking

> with Bible verses, etc., Philip Transou's heirs and the Collegium. He imposes responsibilities on the Collegium which it has never claimed and could never accomplish. The Collegium unanimously decides that no official answer is to be given to this letter. Every member may, if Pastor Schober tries to talk about it, give his opinion according to his own conviction.[39]

By September, Schober's conversations and conduct "toward Dr. Kuehln and the heirs of Philip Transou" had become unbearable and "completely against our [community] orders." Schober was given an official written reprimand by community leaders which alluded to the fragile nature of Schober's relationship to the community during previous times.[40] The reference to Dr. Kuehln in the reprimand established that land speculation losses was not the only problem. Old complaints against Schober were again being raised, for once again his business dealings were encroaching upon the provinces of others.

A 1819 invoice revealed that Schober purchased over $100 worth of shoes and boots for resale—seven pairs of men's wax shoes, twelve pair of grain shoes, three pair of women's "leather sponges" and several other kinds of boots for children.[41] Such articles stretched the definition of Schober's business considerably. In addition, Gottlieb had for several years supplied the community with certain patent medicines and one popular item in particular made of red bark. When Dr. Christian David Kuehln arrived in Salem in 1818, Schober promised to give up his medicines. Once again, seemingly with some weariness, the Overseers had to speak to Schober about "illegal selling." Very little had been said to him in this regard since his Lutheran ordination, and Schober had quietly expanded his operation in direct competition with several Salem enter-

---

[38]Board of Overseers, 10 July 1820, Moravian Archives.

[39]Board of Overseers, 24 July 1820, Moravian Archives.

[40]Board of Overseers, 4 September 1820, Moravian Archives.

[41]Bill of sale from John Bedford and Company, Philadelphia to Reverend Gottlieb Schober, 14 June 1819, Schober Papers, Old Salem Inc. Archives.

prises. He now possessed a small but broad inventory of household and personal goods as well as books, maps, and paper supplies.

All came under the umbrella of "trading for rags for the paper mill." The governing boards, of course, were not fooled. They had long before decided that Schober would never completely conform to community regulations in this regard, but his violations, if kept within reason, could be tolerated by community leaders who could readily observe that the old economic ideals were essentially waning. Doubtless, Schober's activity contributed to the dissatisfaction of many others regarding Salem's closed economic organization. Others also quietly stretched the definition of their business activity beyond authorization, but none so often and as far as Schober. He therefore became, after the death of storekeeper Traugott Bagge in 1800, Salem's best example of an individual businessman, successful in the accumulation of a moderate estate by means of personal initiative.

In addition to these matters, Gottlieb could feel a true sense of satisfaction with several public and private events. In early 1819 he preached for the first time in a Moravian Church. The Hope congregation was without a pastor, and Schober spoke there "to a numerous and attentive audience."[42] In December 1819, he participated in the fiftieth anniversary of the founding of the Single Brothers' House. He was one of only five of the original residents still living in Salem. Two years later he was one of fourteen original Salem citizens celebrating the fiftieth anniversary of Salem's earliest meeting hall.[43] And then in early 1821 there was another wedding in the family. Anna Paulina had almost married Johann Senseman of Salem in 1816, but the lot was negative. Again in the summer of 1820, Peter Kluge of Graceham, Maryland, requested to marry Anna Paulina, but she refused. Then in December 1820, Johann Gottlieb Herman,[44] Salem's former schoolmaster for boys, when he was called as pastor of the Newport, Rhode Island, congregation, proposed marriage to the second daughter of Gottlieb Schober. The lot was affirmative and

---

[42]Salem Diary, 14 February 1819, Fries and others, *Records of Moravians*, 7:3398.

[43]Salem Diary, 27 December 1819, Fries and others, *Records of Moravians*, 7:3406; Salem Diary, 13 November 1821, Fries and others, *Records of Moravians*, 7:3474.

[44]Johann Gottlieb Herman was a native of Niesky, Germany, where he received a strong formal education. He was a teacher in the boys' school at Fulneck, England for six years prior to coming to Salem in 1816 in the same capacity.

Anna Paulina accepted.[45] In January the Schobers welcomed this new son-in-law to the family even while shedding a quiet tear as the bride left Salem for her new home in Rhode Island.

---

[45]Minutes of the Provincial Elders' Conference, 19 December 1820, Fries and others, *Records of Moravians*, 7:3452-53. After the Synod of 1818, the lot was no longer required in the marriage of most Moravians. The marriage of ministers, however, still included the early practice.

CHAPTER 12

Controversy with the Henkels

IN HIS REFORMATION DAY sermon of 1817, Gottlieb Schober articulated a rapidly growing idea among American Lutherans. He voiced the hope that "the spirit of love and union" might be awakened

> among all who believe the divinity of Jesus Christ, the sole mediator between God and man, so that we might come to the blessed time foretold of old when we will live in peace as one flock under one shepherd.[1]

So responsive was his audience in North Carolina that Schober wrote to Pennsylvania Lutherans that "it would be good if the Lutherans and Reformed were to unite with each other," citing as precedent the Plan of Union already operating in Prussia involving the same groups. Schober's Moravian heritage gave him ample foundation for his point of view. Zinzendorf, though badly misunderstood by Pennsylvania Lutherans almost a century earlier, had worked diligently to accomplish similar goals. Now Schober echoed this heritage and found that he was not alone. A Lutheran historian, George Lochman, writing in 1818, said:

> I cannot help expressing my pleasure, in observing that the different denominations are drawing nearer to each other and that bigotry is rapidly

---

[1]Quoted in Donald H. Yoder, "Christian Unity in Nineteenth Century America," *A History of the Ecumenical Movement.* Ruth Rouse and Stephen C. Neill, ed. (Philadelphia: Westminister Press, 1954), pp. 242-43.

declining. In some parts of Germany and in Prussia, the distinction of Lutheran and Reformed is already done away, and both churches consider themselves as one body. And God grant! that this spirit of union and brotherly love may continue to spread! God grant, that all who profess and call themselves Christians may be led into the way of truth and hold the faith in unity of spirit, in the bond of peace, and in righteousness of life.[2]

It must be concluded that Schober was not a maverick, leading North Carolina Lutherans down the road to extinction, despite the judgment of several later local Lutheran historians. This was a national, even international movement within the Lutheran Church, and Schober was its most articulate proponent in the American South.

There is no good evidence of the opposition of the Henkel family—father Paul and sons Philip and David—to ecumenical ideas and the concept of the General Synod until after the censure of David by the North Carolina ministers because of his doctrinal ideas. In fact Schober and Paul Henkel were close friends who exchanged letters of mutual support and encouragement in the work of North Carolina Lutherans.[3] Philip Henkel reviewed and approved Schober's book *Luther*, even with its strong ecumenical statements. But when the North Carolina ministers postponed the ordination of David Henkel, a wound was opened.

In order to justify his own ideas, David Henkel had to find an issue by which he could show that North Carolinians were deviating from historic Lutheranism. That issue was the idea of a General Synod whose concepts were wide enough for both Lutheran and Reformed traditions—and perhaps even other confessional groups. When confessionalism triumphed over ecumenism in the late nineteenth century, Henkel and the Tennessee Synod were cited by some historians as the heroes of the restoration of pure Lutheranism in America.[4] But those same historians do not say that American Lutherans adopted Henkel's ideas, which, it will become evident, were significantly radical at several points. Whatever is the final judgment on this matter, a brief consideration of the Schober-Henkel controversy is integral to an account of Gottlieb's ecumenical efforts.

---

[2]Quoted in Yoder, "Christian Unity in Nineteenth Century America," p. 243.

[3]Paulus Henkel to Gottlieb Schober, Point Pleasant, Mason County, Virginia, 7 August 1816. Schober Papers, Old Salem Inc. Archives.

[4]This judgment was initially made by G. D. Bernheim and not modified in the more recent history of North Carolina Lutherans by Morgan, Brown, and Hall. Lutheran historians writing from a national perspective are more balanced in their perspective.

By the time of the 1821 North Carolina Synod in June, David Henkel had published an attack on the synod, its ministers, and the concept of a General Synod. It was entitled the *Carolinian Herald of Liberty, Religious and Political*, aimed precisely at the Lutheran congregations in North Carolina.[5] He argued forcefully that a General Synod of Lutherans was a step back toward the centralization characterizing Roman Catholicism. Spiritual union of the believer and Christ already existed and that alone was necessary. If the synod materialized

> We may put the light kindled in the Reformation under a bushel; we may draw the veil of death over our eyes; Christian liberty may hide her lovely face, and weep tears of blood; and O! farewell ye happy seats of freedom, where virtue had found an asylum; farewell thou sweet doctrine of free justification, through the crucified. . . .[6]

Henkel then launched into what such a synod *might* do, such as establish a seminary in Pennsylvania and then require all candidates for the ministry to attend. Or a synod might adopt new non-Lutheran hymnbooks or liturgies and force the regional synods to follow suit. "Luther's catechism, and the Augsburgh confession of faith might be omitted without a breach of the [fourth article of the plan-proposal]."[7] He attacked the plan as the beginning of a national church including Lutherans and other denominations.

> Such are the visionary dreams of many in our days; hence they labor with assiduity to promote this cause; and being the heralds of the destruction of party walls, they anticipate in sharing great honors in this new dispensation.[8]

This new arrangement would, Henkel continued, require that doctrinal differences be dropped, and a minister would be forced to believe his own creed and every other one, even if some were in contradiction and therefore in error. It would result in an oppressive established church, robbing Americans of their freedom: "But now, Americans open your eyes! another policy, under the cloak of a brotherhood, is at work; a National Synod is in view." It would be only short steps, Henkel said, until the clergy would

---

[5](Salisbury, North Carolina: Krider and Bingham, 1821).

[6]Henkel, *Carolinian Herald of Liberty*, p. 8.

[7]Henkel, *Carolinian Herald of Liberty*, p. 11.

[8]Henkel, *Carolinian Herald of Liberty*, p. 13.

suborn the populace to send such representatives to Congress subsidiary to their long premeditated scheme; the Constitution might then be rejected, America enslaved, the bloody flag of persecution hoisted—and they, like temporal lords, reigning in the plentitude of power.[9]

After this address, the pamphlet immediately turned to a description of the events surrounding Henkel's censure by the "illegal" synod of April 1819, and his subsequent ordination in June of the same year. His entire case rested on the fact that the April synod did not remove him from the ministry but had postponed his ordination six months by which time the "legal" synod had met and ordained him to the full ministry. Then Henkel attacked the ordained ministers by name, Schober included, as guilty of breach of the Synod Constitution by holding a secret, illegal meeting at which the idea of a General Synod was presented and approved. He further charged that these ministers had departed from Lutheran doctrine on the Lord's Supper because they denied that the corporeal body of Christ was present in the sacrament. Henkel argued that all bodies are corporeal, even spiritual bodies; therefore the real presence was corporeal presence.[10] For these and a number of other reasons, Henkel declared that these ministers were no longer the true Evangelical Lutheran Synod of North Carolina.

All Lutheran churches were invited to participate in the newly organized Tennessee Synod. In a final section, Henkel returned to the doctrine of the presence of Christ in the Lord's Supper. He argued his points from Biblical references and spent considerable time showing how this Lutheran idea was different from the transubstantiation of Roman Catholicism. It was obvious that Henkel believed his case would stand or fall on this point.

By the time of the June 1821 Synod, Henkel's composition had circulated among the ministers. All were upset at the combination of truth, half-truth, falsehood, and innuendo in a propagandistic pamphlet. These ministers believed that they had dealt fairly, even generously, with David Henkel, and had sought to correct his alleged deviations gently so as to preserve his enthusiasm and leadership potential for the good of the church. Now Schober and the others felt that Henkel's tactics were devious and malacious—particularly his combining the weaknesses of the

---

[9]Henkel, *Carolinian Herald of Liberty*, p. 18.

[10]Henkel, *Carolinian Herald of Liberty*, pp. 32- 33.

General Synod plan, which many had recognized and hoped later to strengthen, with distortions in such a way as to portray a power-hungry clergy about to destroy American religious freedom. If Henkel expected Schober and the ministers to continue their gentle and conciliatory treatment of the situation, he was quickly purged of that illusion.

Schober, as secretary of the synod, had in his files a letter from Henkel which proved that he had initially accepted the actions of the 1819 synod. The letter, written 6 May 1819, reported the numbers in Henkel's various congregations and included a footnote relative to the Synod of 1820. "It is agreed upon that the next conference be held in Immanuel's Church Lincolnton in the Rev. Mr. Moser's congregation."[11] There was no indication that the 1819 Synod was "invalid" or "illegal"—evidently that line of thought only emerged later. Therefore Schober came to the synod with his written response almost ready for the press. It was quickly evident that Henkel was not the only Lutheran with a sharp tongue and a pen that made words into weapons. Several read Schober's response, and the synod officially agreed

> to the opinions of the minister, particularly since Rev. Schober himself takes responsibility for his language. It is desirable however that in the future nothing more appear in print from our side; the Henkels may print whatever they wish.[12]

The synod believed that the complaints against David Henkel in 1819, along with the proofs brought forth, should be published with Schober's review in order that the record could be completely public. Once that was accomplished, they did not intend to dignify the controversy further by prolonged debate.

Schober's treatise was not a free-standing publication. He titled it a *Review of a Pamphlet, Issued from the Press of the Western Carolingian in Salisbury, N.C. written by David Henkel. . . .* In the preface he said that Henkel's work was not worth a response,

> but where so many absurdities, pompous bragging, low-bred billigsgate, scurrilous language, scandalous comparisons, perversions of truth, libelous charges, and meanness throughout, are dished up for the digestion of the

---

[11]David Henkel to Gottlieb Schober, 6 May 1819. Schober Papers, Old Salem Inc. Archives. By the time of the 1820 synod Henkel had replaced Daniel Moser as pastor of Immanuel Church, Lincolnton.

[12]Lutheran Synod Minutes, 1821, p. 15-16.

unwary, who are not able to detect poison without assistance, I could not help [but]. . . to review the performance. . . .[13]

Even as Henkel had clearly identified Schober as the leader of events and ideas which he opposed, Schober in turn did not hesitate to indict Henkel with sarcasm and ridicule for attempting to disrupt the church by stirring "the whirlpool of a mudpuddle."

Do not think that for your sake I reluctantly address you, for seven years' experience proves you to be incorrigible. No: what is done here is only done for such readers as have a desire to judge impartially.[14]

After this brisque dismissal at the outset, Schober launched his attack. It was altogether necessary to have read Henkel's work in order to follow Schober's review. He countered Henkel's criticism of the plan for a General Synod by several times turning Henkel's own criticisms back upon himself and his own activities in the new Tennessee Synod.

Every true christian must shudder at your scurrilous language about the desirable union in spirit of all true lovers of Jesus, page 17. . . . You know that no such union as you invent can be effected, or is contemplated; but surely, it would be a millenum, and a desirable one, if the sheep of the flock, guided by and belonging to one shepherd, could, while feeding on his pastures, love one another with all their diversified colors.[15]

This personal section was followed by a review of quarrel between Henkel and Schober over the latter's alleged misuse of the office of postmaster in Salem. Schober labeled the charge as absolutely false and libelous. The language of this section spared nothing in the style of nineteenth century pamphleteering. It was pointed, personal, and left no doubt of the disgust and utter rejection with which Schober regarded Henkel at this time.

In the next section, Schober with equal enthusiasm but less invective defended the now accepted constitution of the General Synod, addressing himself not to Henkel, but to the people. He advocated the education of ministers and missionaries and denied that Pennsylvania would necessarily dominate an educated ministry. He showed that the synod could not

---

[13]Gottlieb Schober, *Review of a Pamphlet, Issued from the Press of the Western Carolingian in Salisbury, N.C., Written by David Henkel* (Salisbury: Bingham and White, 1821), p. 5.

[14]Schober, *Review*, p. 3.

[15]Schober, *Review*, pp. 5-6.

misuse its authority regarding materials of public worship. On each article of the constitution Schober carefully explained and argued the provisions and ideas of the General Synod. He took pains to meet Henkel's objections but was more intent on explaining the intent and strengths of the constitution than in merely defending it. Then it was back to the Henkel situation to rehearse once again the circumstances of David's fight for ordination. Carefully Schober reviewed the sequence of events, including errors he himself made in the printing of a Synod Constitution in the book *Luther.* He also did not hesitate to point out the errors in the Henkel's actions, but quietly. He then addressed David in a series of questions, with emotional heat again beginning to rise, designed to show David's rejection of the synod's action of censure and his determination to be ordained with or without the synod's approval. Schober renewed his charges that Henkel's interpretation of the Lord's Supper was more Roman Catholic than Lutheran. Henkel's arguments "are so far fetched that common sense cannot comprehend them, and are abhorring to the understanding. . . ."[16]

The pamphlet came to a conclusion with a printing of the materials related to doctrinal charges against Henkel at the Synod of April 1819. A long letter from Andrew Hoyl was included, describing Henkel's preaching and advocacy that

> water baptism alone would produce our salvation if we would believe in it; and that a person might receive the baptism of the Holy Ghost, and be and remain a reprobate; and that the Holy Ghost would accompany water baptism; and that ministers of the gospel could forgive sins. . . .[17]

James Hill, another minister, reported that Henkel's preaching on the Lord's Supper,

> from every view of his doctrine I could take, the tenor of it was as palpable transubstantiation as ever was exhibited by a Catholic priest, although probably not in such express terms.[18]

Still another letter told of Henkel's advice to his young people

> not to intermarry among Baptist, Methodists, nor any other profession; . . . so might cows and horses marry. . . [because] there was scripture to prove

---

[16]Schober, *Review,* p. 33.

[17]Schober, *Review,* p. 50.

[18]Schober, *Review,* p. 61.

that marrying in other professions was forbid—and quoted, where it says, "Be Ye equally yoked."[19]

Schober could have included additional charges made by deposition. One man swore that Henkel preached that "he was as righteous as god" and that he repeatedly said from several pulpits that he could forgive sin.[20] Another certified that in 1818 Henkel preached

> if any person or persons received the Lord's Supper as an Emblem or picture [he] is an Idol or Idolitrous Worshipper. But we hold that the Elements are actually Christ's Body and Blood.[21]

Schober rested his case without a final summation. He believed that the evidence was overwhelming and would convince the impartial reader. A concise summary of his point of view was contained in a letter written to Andrew Hoyl about a year *before* the pamphlet itself.

> By your last favour I was delighted to understand how you have exerted yourself to make slanderers explain to the people how the mistake in the Book [*Luther*] has arisen, that you did not succeed, and they refused, will all assist to convince the honest part of the community, what Spirit it is that causes disturbances, and will be of good use hereafter—Mr. R. J. Miller writes that Philip [Henkel] threatened him to put something in Print if the business is not settled according to (his idea) of Justice—To this I have no Objection, for if they want to expose us they will be exposed, and in that case I must publish the papers & depositions filed at our last Synod with your consent, after which no honest Man will decide otherwise than that we ought to have dismissed D[avid Henkel] totally, but from our side we shall not publish any thing, believing as you say that Bounaparte reigned a while & is now in Elba—but I wish you not to cease to be attentive to the movements of Lyars; and that whenever opportunity offers you would assure the Members of the community that we have no other point in view but to keep & preserve our Ministry and Church uncontaminated with impurities—of Popish & Despotic arrogancies & pride—and that the Ministries of our Church may live up to the Doctrine they preach, and abide in Truth. The Rev'd Paul [Henkel] wrote me a letter which I rec'd the same Day I rec'd yours—but says not a Word of all their machinations, and only writes that he was tired of travelling & was going home to rest for the Winter & would come out again in the Spring, his Letter came unsealed, and as I do not know where to send him an answer, I take the Liberty to enclose it to you unsealed, to be forwarded to him. The Contents are only to give him my opinion that we

---

[19]Schober, *Review*, p. 62.

[20]Deposition of Samuel Hawkins, 23 April 1819, David Henkle Papers N338, Southern Historical Collection, University of North Carolina, Chapel Hill.

[21]Deposition of Nathan Davis, 23 April 1819, David Henkle Papers N338, Southern Historical Collection, University of North Carolina, Chapel Hill.

could very well excuse him from being further troubled with visiting us & wish him a quiet accounting Time with a good Conscience.[22]

It was a letter which foreshadowed the events and writings of 1821. The pamphlets indeed exposed the events for public judgment, and, while the arguments continued on a lower key for several years, these outbursts seemed to have a purifying effect. Neither pamphlet was flattering to its author and can only be evaluated as a product of the time—a duel by ministers without guns. On Schober's part, all of his other writings were of higher and more lasting quality. Likewise, Henkel later published better works, including his *Heavenly Flood of Regeneration: or, A Treatise on Holy Baptism* in 1822 and *A Treatise on the Person and Incarnation of Jesus Christ* in 1830.

The Synod of 1822, "because of a public report that we had done D. Henkel injustice" resolved once more to review the matter for the benefit of the various churches in an appendix attached to the synod minutes. This added nothing new but obviously circulated in places untouched by Schober's *Review*. The Tennessee Synod reported petitions from several Rowan County churches "who have publicly renounced the General Synod, and request our Synod to provide a minister for them."[23] But some of these returned to the North Carolina fellowship within a year. Similarly, an itinerant preacher from the North Carolina synod was "received with joy" in Tennessee churches in 1824 and a formal request for affiliation soon arrived.[24] Certainly there was never a doubt about the sentiments of the majority of the Lutheran churches and ministers. In 1821 Gottlieb Schober was elected president of the synod for the first time. He was reelected to this position eight times until age and infirmity forced him to relinquish most of his activity in the pastorate in 1830.

Attempts to reconcile the Tennessee ministers were made in 1823 but to no avail. Finally it was decided to let the matter alone but, since ministers connected with the General Synod were barred from churches belonging to Tennessee, "so we advise our congregations to allow none of their ministers to preach in our churches."[25]

---

[22]G. Shober to Andrew Hoyl, Salem, 6 November 1819, David Henkle Papers N338, Southern Historical Collection, University of North Carolina, Chapel Hill.

[23]Minutes of Tennessee Lutheran Synod, 1822, p.5.

[24]Lutheran Synod Minutes, 1825, pp. 7-9.

[25]Lutheran Synod Minutes, 1824, p. 7.

The doctrinal ideas which separated the Tennessee ministers from some other American Lutherans were summarized in a 1823 letter from Tennessee to the Pennsylvania synod asking a response to these questions.

> 1. Do you believe, that Holy Baptism, administered with natural water, in the name of the Father, and of the Son, and of the Holy Ghost, effects the forgiveness of sins, delivers from death and the devil, and confers everlasting salvation upon all who believe it, as the words and promises of God declare?
>
> 2. Do you believe that the true body and blood of Christ, under the form of bread and wine in the Holy Supper, are present, administered, and received? Do you also believe that the unbelieving communicants receive in this Supper the body and blood of Christ, under the form of bread and wine? We do not ask whether the unbelievers obtain the forgiveness of their sins thereby, but whether they also receive the body and blood of Jesus in this Sacrament.
>
> 3. Do you believe, that Jesus Christ, as true God and man in one person, should be worshipped?
>
> 4. Is it right for the Evangelical Lutheran Church to unite with any religious organization that seeks to deny the doctrines of the Augsburg Confession and Luther's Catechism? Or is it right for Lutherans to go to the Holy Supper with such?
>
> 5. Is your Synod to be henceforth ruled by a majority of the voters?
>
> 6. Does your Synod intend still to adhere to the declaration that Jesus Christ, the Great Head of his Church has given no special direction or order for the establishment of Church Government, as it is declared in the Constitution of the General Synod?[26]

The Pennsylvanians did not respond to this inquiry, nor to a similar one in 1825.

According to the Tennessee minutes, repeated attempts were made toward reconciliation, but the North Carolinians did not respond. A public meeting was set up in 1826 near Organ Church in Rowan County to discuss points of doctrine, but the North Carolinians refused to be drawn into a debate.[27] The schism was a reality; complete fellowship between the two groups was finally restored only a century later in 1921.

In addition to dealing with Henkel's pamphlet, the first North Carolina Synod under Schober's presidency carefully analyzed point by point the General Synod Constitution passed in Hagerstown, Maryland, in 1820. The local synod voted first on each section and then unanimously

---

[26]Socrates Henkel, *History of the Evangelical Lutheran Tennessee Synod* (New Market, Virginia: Henkel & Co., 1890), pp. 59-60.

[27]Henkel, *Tennessee Synod*, p. 70.

accepted the whole document. Charles Storch, the aged leader of North Carolina Lutherans, was elected the ministerial delegate to the October 1821 General Synod meeting with Schober as first alternate in case infirmity prevented Storch from attending. Gottlieb did represent North Carolina and supported the major accomplishments of the synod with enthusiasm.[28]

Plans were begun for the founding of a seminary and for composing an English catechism for the training of youth. Schober was appointed to a committee to work on the latter task, which was completed in 1823 when the recommendation was made to "retain Luther's Catechism for the present, and to report an improved translation of the questions . . . with explanatory additions on the decalogue, infant baptism and the eucharist. . . ."[29] The 1823 General Synod was almost the last. Problems had begun to emerge; some synods feared a loss of autonomy while others were so rationalistic as to depreciate any denominational concept. Samuel S. Schmucker emerged as the principal proponent of the synod, with Schober giving strong support. Obviously the synod needed a cause around which to rally and survive. That cause materialized in 1825 when the first Lutheran seminary in America was founded, opening its doors the following year with Samuel Schmucker as professor and president. Gottlieb Schober was president of the General Synod in that historic session and was immediately named to the seminary's Board of Directors. It was indeed appropriate that Schober's lifelong dedication to education should be capped by this development. Some years later he gave the institution 2,200 acres of land in Surry County, although it cannot be ascertained whether the seminary benefited from the gift.[30]

The new seminary removed another continuing problem. The synod resolved

> that in this Seminary shall be taught, in the German and English languages, the fundamental doctrines of the Sacred Scriptures as contained in the Augsburg Confession.[31]

---

[28]A balanced treatment of the origin and development of the General Synod is Robert Fortenbaugh, *The Development of the Synodical Polity of the Lutheran Church in America, to 1829* (Philadelphia: University of Pennsylvania, 1926).

[29]Schmucker, *The American Lutheran Church*, p. 228.

[30]Among Schobers' estate papers, there is a tax listing for 1835 showing the Lutheran Seminary as owner of the land. North Carolina State Archives, Raleigh, North Carolina.

[31]Minutes of the General Synod, 1825, quoted in Schmucker, *American Lutheran Church*, p. 229.

Here was the victory that moderates like Schober had advocated in 1819 when the plan for a General Synod was developed. Here was the means to combat the syncretistic liberalism which would discard all the historic symbols of Lutheranism. At the same time the priority of Scripture over the Confession was established to disarm those who wished to make the Confession the final word. This seminary in Gettysburg, Pennsylvania, would in years to come provide American Lutherans with a trained native ministry, committed to a solid doctrinal foundation. In 1829 the General Synod removed all doubt of theological foundation when it declared that

> Whilst the grand doctrines of the Reformation are absolutely insisted on, every minister and layman should have full liberty to approach the study of his Bible untrammeled by the shackles of human creeds. The General Synod therefore only requires of those who are attached to her connexion, that they hold the fundamental doctrines of the Gospel, as taught in the Augsburg Confession, and in all minor points leaves them unrestricted.[32]

Schober consistently supported the work of the synod until the end of his ministry. He attended every session of the body until age and infirmity prevented his travel.

The excitement of ecumenical ideas that gripped the North Carolina Synod of 1821 was not confined to cooperation among Lutherans. Robert J. Miller, long a faithful minister in the Lutheran fellowship, asked to be released to return to his native Episcopal Church now that it was more firmly established in the state. At the same time he, along with three official delegates of the Episcopal Church, inquired about a possible closer relationship between the two groups. Adam Empie, a Wilmington minister and one of the delegates, wrote to Miller:

> We pray that both sides may manifest a most conciliatory spirit that has nothing in view but the salvation of souls the prosperity of religion & the glory of God. As for our part we are determined to yield every thing we can in consistency with our consciences our ordination vows the established rules of our Church & the consequent duties that we owe to the Laity to which we belong.[33]

The Lutherans were receptive to the overture. A committee considered the matter and recommended that it would be advantageous and desirable for the two bodies to "be united in a bond of closest friendship."

---

[32]Minutes of General Synod, 1829, p. 15, quoted in Schmucker, *American Lutheran Church*, p. 232.

[33]A. Empie to R. J. Miller, Hillsborough, 4 May 1821. Printed in D. L. Corbitt, ed., "The Robert J. Miller Letters," *North Carolina Historical Review*, (25 October 1948), p. 504.

Each body should send representatives to the meetings of the other, with rights of debate and vote, except in decisions affecting only one of the groups. The Episcopalians promised that Lutheran students of theology who came well recommended would receive free instruction at the New Haven seminary.[34] The 1822 Synod heard a letter saying that the Episcopalian convention had ratified the agreement of cooperation. Schober was one of several Lutheran delegates sent to the Episcopal meeting in 1823, and the Lutheran synod in turn seated Robert Davis, an Episcopalian minister, with full voting rights.

By 1825, however, the cooperative arrangement hit a snag. Schober evidently shared details of this ecumenical venture with some of his Lutheran colleagues in New York. Bishop Ravenscroft in Raleigh soon heard of Schober's action and felt that he misrepresented the relationship between Lutherans and Episcopalians. Schober had evidently indicated that the initiative in the matter came from the Episcopalians. Adam Empie, who earlier had been ready to make great compromises, now counseled Robert J. Miller to disavow Schober's account without, however, offending him or implying that Schober had intended to misstate the facts.[35] Miller's reaction to this request is not known. It was possible that Schober did in fact initiate the discussion of cooperation when his close friend and colleague decided to return to the Episcopal Church. But the extant records indicate that the first delegates to visit another religious body were the Episcopalians in 1821. Whatever the case, the cooperative venture was not mentioned again in synod proceedings.

While most of Schober's time was taken in Lutheran affairs, the livelihood of his family was still earned in Salem. The focus of attention for Gottlieb in this period was the paper mill. The mill was still a profitable venture in itself since the business had been blessed with good managers in recent years. Moreover, the business enabled Schober to maintain a profitable traffic in goods which he sold and traded for rags. Beginning in 1816, the possibility of Schober purchasing the land associated with the mill—which he only leased on an annual basis—was introduced. Salem officials were uncertain of the consequences for the community, since the total tract including mill pond and its watershed

---

[34]Lutheran Synod Minutes, 1821, pp. 10-11.

[35]A. Empie to Rev'd R. J. Miller, Wilmington (N.C.) 8 March 1825, and 31 May 1825 in Corbitt, "The Robert J. Miller Letters," p. 502, p. 504.

amounted to over 150 acres. By this time other Wachovia land outside Salem was being sold to Moravians on a very careful basis; no sale was to interrupt the nature of the community and particularly the community business enterprises. Officials were afraid that if Schober owned the land outright, he might begin other business affairs which would injure the Salem economy. By 1817, the deal appeared probable, but suddenly the matter was dropped when a mutually agreeable price was not reached. Three years later, the Board asked $5 per acre, but at that price Schober was willing to purchase only the thirty-three acres around the very important springs which fed the mill pond and provided the pure water needed for paper manufacture. The Overseers thought this a bad arrangement and preferred either to sell the whole tract or continue to rent it.[36] The frustrations persisted for both sides so that by early 1824

> The Brethren of the Collegium are going to inspect the paper mill tract and take into consideration whether it is more profitable to sell the land at a low price rather than have constant discord and trouble on account of the lease.[37]

They decided to lower the price to $3 per acre for 172 acres of land which Schober had been renting; but he was willing to pay only $2.50. Moreover, this still did not include the vital springs, and for this new land the Collegium insisted on $5. Emmanual believed that this price was the best possible and must have convinced his father because the purchase was completed later that year: 158 acres at $3 and 22.5 at $5.[38] Emmanuel was convinced that more than land was needed to make the mill truly profitable. He wrote Thomas Bartholomew:

> I find great difficulty in carying on paper making in the old way, and I feel more and more inclined to introduce the Machine. . . . Coleman Sellers & Sons of Philadelphia. . .advise us to have a machine with Iron rolls and frame more durable and less liable to get out of repair . . . [would cost] $1100—one made on the same plan with wooden rolls they would charge $900—machines on wooden frames from 5 to 700 Dollars.[39]

And, continued Emmanuel, the arrangement of the mill would need to be changed to accomodate new machinery to best advantage. He described

---

[36]For stages in these negotiations, see Board of Overseers, 13 January, 28 July 1817; 22 January, 24 September 1821, Moravian Archives.

[37]Board of Overseers, 26 January 1824, Moravian Archives.

[38]Congregation Council, 6 May 1824, Moravian Archives.

[39]Emmanual Schober to Thomas Bartholomew, Salem, 27 June 1824, Schober Papers, Old Salem Archives.

the mill and the size of the pond providing power, and then asked Bartholomew's advice on the cost of a total conversion of the mill to modern equipment. If that is too expensive,

> I would sell my establishment—the Mill House with the basement story is 3 stories high—basement story of rock. The other two stories of [??? illeg.] & conveniently arranged stone dam—& two hundred & fifty acres of land attached to it—with abt. 20 or 30,000 lbs. of rags on hand—with a mechanic or a man to manage it would be something new in this county—and a great deal of money could be made at it—*suppen you buy me* out & bring a machine along—I would take $5000 including the stock of rags—or try to sell it for me—or if I cannot sell and a man would undertake to put up a complete machine—I would give him the whole establishment for any time that might be reasonable to pay for the Machine. . . .[40]

Bartholomew's response was not encouraging. His price for used but satisfactory equipment was also over $1,000—a capital outlay which the Schobers felt was prohibitive. Emmanuel continued to correspond with individuals regarding the needed retooling, but no significant investment was made. By 1830 selling the mill was again considered and almost consummated. In 1836 the establishment passed into the hands of another Salem resident, Christian Blum. Over the years it had been the chief producer of Schober's income. But now it was rapidly becoming a liability.

According to tax lists for the years 1824 and 1827, Gottlieb had attained a comfortable estate. He listed a house in Salem, a store, 3,210 acres of land and five taxable slaves. The paper mill does not appear and probably was listed by Emmanuel. Even the tax lists revealed only a part of Gottlieb's total assets. In 1828, Salem renovated the water works for about $1,500; the Overseers approved "that one thousand dollars shall be borrowed from Br. Gottlieb Schober for five years at 5 per cent for the water-works."[41] At his death, Schober's estate amounted to $31,720.68.[42] The heirs were rather surprised that the amount was so small. Peter Wolle explained the discrepancy when he wrote to Emmanuel: "We indeed have reason to lament that so great a portion of our inheritance has

---

[40]Ibid.

[41]Board of Overseers, 22 January 1828, Fries and others, *Records of Moravians*, 8:3845.

[42]Estate Papers of Gottlieb Schober, North Carolina State Archives, Raleigh, North Carolina.

been lost through Biddle and Company. . . ."[43] The financial panic of 1837 weakened the United States Bank of Philadelphia whose president was Nicolas Biddle. Schober evidently had significant deposits or was a shareholder in the institution. In 1839, the bank closed and, after trying to resume business in 1841, declared bankruptcy.[44] Both depositors and stockholders lost heavily.

Family matters during the early 1820s contained both joy and sorrow. The gain of strong sons-in-law in Peter Wolle and Johann Herman was offset by the loss of a daughter, Johanna Sophia Zevely. "Hannah" died quite unexpectedly on 18 November 1821, leaving her husband Vaniman with four young children.

Emmanuel, Gottlieb's only surviving son, had by the early 1820s begun to assume leadership within the family and community. He lived in the Single Brothers' House until the latter closed as a residence in 1823,[45] then bought a small house.[46] He was elected to the Board of Overseers in 1823, but seemed to miss many of the meetings. He spent a good deal of time in Germanton, seat of the county court, where he was likely pursuing the practice of law, although permission for such a vocation had not officially been granted by the Brethren. He was again elected to the North Carolina Senate in 1824, once more following the footsteps of his father, and served a total of six terms in that legislative body. In early 1826 Anna Hanes,[47] a single sister from the Hope community, became Emmanuel's bride and came to Salem to live in the little house on the square.

Anna Paulina Herman moved with her husband from Newport, Rhode Island, to his new pastoral charge in Philadelphia in 1823 and then to Lancaster, Pennsylvania, in 1826. Maria Wolle served with her hus-

---

[43]Peter Wolle to Emmanual Schober, Lititz, 16 August 1843, Schober Papers, Old Salem Inc. Archives.

[44]Hammond, *Banks and Politics in America*, p. 518.

[45]The Single Brothers' Treasury (Ger. Diacony) had been in trouble for a number of years. In addition, control of the young men became increasingly difficult. A series of events which disturbed the congregation's sense of decorum led to the decision to discontinue the House as a communal establishment in 1823. Board of Overseers, 18 November 1822; 27 May, 6 June 1823, Moravian Archives.

[46]The house was built in 1774 by Christian Triebel and stood on modern lot N60 on the corner between the Single Brothers' House and the Miksch house.

[47]Anna Hanes, was born in Rowan County, on 10 January 1799 to Philip and Hannah Hanes, members of the Hope congregation. Anna studied about a year in the Girls' Boarding School of Salem before marrying Emmanual in March 1826.

band, Peter, in Bethania for three years. In 1823, they were called to serve the congregation in Lancaster, Pennsylvania; three years later they moved to Lititz.

Thus the house on the southeast corner of Salem square became quieter as the years passed. Hedwig, one of the younger daughters, was in her twenties. After her formal schooling, she returned home to care for her parents in their declining years. Of course, the children of deceased Nathaniel and Hannah lived close by and without doubt frequently enlivened the home of their grandparents. Events in Salem swept on apace, seeming faster and faster to Gottlieb as his own gait began to slow. More and more frequently he was forced to ask others to preach in his stead. In 1824 a young man named William Jenkins, just beginning in the Lutheran ministry, became Schober's assistant, "gaining unusual approval in the places where he preaches."[48] But the old man was not finished just yet.

---

[48]Bethania Diary, 18 July 1824, Fries and Others, *Records of Moravians*, 8:3725.

Salem Moravian Church, consecrated in 1800
(drawn about 1857 by N. S. Siewers)

CHAPTER **13**

Teaching Them
in Sunday Schools

D URING THE PERIOD of Schober's leadership of the North Carolina Lutheran Synod, he also achieved his greatest effectiveness as a pastor. For twenty years he served Nazareth, Shiloh, Hopewell, and Bethlehem churches (1810-1830)[1] and New Jerusalem from 1815 to 1821. He supplied at various times in the congregations of Pilgrim, St. Luke's, and Beck's, all south of Salem in Davidson County. From his regular churches Schober reported fourteen children baptized in 1822, ten in 1823, and thirteen in 1824. The following year he indicated fifteen children and three adults baptized, twenty-two confirmations, 150 communicants, and one funeral.[2]

By far his most significant contribution for the laypersons in North Carolina was his ever increasing support of the Sunday school. Schober's initial sponsorship of this institution in the state was related in Chapter

---

[1]Nazareth was located north of Salem near Germanton, also first called Beaver Dam Church. Shiloh was ten miles west of Salem near Lewisville, first named Muddy Creek Church. Hopewell was southeast of Salem near the home of Henry Ripple and was often identified as Ripple's Church. Bethlehem was east of Salem and north of later Walkertown. New Jerusalem was west of Salem on the road connecting Salisbury and Mocksville, also called Dutchman's Creek and later Reformation.

[2]Statistics drawn from Lutheran Synod minutes of the years cited.

Ten. Sunday schools immediately assumed an important role in educating children and adults of the backcountry. In 1824 the American Sunday School Union was founded in Philadelphia under the principle that the Sunday school was

> eminently adapted to promote the intellectual and moral culture of the nation, to perpetuate our republican and religious institutions, and to reconcile eminent national prosperity with moral purity and future blessedness.[3]

From the beginning the Union's strategy was "to ignore, whenever possible, doctrinal and political differences; to be antiseptically *undenominational* in purpose and practice." The evangelicals were counseled "to leave their 'distinctive pecularities out of sight and out of mind.' "[4] With such a perspective Schober's enthusiastic support could be anticipated. The interest of the national organization was felt in Wachovia when in 1826 a Reverend Witherspoon, a minister from Hillsborough, visited Salem to encourage the further growth of the schools.[5] The movement immediately gathered momentum in the rural churches of both Moravians and Lutherans. The school at Friedland was typical:

> there is continued interest in the Sunday School begun last spring. On the 9th and 30th of this month small books were given to the children, to encourage them to still more industry. It is pleasant to see about seventy children gather each Sunday. They show a real eagerness to learn. Several of the larger pupils in one week have memorized forty or fifty verses from the New Testament, several short Psalms, two verses from the Hymn Book, and a page from the short *Outline of the Teaching of Jesus*, and can repeat them one after another almost without mistake. We have the names of seventy-seven scholars, and it is seldom that more than eight or ten are absent. The school is opened in the morning at nine o'clock with song and prayer, and lasts until nearly eleven o'clock. Then comes preaching, and usually another meeting. In the afternoon at one o'clock the school begins again, lasting usually until four, but sometimes we are not through until the sixth hour. Several suitable stanzas are sung in closing.[6]

For the youngest children, the Sunday schools were primarily reading schools, beginning with books on the ABC's. More advanced students, as shown above, memorized texts from the Bible. For attendance and memory work, students were given reward "tickets" which were accumu-

---

[3]Resolution of the American Sunday School Union, 1828, quoted in Robert W. Lynn and Elliott Wright, *The Big Little School* (New York: Harper and Row, 1971), p. 1.

[4]American Sunday School Union, 1832, Quoted in Lynn and Wright, *Big Little School*, p. 20.

[5]Salem Diary, 15 April 1826, Fries and Others,*Records of Moravians*, 8:3769.

[6]Salem Diary, 30 July 1826, Fries and Others, *Records of Moravians*, 8:3770.

lated to be exchanged ultimately for books or maybe even a Testament. Study books were available in both English and German; these began with drills on the alphabet and advanced to simple religious stories, then to more complex prayers for children.[7] In addition, most good schools had a circulating library, the only source for such materials in many rural locations. In 1859, of the 50,000 libraries in the United States, 30,000 of them were in Sunday schools.[8]

The initial enthusiasm was sustained by the founding in 1826 of the "Stokes County Sunday School Union" by the visiting Witherspoon and Gottlieb Schober, newly appointed agent of the national body. Thirty-two subscribers paid annual dues of fifty cents or ten dollars for life membership. Schober traveled throughout the county and adjoining areas, advocating this method of bringing education and moral training to children who might otherwise never learn even to read. The results were phenomenal. By December, the Friedberg school had eighty-one students, and the next summer the number rose to 154. Even in Salem, where some Elders voiced doubts about the enthusiasm generated by the movement, the single sisters started a school "where on Sunday afternoon the younger Sisters and older girls who desire to improve in reading and writing are given free instruction. . . ."[9] Other schools were founded in the vicinity at places called Brushy Fork, Pleasant Hill, Pfafftown, Friendship, Mt. Vernon, Spanish Grove, and Hope. The Hope Sunday School Journal indicated in 1829 that

> The Number of enrolled scholars was 39. Classes were regularly arranged, consisting of two reading classes with both divisions [probably male and female], two spelling both divisions and two alphabetic primers. All was harmony and love and the spirit of God reigned. Tickets given out in the reading classes: male 13, female 24. 144 verses recited. May the content thereof be imprinted on their hearts.[10]

While Sunday schools were easy to begin, they were difficult to maintain. Many operated only during the warmer months, and therefore

---

[7]*Erstes Lesebuch für Kinder*, (New York: Amerikanischen Tractat: Gesellschaft, n.d.) A copy of this book once belonging to "Heinrich Wolf" was discovered by this author near Winston-Salem. In the Moravian Archives there is a copy of *The Christian Pilgrim* published by the Sunday and Adult School Union in 1823.

[8]Lynn and Wright, *The Big Little School*, p. 31.

[9]Memorabilia, 1828, Fries and Others, *Records of Moravians*, 8:3833.

[10]Daybook for the Hope Sunday School, Stokes County, North Carolina, 15 March 1829, Moravian Archives.

interest had to be regenerated each spring. As president of the local union, Schober continued to visit the established schools, sometimes preaching an afternoon sermon as well. As an aid to continuity, the celebration of the anniversary of each school was initiated. The largest of these events was the anniversary of the Union itself. In 1829 the first anniversary brought five hundred scholars plus two to three hundred parents and teachers to Salem. Schober spoke to the group, describing "the beginning of Sunday schools in England, in Europe, and in other parts of the world; including this neighborhood."[11]

> It was a pleasant sight to see so many young people from our neighborhood, who through the Sunday Schools not only have an opportunity to learn to read, but also to become acquainted with the word of God.[12]

The following year 1200 students marched in the parade down the streets of Salem.[13] It was a triumphant moment in the life of seventy-four-year-old Gottlieb to step in a lively manner at the head of such a procession. But such enthusiasm could not be sustained. By late 1831 Schober wrote to the secretary of the national organization:

> I wish I could report to your board a lively continuance of the Sunday schools in this County, but it appears as if 6 or 7 are dying out for want of Life in the Teachers. . . . I visit the schools as your Agent as often as possible, and generally preach on the Subject . . . [and] enter into friendly discourses and explain the Lessons to the Little ones who all love me perhaps because I generally give to each reader a Tract—and scripture pictures to the little ones.[14]

Schober further indicated that some religious groups, specifically the Methodists and Baptists, opposed the Sunday school movement. The Methodists attempt "only to effect conversion without imparting necessary knowledge," while the Baptists "are against instructing children, saying they can not become Christians before they are ripe & baptized. . . ."[15] Although the initial enthusiasm of the movement waned in

---

[11]Salem Diary, 29 March 1829, Fries and Others, *Records of Moravians*, 8:3869.

[12]Salem Diary, 29 March 1829, Fries and Others, *Records of Moravians*, 8:3870.

[13]Salem Diary, 28 March 1830, Fries and Others, *Records of Moravians*, 8:3915.

[14]Manuscript addressed to Secretary of American Sunday School Union, 21 November 1831. Schober Papers, Old Salem Inc. Archives.

[15]Ibid.

the late 1830s, it did not die. Many children were taught to read in the institution and had continuing access to the circulating libraries. Schober made provisions in his will for every school in Stokes County to receive $10 from his estate to buy books. At that time ten dollars would buy a set of 100 volumes from the national organization.[16] It was a legacy of which he could be proud.

In addition to his activity for Sunday schools, Schober continued his other pastoral work. He was still preaching with vigor in his churches and in several Moravian congregations. In October 1827, he preached for the first time in Salem "and spoke in an edifying manner."[17] He continued to preside over the synods of North Carolina Lutherans, and in 1827 presented an English translation of extracts from Luther's sermons printed in a German book entitled *Kirchen Postille*. He sought simply to explain clearly Luther's doctrines in a manner which could be understood by the laity. The translation was examined for accuracy, approved, and printed with the synod minutes. That same year, however, Lutheran congregations asked that a younger man be appointed to assist Schober who "is disabled by old age and infirmity."[18] The following year Schober wrote to Samuel Schmucker at the new seminary in Gettysburg asking for a young minister to be sent to North Carolina. He preached the synod sermon in 1828 "to an immense crowd of attentive hearers,"[19] but his sermon at the 1829 ordination of two young ministers was delivered "in a very pathetic and nervous manner." Even though the body was weakening, the mind was still clear. The ideas of that ordination message were appropriate and well developed. In concluding his sermon, however,

> as an encouragement to pious ministers, he described in glowing colours, the unspeakable reward promised, the crown of righteousness, the inheritance that is incorruptible and unfading, and the eternal weight of glory that will be bestowed on all the faithful labourers in the Lord's vineyard.[20]

With an eye on the hereafter and increasingly aware of his advancing age, Schober began to divest himself of responsibilities. He resigned from

---

[16]Lynn and Wright, *The Big Little School*, p. 31.

[17]Salem Diary, 7 October 1827, Fries and Others, *Records of Moravians*, 8:3801.

[18]Lutheran Synod Minutes, 1827, p. 8.

[19]Lutheran Synod Minutes, 1828, p. 2.

[20]Lutheran Synod Minutes, 1829, p. 15.

three of his churches in 1829, promising only to preach occasionally and to administer the Lord's Supper whenever possible. David Rosenmiller, a young minister, arrived in 1830 from the Gettysburg Seminary and assumed these charges. Gottlieb retained one congregation, Hopewell, and was again honored by election as synod president in 1830 and 1831. The latter year he reported six baptisms, eight confirmations, thirty communicants, and a Sunday school of forty children. Still he traveled "every Sunday if the weather is fair," although in a carriage and only eight or ten miles from Salem.[21] In 1832 Schober was excused from synod "on account of age and increasing infirmity."[22] Indeed, there was a new generation of Lutherans: "The Rev'd Father Schober [was] requested to translate [the synod minutes] into the German. . . ."[23] Schober made his final synod appearance in 1835 when the seventy-nine year old patriarch preached his farewell sermon on the text: "Brethren, the grace of our Lord Jesus Christ be with your Spirit."[24]

Even as Gottlieb's Lutheran affairs gradually diminished, so also his name appeared with less frequency in Salem records. There was, however, one thorn which continued to prick the old man even though his income was quite comfortable for his needs. Because the suffocation of personal initiative inherent in Salem's closed economic system was not consistent with ideals of the new nation, more and more citizens came to believe that the system was ultimately self-defeating. Schober in both word and deed had consistently advocated more individual freedom, and when debate on fundamental economic changes began, he was, as usual, squarely in the middle.

The central issue was whether to allow any competition in the mercantile trade, the most consistently profitable enterprise in Salem and from the beginning one of the communal businesses. A direct challenge was, of course, impossible under the circumstances; it was erosion at the edges which began to hurt. In 1825, David Clewell asked to become a master bookbinder in Salem. Several individuals, including Gottlieb Schober, wondered whether a living could be made at that trade in Salem. Besides, stationery and bound blank books were already for sale in town.

---

[21]Report to American Sunday School Union. Manuscript dated 21 November 1831, Schober Papers, Old Salem Inc. Archives.

[22]Lutheran Synod Minutes, 1832, p. 2.

[23]Lutheran Synod Minutes, 1832, p. 8.

[24]Lutheran Synod Minutes, 1835, p. 5.

Brother Schober has presented his problem in the framework of our community regulations. However, we wish very much that he himself would also note his limits and not have other articles for sale which have been reserved for the store solely and which do not fit into his line of trade at all. It is true that Pastor Schober has permission to keep store goods for his rag trade, wherefore Br. Rights and Schulz are going to look through the old minutes and find out how far this privilege extends.[25]

Despite potential problems, Clewell's request was approved, and Gottlieb promised to stay within his trade. Matters were quiet for about three years but then came a letter from Schober to the Overseers accusing Clewell of "collecting rags in the community and its neighborhood and sending them to Pennsylvania and this infringing upon [Schober's] business." Instead of supporting Gottlieb, the Overseers advised "that he too should offer money for rags. We cannot force people to accept those compensations for rags that Pastor Schober offers."[26] It was obvious that the freedom of competition that Schober had long sought, now worked against him. Some of his profit was made in the barter of articles which he bought wholesale and traded at retail values. To pay cash for rags hurt profits. Schober's reaction was predictable and not particularly a compliment to his character. He protested bitterly of Clewell's violations of regulations. The vehemence of Schober's attack also showed his advancing age, "arousing deep pity" in the Elder's Conference. In light of Gottlieb's "distressed state of mind" the Elders felt constrained to talk with him quietly rather than exchange letters.[27] But the fundamental issue was forced into the open. Less than sixty days after Schober's initial outburst, the Overseers were discussing the possibility of a second store or opening up the trade to limited competition. Gottlieb was not the only Salem citizen who was pushing the regulations to the limit and beyond:

Upon consideration of the small private dealings which are being made in the community, the Collegium decided to have a private talk with all those brethren concerned by it and point out to them the great advantage which they all enjoy through the Community Treasury, which they seem to forget. Accordingly, H. Blum and E. Schober are going to talk to Pastor Schober, Herbst and Benzien to Br. [Will] Fries, Thomas Schulz and J.J. Blum to the milliners in the Sister's House, and Thomas Schulz and Benzien to David Clewell. We doubt the general success of these talks.[28]

---

[25]Board of Overseers, 11 July 1825, Moravian Archives.

[26]Board of Overseers, 26 November 1828, Moravian Archives.

[27]Elder's Conference, 12 November 1828, Moravian Archives.

[28]Board of Overseers, 26 January 1829, Moravian Archives.

As expected, the conversations were of little value. Schober would agree to limit his trade only if Clewell was also restricted. But the Overseers would not agree because "Schober's paper is inferior in quality to that of Clewell and he is not willing to pay as much for rags as does David Clewell." We believe, they concluded, that "this should stimulate Pastor Schober to supply us with better paper."[29] Yet the Overseers recognized that the real issue was the monopoly system itself. And only the people themselves could finally decide that matter. A meeting of all adult members was planned at which the advantages of the system, such as the providing of necessary community services through the profits of community enterprises, would be presented. There would follow an open discussion, then

> a secret vote can be taken determining whether the public is willing to check the mentioned encroachments according to the old tradition and if this restraint should not be found possible, what practicable answers are to be taken which would enjoy the active support of the people of the community.[30]

This statement revealed the realism and insight of the Board. The system could not be maintained by sanctions; only voluntary cooperation would prohibit violators from making a profit and continuing to do business. Several community meetings were held, but the issue was too complicated. The livelihoods of many people would be affected regardless of the decision. Some wanted complete abolition of monopolies, others preferred private stores paying "recognition fees" to the treasury, and still others advocated a second community store simply to provide competition for the benefit of citizens without a loss of profits for the treasury.

By August, no solution had been reached, although several Brothers volunteered to open a private store, or manage a second store for the Community Treasury. Desperately the Overseers tried to hold on to the old ideals, while individuals measured the actions of others against the rules and found them wanting.[31] To abolish all monopolies meant higher congregation dues, i.e. taxes, but to keep the old ways and tolerate the violations meant that community enterprises would likely lose profits.

---

[29]Board of Overseers, 9 February 1829, Moravian Archives.

[30]Board of Overseers, 23 February 1829, Moravian Archives.

[31]Board of Overseers, 7 September 1829, Moravian Archives.

The Congregation Council finally decided that a second store operated by the Community was the best solution.[32] But it took another year to convince the Overseers that this was really the best step. Then within a few months Will Fries and Christian Blum requested to sell small items such as molasses, sugar, coffee, paint, nails, glass, stationery, and books.

> Inquiry had been made of Pastor Schober, who has had stationery for sale for some time, and he says that if J. Chr. Blum is granted permission to sell the various articles mentioned, he would have to expand his trade along other lines also, especially since Br. Clewell, the bookbinder has paper and blank books for sale. It was evident that if Brother J. Christian Blum were to have permission to sell all the various articles connected with book-printing, one could not refuse other trades equal privileges. It would be so with Brother Fries, if, in addition to the articles released for the Toy Shop and his tobacco business, we should permit him to carry other articles for sale. Thus, on all sides, there would be infringements into the privileges of others and those of the Congregation Diacony stores which in these times of straitened livelihood would be ruined, as well as our Diacony system for the good of the whole congregation. . . .[33]

Despite this decision, the opening of a second store was the beginning of the end of the monopoly. In 1833, one store reported annual profit of $2.69 and the other a loss of $1,105. According to the Elders, Salem residents were not patronizing their own establishments, preferring the lower prices of several new stores recently opened in Salem's vicinity. Managers were changed, and profits began to pick up only to have the financial slump of 1837 cause another deficit of $1,135. The governing boards finally studied the long-term profit record of the store and found that the average annual profit from 1817-1827 was $792, while the years 1827-1837 averaged an annual loss of $132.[34] The stores were immediately offered for sale. Although the total monopoly system was not abolished for another decade, its effectiveness was compromised so that the arrangement was moribund. By that time Schober and others who had chafed under the system were dead, but the spirit which they had embodied was very much alive.

After 1831 the days of feuding were over for Gottlieb. He could afford for others to assume positions of leadership and influence, particularly

---

[32]Congregation Council, 8 October 1829, Moravian Archives.

[33]Board of Overseers, 28 November 1831, Moravian Archives. Part of quotation in Fries and Others, *Records of Moravians*, 8:3994-95.

[34]Board of Overseers, 31 July 1837; Elder's Conference, 2 August 1837, Moravian Archives.

since some of them were his own flesh and blood. Emmanuel was heavily involved as a local attorney and was also serving on the Board of Overseers. As Captain of the Salem Light Infantry Company he was responsible for defending the town in emergency. When sickness forced Gottlieb to relinquish the office of Postmaster, Emmanuel also assumed that task. Peter and Maria Wolle were still in Pennsylvania where they served the Philadelphia congregation. On a visit to Salem in 1832, Peter preached for the Sunday School Anniversary in Gottlieb's stead. Johann and Paulina Herman came in 1834, bringing three daughters whom the grandparents had never seen. Both of these sons-in-law would in later years be named bishops in the Unity and assume positions of leadership in both Europe and America. Hedwig was still at home and had assumed a special place in her parents' hearts for her unselfish assistance in these latter years. Thus Gottlieb and Maria could reflect with pride upon their family. In turn the children and grandchildren honored them on a special occasion in 1832.

> On December 17 the 50th wedding anniversary of Br. Gottlieb and Sr. Maria Magdalena Schober was observed, attended by children and children's children and many friends. A lovefeast was held to which the Married People, Widows, and Widowers Choirs and relatives in the other choirs were invited.[35]

Maria Schober had never involved herself in community affairs at levels of leadership. Yet her faithfulness was well known and respected by all who knew her. She certainly had a mind of her own and disagreed on occasion with her outspoken husband. All evidence would indicate a happy relationship which was only broken by Maria's death on 13 June 1835, only five days before her seventy-seventh birthday. Although Gottlieb lived for another three years, there is no record of public activity. According to his memoir, these last quiet years were spent preparing for the end.

> He concerned himself much with his homegoing and spoke of his hope of eternal life. In such speech he often declared himself very sinful and placed his trust simply on the redemptive power of Jesus.[36]

Shortly before the end, he told a visiting friend: "When you hear that I am gone, know that I have gone to the Saviour." In June 1838, a conta-

---

[35]Salem Diary, 17 December 1832, Moravian Archives.

[36]Memoir of Gottlieb Schober, Moravian Archives.

gious fever swept through Salem, touching both young and old. The children were able to withstand illness without lingering effects, but it weakened several of the older people like Gottlieb.

> On the night of the 28th he was only slightly conscious and remained completely unconscious on the following day. After he had slept through one more night it was evident on the morning of the 29th that the Lord had given him the sign.
> It happened to him then according to his urgent prayer and under a feeling of the nearness of God who gave a blessing to his homegoing. Shortly when again the death watch was held at his bed, his breath stopped at 10 AM almost unnoticed. He went to sleep in an exceptionally gentle way after a pilgrimage of 81 years, seven months, and twenty-eight days.[37]

On 1 July a large congregation gathered to pay final respect to Gottlieb Schober. The Salem minister, William H. Van Vleck, spoke first in German, then in English on the text from Revelation 22:3.[38] Referring to the New Jerusalem, the passage states: "And there shall be no more curse; but the throne of God and of the Lamb shall be in it; and his servants shall serve him: . . . ." He was buried in God's Acre.

When the Lutheran synod next met, the president acknowledged simply and truthfully:

> His life was spent in untired activity and useful labors until old age admonished him to seek retirement. The Church, the benevolent societies, especially the Education and Sunday School cause, all have lost a liberal and efficient member and patron. May his memory long be cherished and respected among us, and his exemplary activity and liberality be imitiated.[39]

---

[37]Memoir of Gottlieb Schober, Moravian Archives.

[38]Salem Diary, 1 July 1838, Fries and Others, *Records of Moravians*, 9:4389.

[39]Lutheran Synod Minutes, 1839, President's address, appendix, p. 1.

A Vision
of Discipleship

> To serve God simply means to do what God has commanded and not to do what God has forbidden. And if only we would accustom ourselves properly to this view, the entire world would be full of service to God, not only the churches but also the home, the kitchen, the cellar, the workshop, and the field of townsfolk and farmers. For it is certain that God would have not only the church and world order but also the house order established and upheld. All, therefore, who serve the latter purpose ... are jointly serving God; for so He wills and commands.
> . . . .
> In this way a man could be happy and of good cheer in all his trouble and labor; and if he accustomed himself to look at his service and calling in this way, nothing would be distasteful to him.[1]

These words could have been written by Gottlieb Schober; they were in fact contained in a sermon by Martin Luther in 1532. Just as Luther believed that vocations practiced in faith were as surely God's call as any minister who celebrated Holy Communion, so Schober tried to embody that idea in living. He possessed from his early years a vision of discipleship. Even though that vision changed and matured in later life, the essence remained the same: to serve God.

---

[1]Ewald M. Plass, comp. *What Luther Says: An Anthology* (St. Louis, Missouri: Concordia Publishing House, 1959), 2:560.

Frustrated in his early aspiration for service in the church, and unwilling to forsake the security of Salem for the risks of secular society, young Schober took the only true opportunity he had. He used his talents to achieve financial security. Success reenforced his sense of call, and, when no longer forced to occupy his mind and hands with a livelihood for himself and his family, he readily turned those same talents to the service of the church. First he became an attorney, handling Moravian legal affairs and problems without compensation. Gradually, however, Gottlieb became dissatisfied with the manner in which Salem was administered. Too many leaders lacked vision, he believed, and were unwilling to accept the challenges of social and economic change which would maintain Salem's viability as a community. Too often they relied upon a formal utilization of the lot, subordinating other concepts of divine leadership. While Schober's criticisms may appear harsh, two things should be remembered. First, Gottlieb was committed without reservation to the principles upon which the Unity was established, and therefore his criticisms, right or wrong, were intended in a constructive manner. Secondly, the early nineteenth century was a difficult period for the Moravian Church in general and weaknesses in individual congregations should not be surprising. Two respected Moravian historians, J. Taylor Hamilton and Kenneth G. Hamilton, describe 1801-1857 as "Years of Decline and Renewal." Early in that period, "those in office ... tended to regard change with disfavor and to fear any attempt to introduce innovations as revolutionary."[2] The groundwork for Moravian renewal was laid in the Unity Synod of 1848 and completed in the Synod of 1857 when the principles of decentralized government were adopted.[3] This principle was at the heart of Schober's criticism. More local authority would improve the ability of individual congregations to meet local needs without compromising vital concepts. After 1857, the Moravian Church began to assume its modern form.[4] It is appropriately symbolic that presiding over the Unity Synod of 1848 as it laid the foundation of Moravian renewal was Bishop John G. Herman, son-in-law of Gottlieb Schober and husband of Anna Paulina.

---

[2]Hamilton and Hamilton, *History of the Moravian Church*, p. 176.

[3]Hamilton and Hamilton, *History of the Moravian Church*, pp. 184-85, pp. 316-17.

[4]Hamilton and Hamilton, *History of the Moravian Church*, 315ff.

Perhaps Schober's frustration was a factor in his acceptance of ordination from Lutheran ministers in 1810 and his attempt to fulfill his expression of service to God within that communion. He served as a pastor to humble folk, but more importantly his vision of the Church of Christ matured into an unusually perceptive concept. His ecumenism was not unique even in his own time and certainly its roots were deep in his Moravian heritage, but few of his day advocated Christian unity and cooperation so forthrightly and worked so diligently for the realization of those goals. Equally important, Schober preached that an ignorant ministry and laity limited God's ability to accomplish his goals with mankind. Seminaries and Sunday schools could change that and hasten the time when the Kingdom of God would be a reality.

Schober's efforts to live fully his Christian life and calling did not mean that he was without faults. The recognition of his own failings as he approached death was not empty rhetoric. He knew that his temper was uncontrollable at times. He knew that his words and actions had hurt people beyond the recall of a simply apology. He knew that temptations of creature comforts clouded his judgments on important issues. For these and other failures known only to himself he could only rely on a faith in divine love and mercy.

To interpret Gottlieb Schober, even "warts and all," as the fulfillment of a vision of discipleship is to assign the best possible motives to his actions. Some would see him as a monumental ego, cocky and impertinent even in adulthood, greedy for material prosperity, always dissatisfied unless he was in the spotlight, and livid with rage if anyone dared to question his opinion or judgment. The residents and officials of Salem on several occasions wondered whether he was more liability than asset. The answer probably lies in the fact that Salem itself was in the process of evolution.

The changes in the nature of the community which had begun while Gottlieb was alive accelerated in the years following his death. In the 1830s, the increasing use of slave labor, despite efforts of congregation leaders to restrict it, soon made Salem indistinguishable from hundreds of other small villages in the antebellum South. The financial crisis of 1837 inflicted mortal wounds on the remaining communal enterprises. In 1840, the monopoly in storekeeping was abandoned, the tannery was sold to its operator, and the tavern was managed by a non-Moravian. Nine years later the entire monopoly system was discarded in favor of open competition in a free enterprise system.

By this time, Salem citizens were aware that the last vestige of the old theocratic organization, the lease system, could not long endure. It became "more and more apparent that we had for some time contented ourselves with the shadow after the substance had virtually been withdrawn."[5] As the governing boards struggled for an equitable solution, the North Carolina Legislature in 1849 divided Stokes County to create Forsyth County. Salem already stood near the center of the new unit and was therefore the logical choice as county seat. Against the counsel of church leaders, the Congregation Council voted to sell fifty-one acres of land to the Forsyth Commissioners at five dollars per acre. The southern edge of the tract was located five hundred feet from Salem's northern boundry; on this land, named in honor of revolutionary hero, Joseph Winston, the buildings for the new county were erected. Only a few years later the lease system was dissolved, lease holders were allowed to buy their lots, and other new lots were sold at auction.[6]

In short, from a theocratic community in which individuals confidently believed that God was involved in the management of their lives, Salem was moving slowly toward the kind of civil community more characteristic of the American scene. These civil communities, while maintaining many of the old social and economic values, relied more on the human ability to discover correct action than on continual divine guidance. Salem did not, of course, immediately become a secular town as the theocratic concept faded. Towns are made of people and Salem's people were mostly dedicated Moravians for many years. But the civil community was changing nevertheless. Concurrently, the religious dimension of Salem was also in transition. Moravians had been a recognized Church from at least the early 1700s, if not before. Now they began to reveal more clearly the characteristics of a denomination, again reflecting the trends of American religious history. The denomination is a nineteenth century American development, characterized by a political context of religious freedom, voluntary membership, and a purposive missionary activity aimed at increasing the group's size.[7] As Moravians

---

[5]Memorabilia of the Salem Congregation, 1856, Moravian Archives.

[6]The full account of the changes in Salem is contained in Jerry L. Surratt, *From Theocracy to Voluntary Church and Secularized Community: A Study of the Moravians in Salem, North Carolina 1772-1860* (Ann Arbor: University Microfilms, 1968).

[7]See Sidney E. Mead, *The Lively Experiment: The Shaping of Christianity in America*

became more voluntaristic, they became more denominational. The congregation in Salem was now a voluntary body—only those citizens of Salem who desired to join were members of the body.

Gottlieb Schober was much involved in the early portion of this evolution, and in many ways he epitomized its essence. He would not have been displeased with the developments after his death and with the character which the community and the Church ultimately assumed. According to a newspaper obituary,[8] he was the last survivor of the early inhabitants of Salem. In spirit, however, perhaps he was the first of a new generation of pioneers.

(New York: Harper and Row, 1963) and Sidney E. Mead, "Denominationalism: The Shape of Protestantism in America," *Church History*, 23:291-320.

[8]Newspaper clipping in the fly-leaf of Gottlieb Schober's Bible, exact source unknown. Moravian Archives.

BIBLIOGRAPHY

Manuscript Sources

Archives of the Moravian Church in America, Northern Province, Bethlehem, Pennsylvania.

    Book Inventory for Nazareth Hall, 30 April 1771. Translation by Del-Louise Moyer.

    Draft for the House Regulations of the Educational Institution at Nazareth, n.d. Translation by Del-Louise Moyer.

    Memoir of Andreas Schober

    Memoir of Hedwig Schober, nee Schubert

Archives of the Moravian Church in America, Southern Province, Winston-Salem, North Carolina.

    Board of Overseers Minutes, Salem, 1772-1840, Translation by Erika Huber.

    Helfer Conferenz Minutes, Salem, 1772-1811, Translation by Erika Huber.

    Congregation Council Minutes, Salem, 1772-1840, Translation by Erika Huber.

    Elders' Conference Minutes, Salem, 1772-1840, Translation by Edmund Schwarze.

    Fries, Adelaide L. History of the Single Sisters' House. Typescript.

    _____ Daybook for the Hope Sunday School, Stokes County, North Carolina, 1829, Typescript.

    Memoirs of the Schober Family Members.
      Gottlieb Schober

Maria Magdalena Schober, nee Transou
Nathaniel Schober
Johanna Sophia Vaniman, nee Schober
Emmanuel Schober
Anna Paulina Herman, nee Schober
Hedwig Elizabeth Schober
Philip Transou
Magdalena Transou, nee Gander

Gottlieb Schober Papers

North Carolina State Archives, Raleigh, North Carolina.

Estate Papers of Gottlieb Schober

Legislative Papers of the Senate of North Carolina, 1789.

Stokes County Deed Book, 1, 2, 5, 7, 10

Old Salem, Incorporated Archives

Gottlieb Schober Papers. Some Translation by Grace Dollnitz and by Elizabeth Marx.

University of North Carolina at Chapel Hill Library, Southern Historical Collection.

David Henkle Papers No. 338.

Lenoir Family Papers No. 426.

Printed Sources

Africa, Philip, "Slaveholding in the Salem Community, 1771-1851," *North Carolina Historical Review,* 54 (July 1977): 271-307.

Ahlstrom, Sydney E., "The Romantic Religious Revolution and the Dilemmas of Religious History," *Church History,* 46 (June 1977): 149-70.

Atherton, Lewis E., *The Southern Country Store.* Baton Rouge: The Louisiana State University Press, 1949.

Bernheim, G. D. *History of the German Settlements and of the Lutheran Church in North and South Carolina.* Philadelphia: The Lutheran Book Store, 1872.

Bishop, J. Leander. *A History of American Manufactures from 1608 to 1860.* 3 volumes. Philadelphia: Edward Young and Company, 1866.

Brickenstein, John C. "The Second 'Sea Congregation,' 1743," *Transactions of the Moravian Historical Society.* 1:107-24.

The British Museum General Catalogue of Printed Books. Photolithograph edition to 1955. London: Trustees of the British Museum, 1965.

Clark, Walter, ed. *The State Records of North Carolina,* 16 volumes. Winston, Goldsboro, & Raleigh: State of North Carolina, 1886-1907.

Corbitt, D. L., ed. "The Robert J. Miller Letters," *North Carolina Historical Review.* 25 (October 1948): 485-521.

DeVoe, Shirley S. *The Tinsmiths of Connecticut.* Middletown: Wesleyan University Press, 1968.

Douglass, Elisha P. *The Coming of Age of American Business.* Chapel Hill: University of North Carolina Press, 1971.

Erstes Lesebuch für Kinder. Neu York: Amerikanischen Tractat: Gesellschaft, n. d.

Ettinger, A. A., ed. *Two Centuries of Nazareth, 1740-1940.* Nazareth PA: Nazareth Bi-Centennial, Inc., 1940.

Fortenbaugh, Robert. *The Development of the Synodical Polity of the Lutheran Church in America, to 1829.* Philadelphia: University of Pennsylvania Press, 1926.

Fries, Adelaide L. *Customs and Practices of the Moravian Church.* Revised Edition. Winston-Salem: Board of Christian Education and Evangelism, 1973.

_____ "An Early Fourth of July Celebration," *Journal of American History.* 9 (July 1915): 469-74.

_____ "First Paper Mill in Salem Started in 1791," *Employment Security Commission Quarterly.* 6 (Winter 1948): 30-32.

_____ trans. and ed. *Records of the Moravians in North Carolina.* Volumes 1-6. Raleigh: North Carolina Historical Commission, 1927-1943; Volume 7. Raleigh: State Department of Archives and History, 1947.

_____ *Forsyth County.* Winston NC: Stewart Printing House, 1898.

_____ Stuart T. Wright and J. Edwin Hendricks. *Forsyth: A County on the March.* Revised edition. Chapel Hill: University of North Carolina Press, 1976.

Gambosi, Marily. *A Day of Solemn Thanksgiving: Moravian Music for the Fourth of July, 1783, in Salem, North Carolina.* Chapel Hill: University of North Carolina Press, 1977.

Griffin, Frances. *Less Time for Meddling: A History of Salem Academy and College, 1772-1866.* Winston-Salem NC: John Fries Blair, Publisher, 1979.

Hacker, H. H. *Nazareth Hall.* Bethlehem PA: Times Publishing Co., 1910.

Hamilton, J. Taylor and Kenneth G. Hamilton. *History of the Moravian Church: The Renewed Unitas Fratrum, 1722-1957.* Bethlehem PA: Moravian Church in America, 1967.

Hamilton, Kenneth G., trans. and ed. *The Bethlehem Diary, 1742-1744.* Bethlehem, Pennsylvania: Archives of the Moravian Church, 1971.

_____ trans. and ed. *Records of the Moravians in North Carolina,* volumes 10-11. Raleigh: State Department of Archives and History, 1966 and 1969.

Hammond, Bray. *Banks and Politics in America from the Revolution to the Civil War.* Princeton: Princeton University Press, 1957.

Hazen, Edward. *The Panorama of Professions and Trades.* Philadelphia: Uriah Hurt and Son, 1836.

Hembury, D. M. "Baptismal Controversies, 1640-1900," *Christian Baptism,* A. Gilmore, editor. Philadelphia: Judson Press, 1959.

Henkel, David. *Carolinian Herald of Liberty, Religious and Political, An Oration.* Salisbury NC: Krider & Bingham, 1821.

——————— *Heavenly Flood of Regeneration, or, A Treatise on Holy Baptism.* Salisbury NC: Bingham & White, Printers, 1822.

Henkel, Socrates. *History of the Evangelical Lutheran Tennessee Synod.* New Market VA: Henkel and Co., 1890.

Hunter, Dard. *Papermaking in Pioneer America.* Philadelphia: University of Pennsylvania Press, 1952.

Jacobs, Henry E. *Book of Concord.* Philadelphia: United Lutheran Publication House, 1882.

James, Hunter. *The Quiet People of the Land: A Story of the North Carolina Moravians in Revolutionary Times.* Chapel Hill: University of North Carolina Press, 1976.

Johnson, Guion G. *Ante-Bellum North Carolina: A Social History.* Chapel Hill: University of North Carolina Press, 1937.

Journals of the Senate and the House of Commons of the General Assembly of North Carolina, 1790-1860. Raleigh: State of North Carolina, 1861.

Jung-Stilling, Heinrich. *Scenes in the World of Spirits,* G. Schober, translator. New Market VA: Ambrose Henkel and Co., 1815.

Korner, Jules G., Jr. *Joseph of Kernersville.* Durham NC: Seeman Printery, 1958.

Kurzer Bericht von den Conferenzen der Vereinigten Evangelisch Lutherischen Predigern und Abgeordnetan in dem Staat Nord-Carolina vom Jahr 1803, bis zum Jahr 1810. Neu-Market VA: Ambrostus Henkel, 1811.

Lefler, Hugh T. and Albert R. Newsome. *North Carolina: The History of a Southern State.* Third edition. Chapel Hill: University of North Carolina Press, 1973.

Levering, Joseph M. *The History of Bethlehem, Pennsylvania, 1741-1892.* Bethlehem PA: Times Publishing Co., 1903.

Lewis, A. J. *Zinzendorf: Ecumenical Pioneer.* London: Westminster Press, 1962.

Lineback, Julius A. "The Single Brethren's House of Salem, North Carolina," *Salem's Remembrancers.* Winston-Salem NC: Wachovia Historical Society, 1976.

Lynn, Robert W. and Elliott Wright. *The Big Little School.* New York: Harper and Row, 1971.

Mead, Sidney. "Denominationalism: The Shape of Protestantism in America," *Church History,* 23, (December 1954): 291-320.

——————— *The Lively Experiment: The Shaping of Christianity in America.* New York: Harper and Row, 1963.

Moon, R. O. *Jung-Stilling: His Biography.* London: G. T. Foulis and Co., 1938.

Morgan, Jacob L., Bachman S. Brown, and John Hall. *History of the Lutheran Church in North Carolina.* N. P. United Evangelical Lutheran Synod of North Carolina, 1953.

Peschau, F. W. E., trans. *Minutes of the Evangelical Lutheran Synod and Ministerium of North Carolina, 1803-1826.* Newberry SC: Aull and Houseal, 1894.

Pickering, Octavius and Charles W. Upham. *The Life of Timothy Pickering*. 4 Volumes. Boston: Little, Brown and Company, 1867-1873.

Plass, Ewald M., comp. *What Luther Says: An Anthology*. 3 Volumes. Saint Louis MO: Concordia Publishing House, 1959.

Reichel, Levin T. *A History of Nazareth Hall*. Philadelphia: J. B. Lippencott Co., 1855.

Reichel, William C. *Historical Sketch of Nazareth Hall from 1755-1869*. Philadelphia: J. B. Lippencott Co., 1869.

Rights, Douglas L. trans. and ed. *Records of the Moravians in North Carolina*, Volume 8. Raleigh: State Department of Archives and History, 1954.

Rondthaler, Edward. "The Use of the Lot in the Moravian Church," *Salem's Remembrancers*. Winston-Salem NC: Wachovia Historical Society, 1976.

Sabin, Joseph. *Bibliotheca Americana*. 29 volumes. New York: J. Sabin and other publishers, 1868-1936.

Sakolski, A. M. *The Great American Land Bubble*. New York: Harper and Bros., 1932.

Schmucker, Samuel S. *The American Lutheran Church*. Philadelphia: E. W. Miller, 1852.

Schober, Gottlieb. *A Comprehensive Account of the Blessed Reformation of the Christian Church by Doctor Martin Luther*. Baltimore: Schaeffer and Maund, 1818.

_____ *Review of a Pamphlet, Issued from the Press of the Western Carolingian in Salisbury, N. C., written by David Henkel*. Salisbury NC: Bingham and White, 1821.

Smith, Minnie J. trans. and ed. *Records of the Moravians in North Carolina*, Volume 9. Raleigh: State Department of Archives and History, 1964.

Succinct Information of the Transactions of the German and English Lutheran Synod for North Carolina and Adjacent States. Various printers for the Synod, 1811-1838.

Surratt, Jerry L. *From Theocracy to Voluntary Church and Secularized Community: A Study of the Moravians in Salem, North Carolina, 1772-1860*. Ann Arbor: University Microfilms, 1968.

_____ "The Role of Dissent in Community Evolution among Moravians in Salem, 1772-1860," *North Carolina Historical Review*, 52 (July 1975): 235-55.

Walker, Williston. *A History of the Christian Church*. Revised Edition. New York: Charles Scribner's Sons, 1959.

Warville, Jacques Pierre Brissot de. *New Travels in the United States, Performed in 1788*. New York: T & J Swords, 1792.

Weinlick, John R. *Count Zinzendorf*. Nashville: Abingdon Press, 1956.

Wenhold, Lucy Leinback. "The Salem Boarding School between 1802 and 1822," *North Carolina Historical Review*, 27 (January 1950): 32-45.

[Wilcocks, Thomas]. *A Choice Drop of Honey from the Rock Christ or a Short Word of Advice to all Saints and Sinners*. Ca. 1665. Reprinted by G. Shober. New-Market VA: Ambrose Henkel and Co., 1811.

Yoder, Donald H. "Christian Unity in Nineteenth Century America," *A History of the Ecumenical Movement, 1517-1948*. Ruth Rouse and Stephen C. Neill, editors. Philadelphia: Westminster Press, 1954.

[Zinzendorf, Nicolas L.] *Maxims, Theological Ideas and Sentences out of the Present Ordinary of the Brethren's Churches . . . from the year 1738 till 1747.* Extracted by J. Gambold. London: J. Beecroft, 1751.

——————— *Nine Public Lectures on Important Subjects in Religion.* Trans. and ed. George W. Forell. Iowa City: University of Iowa Press, 1973.

INDEX

Abbeville SC, 136
Alamance County, 120n
Alcohol abuse in Salem, 26-27, 73, 84, 86, 91, 114
Alexander, Evan, 66n, 95
American Revolution: and Salem, 22-24, 24n, 40, 94
American Sunday School Union, 212-14
Anabaptists, 170
Apprentice system in Salem, 22-23, 57, 117
Arndt, J. G., 137
Arnett, Valentine, 76
Augsburg Confession: and the Henkels, 186-87, 202; ideas of, 170, 203-204; and Lutherans, 138, 156, 172, 188, 195; and Moravians, 138, 156; and Schober, 143, 151, 170-72, 185
Aust, Gottfried, 64
Aust, Mary, 64-66, 66n
Austwärtige membership in Salem, 129-30

Bachman, Johann, 86, 174
Bagge, Charles, 73, 94
Bagge, Traugott, 29n, 38, 73, 92, 106, 120; comparison with Schober, 60, 72, 93, 191; and Revolutionary opinion, 24n; as store manager, 29-30
Bank of Cape Fear, 179
Banking in North Carolina, 109-10, 124, 125
Barnwell SC, 136
Baptism: of believers, 146; of infants, 145-50, 166, 169, 171; regeneration by, 184, 186-87, 189, 202
Baptists, 143, 143n; criticism of, 147, 199; and Moravians, 138-39; and Sunday schools, 214
Bartholomew, Thomas, 206-207
Beck's Lutheran Church, 165, 211
Bell, Joseph E., 168, 174, 183-86
Benzien, Christian L., 38; counseling Schober, 108, 115, 130-33, 217; as Wachovia administrator, 103, 121-22
Bernhardt, Christian E., 137
Bethabara, 16, 17, 30, 46, 47, 55, 57
Bethania, 16, 33, 41, 46, 55, 56, 65, 106, 132, 180, 209
Bethlehem Lutheran Church, 140, 211, 211n, 216
Bethlehem PA, 5, 7, 8, 9, 28, 34, 178
Biddle, Nicolas, 208
Billing, Joseph, 75

/M/P GOTTLIEB SCHOBER OF SALEM

Designed by Haywood Ellis

Composition by Omni Composition Services, Macon, Georgia
 typeface—11/13 Garamond; heads in Korinna Bold
 the text was "read" by a Hendrix Typereader II OCR Scanner
 and formatted by Mary M. Baker on an Addressograph Multigraph
 Comp/Set 5404, then paginated on an A/M Comp/Set 4510

Production specifications:
 text paper—60 pound Warren's Olde Style
 cover—Holliston Roxite B 53540
 and jacket—100 pound enamel

Printing (offset lithography) by Omnipress of Macon, Inc., Macon, Georgia
Binding by John H. Dekker and Sons, Inc., Grand Rapids, Michigan